THE GERM-CELL CYCLE
IN ANIMALS

BY

ROBERT W. HEGNER, Ph.D.

ASSISTANT PROFESSOR OF ZOÖLOGY IN THE UNIVERSITY
OF MICHIGAN

AUTHOR OF "AN INTRODUCTION TO ZOÖLOGY"
AND "COLLEGE ZOÖLOGY"

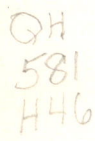

New York
THE MACMILLAN COMPANY
1914

All rights reserved

COPYRIGHT, 1914,
BY THE MACMILLAN COMPANY.

Set up and electrotyped. Published September, 1914.

Norwood Press
J. S. Cushing Co. — Berwick & Smith Co.
Norwood, Mass., U.S.A.

PREFACE

This book is the result of a course of lectures delivered during the past school year before a class in Cellular Biology at the University of Michigan. Many of the most important recent additions to our knowledge of heredity have resulted from the study of the germ cells, especially those of animals. This study is now recognized as one of the chief methods of attacking certain problems in genetics and must be employed in correlation with animal breeding before we can hope to obtain an adequate explanation of the results of hybridization. Fortunately the cytological studies of the germ cells, both observational and experimental, have kept pace with the rapid advances in our knowledge of plant and animal breeding which have been made since the rediscovery of Mendel's investigations in 1900. The term "Germ-Cell Cycle" is meant to include all those phenomena concerned with the origin and history of the germ cells from one generation to the next generation. The writer has, with few exceptions, limited himself to a consideration of the germ cells in animals because the cycle is here more definite and better known than in plants.

It is obvious to any one familiar with this subject that only a few of the many interesting phases of the problems involved can be considered in a work of this size, and those for which space can be found must be limited in their treatment. For this reason some periods in the germ-cell cycle are only briefly mentioned, whereas others are more fully discussed. The latter are naturally those in which the writer is most interested and with which he is best acquainted. Furthermore, the attempt is made to present the data available in such a way as to make it intelligible to those who have not been able to follow in detail the progress of cytology during the past few years. This can only be accomplished by introducing many facts that are well known to cytologists and zoölogists in general, but are necessary for the presentation of a complete account of the subject.

Much of the recent cytological work done on germ cells has emphasized the events which take place during the maturation of the eggs and spermatozoa, that is, the periods of oögenesis and spermatogenesis. These are, of course, very important phases of the germ-cell cycle, but they should not be allowed to overshadow the rest of the history of the germ cells. Contrary to the usual custom, the period that is emphasized in this book is not the maturation of the germ cells, but the segregation of the germ cells in the developing egg and the visible substances (keimbahn-determinants) concerned in this process.

It has been impossible to include in this book as much illustrative material as desirable, but the bibliography appended indicates what data exist and where they may be obtained. This list of publications has been arranged according to the method now in general use among zoölogists; the author's name and the date of the appearance of the contribution in question are bracketed in the text wherever it has been considered necessary, and reference to the list at the end of the book will reveal the full title and place of publication of the work, thus avoiding cumbersome footnotes. The figures that have been copied or redrawn are likewise referred in every case to the original source. Many of them have been taken from the writer's previous publications and a few have been made especially for this work. The writer has likewise drawn freely upon the text of his original investigations already published.

Ann Arbor, Michigan,
April 16, 1914.

TABLE OF CONTENTS

CHAPTER I

PAGE

INTRODUCTION 1

The Cell, 2; Cell Division, 13; Methods of Reproduction, 17; The Germ Cells, 19; The Life Cycles of Animals, 22.

CHAPTER II

GENERAL ACCOUNT OF THE GERM-CELL CYCLE IN ANIMALS 25

Protozoa, 25; Metazoa, 28.

CHAPTER III

THE GERM-CELL CYCLE IN THE PÆDOGENETIC FLY, MIASTOR 51

CHAPTER IV

THE SEGREGATION OF THE GERM CELLS IN SPONGES, CŒLENTERATES, AND VERTEBRATES . . . 69

1. Porifera, 69. 2. Cœlenterata, 80. 3. Vertebrata, 98.

CHAPTER V

THE SEGREGATION OF THE GERM CELLS IN THE ARTHROPODA 106

1. The Keimbahn in the Insects, 106; Diptera, 107; Coleoptera, 109 (In Chrysomelid Beetles, 109; Origin of Nurse Cells, 119; Cyst Formation in Testis, 125; Amitosis, 133; Differentiation of Nuclei in Egg, 141); Hymenoptera, 143. 2. The Keimbahn in the Crustacea, 163.

CHAPTER VI

THE SEGREGATION OF THE GERM CELLS IN NEMATODES, SAGITTA, AND OTHER METAZOA . . . 174

1. The Keimbahn in the Nematodes, 174. 2. The Keimbahn in *Sagitta*, 179. 3. The Keimbahn in Other Animals, 183.

CHAPTER VII

THE GERM CELLS OF HERMAPHRODITIC ANIMALS . . 189

CHAPTER VIII

KEIMBAHN-DETERMINANTS AND THEIR SIGNIFICANCE . 211

A. The Genesis of the Keimbahn-Determinants, 211 (*a*, Nuclear, 213; *b*, Cytoplasmic, etc., 224; *c*, Discussion, 228). *B*. The Localization of the Keimbahn-Determinants, 235. *C*. The Fate of the Keimbahn-Determinants, 240.

CHAPTER IX

THE CHROMOSOMES AND MITOCHONDRIA OF GERM CELLS 245

The Chromosome Cycle in Animals, 245. The Mitochondria of Germ Cells, 275.

CHAPTER X

THE GERM-PLASM THEORY	290
REFERENCES TO LITERATURE	311
INDEX OF AUTHORS	337
INDEX OF SUBJECTS	341

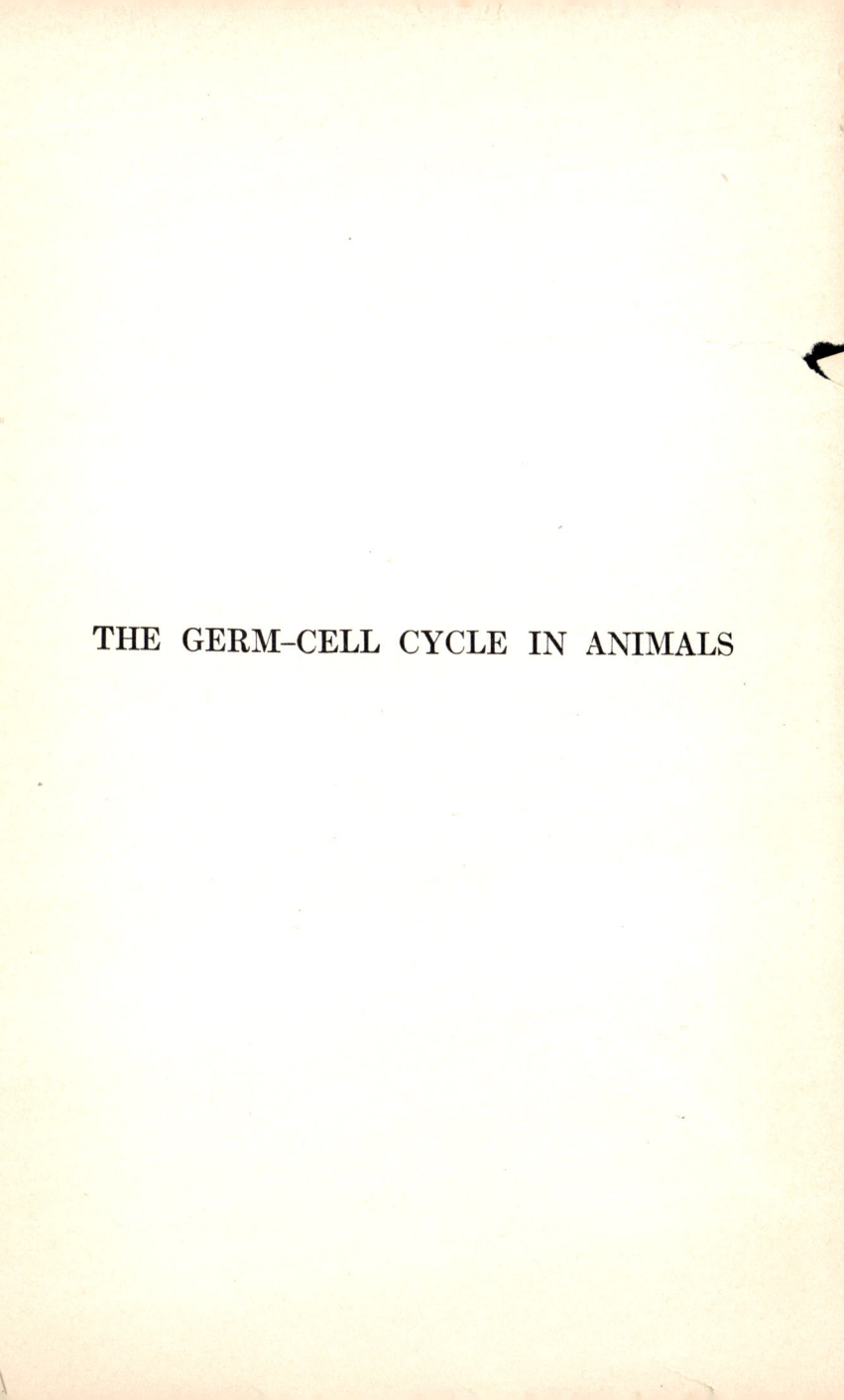

THE GERM-CELL CYCLE IN ANIMALS

GERM-CELL CYCLE IN ANIMALS

CHAPTER I

INTRODUCTION

Since the enunciation by Harvey of the aphorism *Omne vivum ex ovo* in the seventeenth century, the statement has frequently been made that every animal begins its individual existence as an egg. While this is not strictly true, since no eggs occur in the life history of many one-celled animals (Protozoa), and a large number of multicellular animals (Metazoa) are known to develop from buds or by fission, still the majority of animals arise from a single cell — the egg (Fig. 4, *A*). In most cases this egg, or female sex-cell, is unable to develop in nature unless it is penetrated by a spermatozoön or male sex-cell (Fig. 4, *B*). The single cell resulting from the fusion of an egg and a spermatozoön is known as a zygote. One of the most remarkable of all phenomena is the development of a large, complex organism from a minute, and apparently simple, zygote.

According to the older scientists, a miniature of the adult individual was present in the egg, and development consisted in the growth and expansion of rudiments already *preformed*. This belief could not continue to exist after Caspar Wolff's brilliant researches proved that adult structures arise gradually from apparently undifferentiated material; that is, development is *epigenetic*. Epigenesis, however, does not explain development; it simply maintains that it occurs.

During the years since the theory of epigenesis was proposed a new theory of preformation has entered into our conception of development, a theory which we may designate as *predetermination*. We know from our microscopical studies that the germ cells possess a certain amount of organization, and that the zygote contains certain structures contributed by the egg and other structures brought into the egg by the spermatozoön. Hence, to a certain extent, development is predetermined, since the initial structure of the zygote determines the characteristics of the individual that arises from it. On the other hand, development is also epigenetic, and our modern conception includes certain features of each theory.

THE CELL. A brief account of the structure, physics, and chemistry of the cell will serve to give us some idea of the condition of the zygote from which the individual arises, and will help us to understand certain events in the germ-cell cycle to be discussed later.

The cell is the simplest particle of matter that is able to maintain itself and reproduce others of its kind. The term 'cell' was applied by Hooke in 1665 to the cell-like compartments in cork. Cells filled

INTRODUCTION

with fluid were slightly later described by Malpighi. In 1833 Robert Brown discovered nuclei in certain plant cells. What is known now as the CELL THEORY is usually dated back to the time of the botanist Schleiden (1838) and the zoölogist Schwann (1839), whose investigations of the cellular phenomena in animals and plants added greatly to the knowledge of these units of structure. At this time the cell-wall was considered the important part of the cell, but continued research proved this idea to be erroneous. Schleiden called the substance within the cells plant slime. Later (1846) von Mohl gave the term protoplasm to the same substance. The substance within the animal cell was named sarcode by Dujardin. The similarities between the protoplasm of plants and the sarcode of animals were noted by Cohn, and animal cells without cell-walls were observed by Kölliker (1845). It was not, however, until 1861 that Max Schultze finally established the fact that plant protoplasm and animal sarcode are essentially alike, and defined the cell as a mass of protoplasm containing a nucleus. Schultze's researches serve as the starting point for modern studies of cellular phenomena, but the definition furnished by him must be modified slightly, since we now know that many cells exist without definite nuclei. These cells, however, are provided with nuclear material scattered throughout the cell body (the so-called distributed nucleus). Our definition must be changed to read, *a cell is a mass of protoplasm containing nuclear material.* Changes likewise have taken place in the Cell Theory; we no longer consider cells as isolated units and the multicellular animal as equivalent to the sum of its constituent cells, but recognize the influence of the cells upon one another, thus reaching the conclusion that the metazoön represents the sum of the individual cells plus the results of cellular interaction.

Cells vary considerably in size, ranging from those we call Bacteria, which may be no more than $\frac{1}{25000}$ of an inch in length, to certain egg cells which are several inches long; the latter, however, owe their enormous size to the accumulation of nutritive substances within them. An average cell measures about $\frac{1}{2500}$ of an inch in diameter. Cells vary in shape as well as in size; egg cells are frequently spherical, but most cells are not, since they are surrounded by other cells which press against them. A diagram of a typical cell is shown in Fig. 1.

Authorities are not agreed as to the structure of protoplasm; to some it appears, as shown in Fig. 1, to consist of a network of denser fibers called spongioplasm (s) traversing a more liquid ground substance, the hyaloplasm. Others consider protoplasm to be alveolar in structure, thus resembling an emulsion, whereas another group of zoölogists maintain that while protoplasm may appear to be fibrillar or alveolar, its essential basis consists of multitudes of minute granules. Wilson's view is the one usually adopted at the present time; that is, the protoplasm of the same cell may pass successively "through homogeneous, alveolar, and fibrillar phases, at different periods of growth and in different conditions of physiological activity," and that "apparently homogeneous protoplasm is a complex mixture of substances which may assume

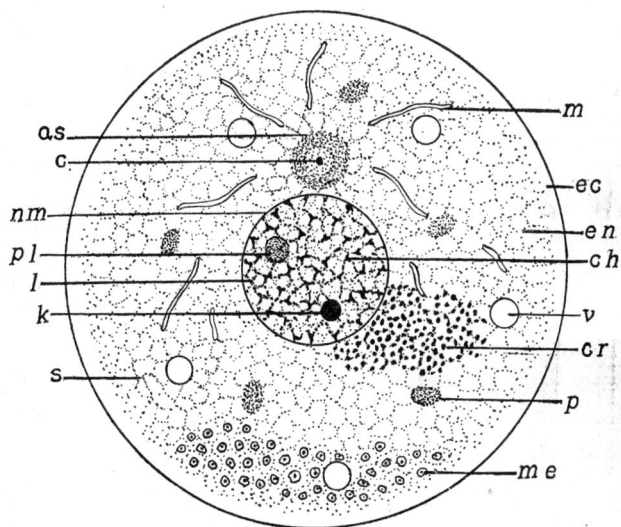

Fig. 1.—Diagram of a cell. as = attraction-sphere; c = centrosome; ch = chromatin reticulum; cr = chromidia; ec = ectoplasm; en = endoplasm; k = karyosome; l = linin; m = mitochondria; me = metaplasm; nm = nuclear membrane; p = plastid; pl = plasmosome or nucleolus; s = spongioplasm; v = vacuole.

various forms of visible structure according to its modes of activity."

The physical properties of protoplasm are not well known, since most of our studies have been made with fixed material. We know that protoplasm may exist as a gel or a sol, and that it is intermediate between true solids and true liquids, with many of the properties of each and a number of properties peculiar to itself. No doubt the protoplasm differs in its physical nature in different cells. In the egg of the starfish, *Asterias*, Kite (1913) has shown that the cytoplasm is a translucent gel of comparatively high viscosity and is only slightly elastic; pieces become spherical when separated from the rest of the egg. Scattered throughout this gel are minute granules (microsomes) about $\frac{1}{1000}$ mm. in diameter which cannot be entirely freed from the matrix. What appear to be alveoli contain globules which possess many of the optical properties of oil drops; these are suspended in the living gel. The cytoplasm of the starfish egg is not therefore alveolar in structure as usually stated, but is rather of the nature of a suspension of microsomes and globules in a very viscous gel. The nuclear membrane is a highly translucent, very tough, viscous solid, and not a delicate structure as ordinarily conceived. The nucleolus is a quite rigid, cohesive, granular gel suspended in the sol which makes up the rest of the nuclear material. Dividing male germ cells of certain insects (squash bugs, grasshoppers, and crickets) revealed the fact that the chromosomes are the most highly concentrated and rigid part of the nuclear gel; that the spindle fibers are elastic, concentrated threads of nuclear gel; and that the metaphase spindle fibers seem to be continuous with the ends of the chromosomes.

The ground substance of the nucleus is a sol termed nuclear sap or karyolymph. In the so-called 'resting' nucleus a network of fibers may be observed similar to the spongioplasm in the cytoplasm; these consist of a substance named linin because it usually occurs in threads (Fig. 1, *l*). Distributed along the linin fibers are granules of a substance which stains deeply with certain dyes, and for this reason is known as chromatin (*ch*). These chromatin granules may unite to form larger spherical masses, the karyosomes or chromatin-nucleoli (*k*), and during mitotic nuclear division constitute the chromosomes (Fig. 3, *C*). In many cells one or more bodies resembling the karyosomes somewhat, but differing from them chemically and physiologically, are present; these are the true nucleoli or plasmosomes (Fig. 1, *pl*). Embedded in the cytoplasm near the nucleus may often be seen a granular body, the centrosome (*c*), which is thought to be of great importance during mitotic cell division. The protoplasm surrounding the centrosome is usually a differentiated zone, the attraction-sphere (*as*), consisting of archoplasm. The chromatin which may be seen in the cytoplasm of certain cells is as a rule in the form of granules called chromidia (*cr*). Certain other cytoplasmic inclusions that have attracted considerable attention within the past fifteen years exist as granules, chains, or threads, and are known as mitochondria, chondriosomes, plastosomes, etc. (*m*). Various sorts of plastids (*p*), such as chloroplastids and amyloplastids, may be present, besides a varying number of solid or liquid substances, collectively designated as metaplasm (*me*) or paraplasm, which are not supposed to form part of the living substance; these are pigment granules, fat globules, excretory products, vacuoles (v), etc.

It has been found possible to explain many cellular activities and even the results obtained by experimental animal breeding by studies of the physics and chemistry of protoplasm. An exhaustive account of the subject is impossible and even unnecessary here, but the importance assigned to the physicochemical explanation of life phenomena requires a brief statement. Kossel has separated the cellular constituents into two main groups. (1) Primary constituents are those necessary for life; these are water, certain minerals, proteins, nucleoproteins, phosphatides (lecithin), cholesterin, and perhaps others. (2) Secondary constituents are not essentially necessary and do not occur in every cell; they are usually stored up reserve material or metabolic products representing principally what we have termed metaplasm.

Water which constitutes about two-thirds of the animal is necessary for the solution of various bodies, the dissociation of chemical compounds, the exchange of materials, the removal of metabolic products, etc. Mineral substances are present in all animal tissues, and different tissues are characterized by the presence of different minerals. The principal ones are potassium, sodium, calcium, magnesium, iron, phosphoric acid, sulphuric acid, and chlorine. The other constituents are of a colloidal nature, and its richness in colloids is one of the chief characteristics of protoplasm. To understand the activities of protoplasm we must therefore know something of the physics and chemistry of colloids.

Colloids (from *colla* = glue) do not diffuse, or diffuse very slowly, through animal membranes; in this respect they differ from crystalloids, which diffuse comparatively rapidly through animal membranes. Wolfgang Ostwald recognized two sorts of colloids: (1) suspension colloids, which are mixtures of solid and liquid phases, are non-viscous, and easily coagulated by salts, *e.g.* a mixture of finely divided metal and water; and (2) emulsion colloids, which are composed of two liquid phases, are viscous, and coagulated by salts with difficulty. Protoplasm is rich in emulsion colloids; these may exist as liquid sols, or more solid gels. In either case they consist of fine colloidal particles. According to another classification colloids may be separated into reversible and irreversible; the former may change from the sol to the gel state and back again, but the latter are unable to do this. Protoplasm is a reversible colloid, and many cellular structures appear to originate through the gelation of liquid colloids. Since protoplasm is a sol or gel due to water, it is a hydrosol or hydrogel, and because of its water content is said to be hydrophylic. It contains crystalloids and its chemical reactions take place in a dilute solution of electrolytes; these are substances which dissociate, at least in part, into their constituent ions when in solution, and the ions are electrically charged. For example, $NaCl$ dissociates into electro-positive Na ions (cations) and electro-negative Cl ions (anions). Colloidal particles are likewise electrically charged, those of acid colloids usually negatively and those of alkaline colloids positively. The union and separation of particles and their consequent rearrangement cause gelation, liquefaction, etc.; it is thus evident that many physiological activities may be due to the electrical charges of ions instead of the chemical nature of the particles themselves. Cellular structures therefore depend upon the tendency of colloidal particles to form aggregates (gelation, coagulation), and more or less upon the electrically charged nature of the particles.

The most characteristic chemical constituents of protoplasm are the proteins. The most common proteins in the body show on the average the following percentage of elements: —

Carbon	50 –55 %
Hydrogen	6.5– 7.3%
Nitrogen	15 –17.6%
Oxygen	19 –24 %
Sulphur	.3– 2.4%

Proteins may be separated into three groups: (1) simple proteins, such as protamines, albumins, and globulins; (2) conjugated proteins, the glucoproteins, nucleoproteins, and chromoproteins; and (3) the products of protein hydrolysis, infraproteins, proteoses, peptones, and polypeptides. These have been studied both by microchemical and macrochemical methods. In the former method reagents are applied to the microscopic objects and the changes in color, etc., indicate its constitution; *e.g.*, iron and phosphorus may be detected in this way. Parts showing affinity for acid stains like eosin are said to be acidophile or oxyphile; those showing affinity for basic dyes, like methylene blue, are called basophile. The chromatin is basophile, whereas the linin and cytoplasm are oxyphile. In macrochemistry large quantities of the substances are collected and examined by ordinary laboratory methods.

Because of the importance that has been assigned to the chromatin, this substance is particularly interesting. Chromatin consists of nuclein, which is a conjugated protein containing nucleic acid, the latter being an organic acid, rich in phosphorus; it is hence called nucleoprotein. Nucleoproteins are found chiefly in the nucleus but also occur in the cytoplasm. They may differ from one another in their protein content as well as in the character of their nucleic acid constituent. When treated with dilute acids nuclein is obtained, and when this is further subjugated to caustic alkali it decomposes into protein and nucleic acid. The nucleic acids which have been principally studied are those derived from the thymus gland, and from the spermatozoa of salmon, herring, and other fish; they are probably all the same. Levene (1910) recognizes three sorts of nucleic acid, of which the most complex is termed thymonucleic acid. This consists of

two purine bases, guanine and adenine;

two pyrimidine bases, thymine and cytosine;

a hextose (carbohydrate); and
phosphoric acid.

Its formula, according to Schmiedeberg, is $C_{40}H_{56}N_{14}O_{16} \cdot 2\ P_2O_5$, and according to Steudel, $C_{43}H_{57}N_{15}O_{12} \cdot 2\ P_2O_5$. Considerable progress has been made, especially by Emil Fischer and his students, in the synthesis of protein-like bodies. Many complex polypeptides have been built up which resemble peptones in many of their reactions and when injected into living organisms appear to be utilized in metabolism in much the same way as are native proteins.

We are still, however, very far from an adequate understanding of the nature of chromatin. Della Valle (1912), for example, after an exhaustive study of the physico-chemical properties of chromatin both in the resting nucleus and in the dividing cell, has concluded that this substance resembles that of fluid crystals. "Consequently all of the phenomena presented by the chromosomes; their mode of origin, differences in size, state of aggregation, form, structure, colorability, optical characteristics, variations in form, longitudinal division and the phenomena which follow this mode of scattering, demonstrate that the chromosomes are crystalloids."

Two other primary constituents of protoplasm may be mentioned briefly. The phosphatide, lecithin, belongs with cholesterin to a group of compounds called lipoids. It consists of glycerophosphoric acid plus certain fatty acid radicles, such as stearic acid, oleic acid, etc., and a nitrogenous base (cholin). It probably plays some part in cell metabolism, may furnish material for building up nucleins, and according to Fauré-Frémiet is concerned in the formation of mitochondria. Cholesterin is considered a waste product of cell life, although it is known to inhibit hæmolysis produced by certain bodies and is thus a protective against toxins, and may have other functions. We should look forward with great interest to the results of investigations that are now being carried on by biochemists, since we depend upon them for an explanation of many of the phenomena of life, cellular differentiation, and heredity. We even hope that they may be able to create compounds in the laboratory that we may consider living organisms. However, the task does not seem to be so simple to the biochemist, who should know, as it does to the biologist. Nevertheless, as Jacques Loeb has said, we should "either succeed in producing living matter artificially, or find the reasons why this should be impossible."

CELL DIVISION. Cells may increase in number by direct (amitotic) or indirect (mitotic or karyokinetic) division. There is no doubt that mitosis occurs, but not all investigators are convinced that cells ever divide amitotically. Direct division was once considered the only method of cell multiplication. It was described as a simple division of the nucleus into two parts (Fig. 2), preceded by a division of the nucleolus into two, and succeeded by a constriction of the entire cell; the result was two daughter cells each with one nucleus containing one-half of the nucleolus. As we shall see later (Chapter V), amitosis has been described in cells of the germ-cell cycle, and must therefore be reckoned with in any discussion of the physical basis of heredity.

Mitosis or karyokinesis involves a rather complicated series of processes which cannot be fully discussed here but will be outlined very briefly with the aid of Fig. 3.

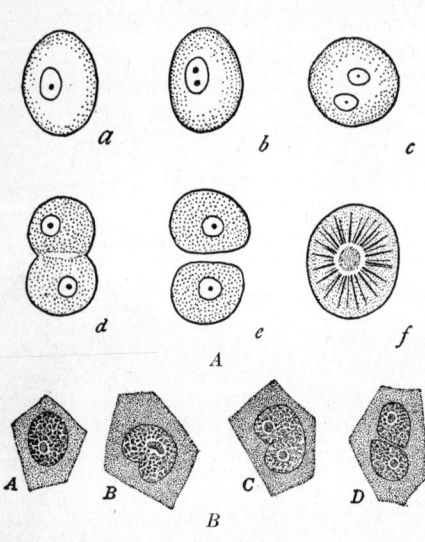

FIG. 2. — Amitosis. *A*. Division of blood-cells in the embryo chick, illustrating Remak's scheme. *a–e* = successive stages of division. (*From Wilson, 1900.*) *B*. Amitotic nuclear division in the follicle cells of a cricket's egg. (*From Dahlgren and Kepner, 1908.*)

(*a*) During the *prophase* the chromatin granules which are scattered through the nucleus in the resting cell (*A*) become arranged in the form of a long thread or *spireme* (*B*). At the same time the centrosomes move apart (*A, c*; *B, a*), and a spindle arises between them (*C*). While this is going on, the nuclear membrane generally disintegrates and the spireme segments into a number of bodies called chromosomes (*C*); these take a position at the equator of the spindle, halfway be-

INTRODUCTION

tween the centrosomes (D, ep). The stage shown in Fig. 3, D, is known as the *amphiaster;* at this time

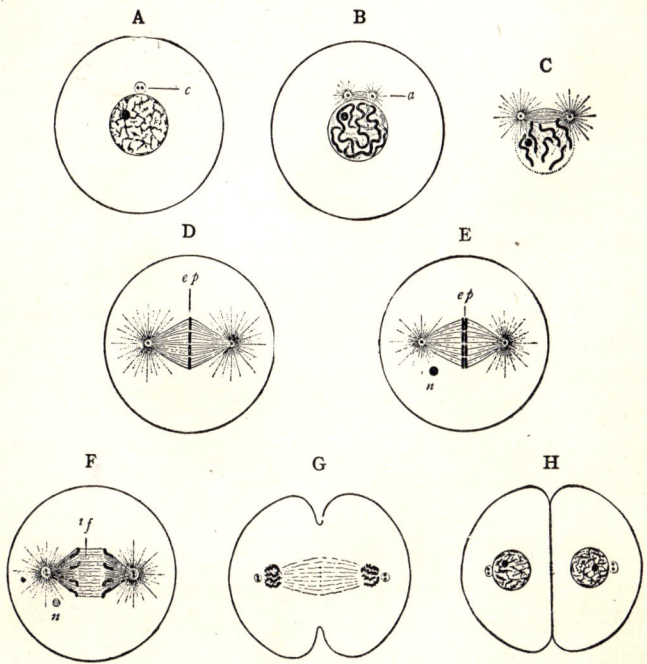

Fig. 3. — Mitosis. Diagrams illustrating mitotic cell division. (*From Wilson.*) A, resting cell; B, prophase showing spireme and nucleolus within the nucleus and the formation of spindle and asters (a); C, later prophase showing disintegration of nuclear membrane, and breaking up of spireme into chromosomes; D, end of prophases, showing complete spindle and asters with chromosomes in equatorial plate (ep); E, metaphase — each chromosome splits in two; F, anaphase — the chromosomes are drawn toward the asters, if = interzonal fibers; G, telophase, showing reconstruction of nuclei; H, later telophase, showing division of the cell into two.

all of the mechanism concerned in mitosis is present. There are two *asters*, each consisting of a centrosome surrounded by a number of radiating astral rays, and a spindle which lies between them. The chromosomes lie in the equatorial plate (ep).

(b) During the second stage, the *metaphase*, the chromosomes split in such a way that each of their parts contains an equal amount of chromatin (E, ep). As we shall see later, this is one of the most significant events that takes place during mitosis.

(c) During the *anaphase* (F) the chromosomes formed by splitting move along the spindle fibers to the centrosomes. As a result every chromosome present at the end of the prophase (D) sends half of its chromatin to either end of the spindle. The mechanism that brings about this migration is as yet somewhat in question. Fibers are usually left between the separating chromosomes; these are known as interzonal fibers (F, if).

(d) The *telophase* (G, H) is a stage of reconstruction from which the nuclei emerge in a resting condition; the chromatin becomes scattered through the nucleus, which is again enveloped by a definite membrane (H); the centrosome divides and, with the centrosphere, takes a position near the nucleus. Finally the cycle is completed by the constriction of the cell into two daughter cells.

There are a number of differences between the sort of mitosis just described and that which occurs during the maturation of the egg and spermatozoön; these and certain other phases of cell division will be considered in their appropriate places in succeeding chapters.

METHODS OF REPRODUCTION. In the beginning paragraph of this chapter it was stated, with reservations, that every individual develops from an egg. Before we can discuss the germ-cell cycle intelligently, however, we must consider the exceptions to this rule, and outline as briefly as possible the various methods of reproduction which are known to occur among animals. Reproduction is the formation of new individuals by division; this is frequently preceded by conjugation (in the PROTOZOA) or fertilization (in both the PROTOZOA and the METAZOA).

Three principal methods of reproduction occur in the PROTOZOA. (1) *Binary fission* appears to be the most primitive. The individual divides into two parts which are similar in size and structure; these grow into cells like the original parent. Many CILIATA, FLAGELLATA, and RHIZOPODA normally reproduce in this way. (2) *Budding* occurs when a small outgrowth or bud separates from the parent cell. This method occurs among the SUCTORIA, RADIOLARIA, HELIOZOA, CILIATA, and MYXOSPORIDIA. (3) *Sporulation* results from the division of the nucleus of the parent into many daughter nuclei and a subsequent division of the cell into as many "spores" as there are nuclei. This process is characteristic of the SPOROZOA and also is found among the RHIZOPODA. *Conjugation* is of frequent occurrence in the PROTOZOA. Two or more individuals may become connected without fusion of nuclei or cytoplasm, thus forming colonies; a pair of individuals may unite either temporarily or permanently with fusion of the cytoplasm only; or both cytoplasm and nuclei of such a pair may fuse or be interchanged.

METAZOA reproduce either sexually or asexually. *Asexual reproduction* is reproduction without the aid of sex cells. It takes place as a rule by means of buds or by fission as in many polyps, sponges, flat-worms, segmented round-worms, and bryozoans. Even the tunicates, which occupy an advanced position in the animal series, form buds. Some of the sponges produce internal buds called gemmules, and certain bryozoans form similar bodies known as statoblasts. *Sexual reproduction* requires that the individual develop from a mature egg. As a rule the egg must be fertilized by the union with it of a spermatozoön, thus forming a zygote; but the eggs of many animals develop without being fertilized; that is, they are *parthenogenetic*. In rare cases such parthenogenetic eggs may be produced, as in the fly *Miastor* (see Chapter III), by immature individuals. When this occurs, reproduction is said to be *pædogenetic*.

The *sex* of an animal is judged by the kind of sex cells it produces, — eggs by the female and spermatozoa by the male, — and when the individuals of a single species are differentiated as either males or females, the species is said to be *diœcious* and the individuals *gonochoristic*. In many species there is but a single sort of individual which produces both eggs and spermatozoa; such species are *monœcious*, and the individuals are *hermaphroditic*.

The Germ Cells. Eggs and spermatozoa differ from each other both morphologically and physiologically. *Eggs* are usually spherical or oval in shape (Fig. 4), although they may vary greatly from the typical form and may even be ameboid as in certain cœlenterates. In size they range from that of the mouse, which is only about 0.065 mm. in diameter, to that of birds, which are several inches long. The large volume of the latter is due to the presence of an enormous amount of nutritive material, and the general statement may be made that the size of an egg does not depend so much upon the size of the animal as upon the amount of yolk stored within it. The egg nucleus, which is frequently very large and clear, is known as the germinal vesicle; and its nucleolus has often been referred to as the germinal spot. Embedded within the cytoplasm of the ovum are several bodies besides the yolk globules. A "yolk nucleus" may be present; mitochondrial granules or rods may occur; and special inclusions, which become associated with the primordial germ cells and have been named keimbahn-determinants, have been recorded in many cases. Considerable evidence has accumulated that the egg substance is not a homogeneous, isotropic mixture, but is definitely organized, and that this organization is related to the morphology of the embryo which is to develop from it; hence we speak of the *promorphology* of the egg. Eggs are said to possess polarity, and even the oögonium as it lies in the ovary is definitely oriented with respect to its chief axes.

20 GERM-CELL CYCLE IN ANIMALS

The principal poles are dissimilar; the end of the egg containing most of the cytoplasm and nearer which lie the nucleus and centrosome is known as the animal pole; the other end, which is often crowded

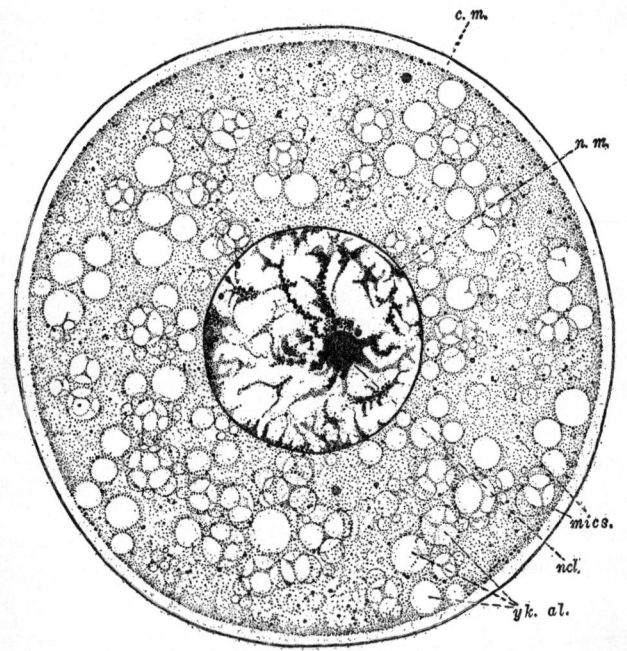

FIG. 4. — Germ cells. Ovarian ovum of a cat just before maturity. *c. m.* = cell membrane; *mics.* = microsomes; *ncl* = nucleolus; *n. m* = nuclear membrane; *yk. al.* = yolk alveoli. (*From Dahlgren and Kepner.*)

with the yolk globules, is called the vegetative pole. The subject of the organization of the egg will be referred to more in detail later (Chapter VIII).

The male sex cells or *spermatozoa* differ very strikingly from the eggs. They are usually of the

INTRODUCTION

flagellate type (Fig. 4a), consisting of a head, largely made up of chromatin, a middle piece, and a vibratile tail. Spermatozoa are comparatively minute, ranging in size from those of *Amphioxus*, which are less than 0.02 mm. long, to those of the amphibian, *Discoglossus*, which reach a length of 2.0 mm. According to Wilson it would take from 400,000 to 500,000 sea urchin spermatozoa to equal in volume the egg of the same species. It is not surprising, therefore, to find that the number of spermatozoa produced by a single male may be hundreds of thousands times as great as the number of eggs developed in a female. Eggs are, as a rule, incapable of locomotion, but spermatozoa are active, swimming about by means of their tails until they reach the passive eggs which they are to fertilize. Since generally only one spermatozoön fuses with an egg, it is obvious that most of them never perform the function for which they are specialized; but apparently an enormous number are formed to make the fertilization of the eggs more certain.

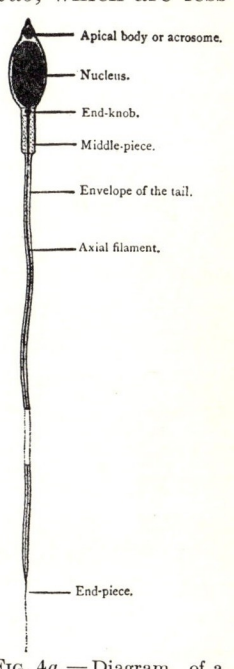

Fig. 4a. — Diagram of a flagellate spermatozoön. (*From Wilson, 1900.*)

The experiments of Loeb and Bancroft (1912) on spermatozoa have shown that when the living spermatozoa of the fowl are placed in a hanging drop of white of egg or in yolk they undergo a transformation into nuclei. The possibility that a spermatozoön may give rise to an embryo without the help of an egg is recognized, but this has not yet been accomplished.

THE LIFE CYCLES OF ANIMALS. The life cycle of an animal has considerable influence upon the course of the germ-cell cycle. In all animals that are produced by the sexual method the beginning stage in the life cycle is a mature egg, either fertilized or unfertilized according to the species. Animals which develop asexually, on the other hand, begin their cycle with the first recognizable evidence of budding or fission. As a rule budding or fission are sooner or later interrupted by the formation of sex cells, hence the life cycle of such animals may be considered to extend from the mature egg to that stage in the life history of the species when mature eggs are again produced. Such a life cycle consists really of two or more simple life cycles represented by individuals differing from one another in both structure and method of reproduction. As examples of some of the principal types of life cycles we may select certain insects and cœlenterates.

A very simple life cycle is that of the wingless insects of the order APTERA. The young, when they hatch from the egg, are similar in form, structure, and habits to the fully grown individual and undergo no perceptible changes, except increase in size, until they become sexually mature adults. In certain other groups of insects, such as the grasshoppers, the newly hatched young resemble the adult in many ways, differing principally in the absence of wings. The young Rocky Mountain locust (*Melanoplus spretus*), for example, changes its exoskeleton (molts) five times before the adult condition is attained. After each molt there are slight changes in color, structure, and size, the most notable difference being the gradual acquirement of wings. In still other orders of insects a larva hatches from the egg; this larva, on reaching its full growth, changes in shape and structure, becoming a quiescent pupa, from which after a rather definite interval an adult emerges.

A combination of two simple life cycles to form one complex cycle occurs in certain hydroids. The eggs of these species produce free-swimming embryos which become fixed to some object and develop into polyps. These polyps form other polyps like themselves by budding, but finally give rise to buds which become jelly-fishes or medusæ. Instead of remaining attached to the parent colony the medusæ, as a rule, separate from it and swim about in the water; they later give rise to eggs which, after being fertilized, develop as before into polyps. There are thus in this species two life cycles combined, that extending from the egg to the time when the colony forms medusa-buds, and that beginning with the medusa-bud and ending with the mature egg. Such an alternation of an asexual and a sexual generation is known as metagenesis.

There is another sort of alternation which normally occurs in many species, and that is the alternation of individuals developing from parthenogenetic eggs with those from fertilized eggs. In the aphids, or plant lice, for example, the race in the northern part of the United States passes the winter in the shape of fertilized eggs. All of the individuals which hatch from these eggs in the spring are females called stem-mothers. The stem-mothers produce broods of females from parthenogenetic eggs, and these in turn give rise to other broods of females in the same manner. Thus throughout the summer, generation after generation of parthenogenetic females appear; but as autumn approaches females develop whose eggs must be fertilized, and males are also produced. The eggs of these females are fertilized by spermatozoa from the males, and the zygotes thus formed survive the winter, producing stem-mothers the following spring.

CHAPTER II

GENERAL ACCOUNT OF THE GERM-CELL CYCLE IN ANIMALS

It will be impossible to present in this chapter even a general account of all the variations in the germ-cell cycle that are known to occur in animals. It will be necessary, therefore, to restrict ourselves to the series of events that occurs in the majority of animals, mentioning as many of the more notable variations and exceptions as possible without causing confusion. It also seems advisable to consider the germ-cell cycles in the PROTOZOA and the METAZOA separately.

PROTOZOA. Weismann, in his classical essays on the germ-plasm, argues in favor of the view that the PROTOZOA are potential germ cells, and, since new individuals arise by division of the parent cell into two or more parts, that natural death does not occur. The PROTOZOA are consequently also potentially immortal. The METAZOA, on the other hand, possess a large amount of somatic substance which always dies a natural death. It has often been pointed out that a PROTOZOÖN, although consisting of but a single cell, performs most of the physiological activities characteristic of the larger, complex METAZOA, and that certain parts of the PROTOZOÖN are recognizably concerned with the performance of certain definite functions. The fundamental difference, then, between the one-celled and the many-celled animals is that the differentiated structures in the former are not separated from one another by cell walls as in multicellular organisms.

Whether all PROTOZOA possess a body which can be considered as specialized and set aside for reproduction purposes, as the germ-plasm theory requires, is a question upon which authorities differ. In certain cases it seems possible to distinguish between germinal and somatic protoplasm without any difficulty. The life history of the fresh water rhizopod, *Arcella vulgaris* (Fig. 5), will serve to illustrate this (Hertwig, 1899; Elpatiewsky, 1907; Swarczewsky, 1908; Calkins, 1911). The single nucleus of the young *Arcella* divides to form two primary nuclei (N); chromatin from these migrates out and forms a layer near the periphery (Ch) —the "chromidial net" of Hertwig. This chromatin substance in the mature individual produces hundreds of secondary nuclei (n), each of which is cut off, with

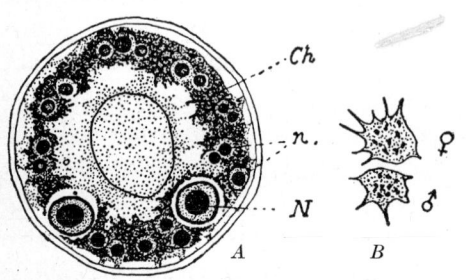

FIG. 5.—Reproduction in *Arcella vulgaris*. *A*. Formation of secondary nuclei. Ch = chromidia; n = secondary nuclei; N = primary nucleus. (*From Hertwig, 1899.*) *B*. Two gametes. (*From Elpatiewsky, 1907.*)

a small amount of the surrounding cytoplasm, from the others, thus becoming a swarm spore. The swarm spores escape from the mouth of the parent cell; whereas the two primary nuclei and a portion of the cytoplasm not used up in the formation of the swarmers die. The swarmers are not all alike, being of two sizes; the larger, which may be called macrogametes, and which correspond to the eggs of the METAZOA, fuse with the smaller microgametes. The zygotes which result develop into normal *Arcellæ*. The swarmers may be supposed to represent the germinal protoplasm, of which, as in metazoan germ cells, the chromatin content may be considered the essential portion. The conditions during reproduction in other PROTOZOA may also be explained in this way, so that germinal and somatic protoplasm can be distinguished as in the METAZOA.

The discovery of the chromidia in PROTOZOA led to the formulation of the hypothesis of binuclearity. Believers in this hypothesis maintain that each cell contains both a somatic and propagatory nuclear material which, as a rule, are united into one amphinucleus. The somatic nuclear material controls vegetative functions; the propagative portion serves only for the propagation of new individuals. Separation occurs rarely except in certain PROTOZOA, where, as in *Paramecium*, the propagative substance is represented by the micronucleus, the somatic by the macronucleus. Since the chromatin is the essential substance concerned in the binuclearity hypothesis, the term dichromaticity has been suggested as more appropriate, and the two kinds of chromatin involved have been called *idiochromatin*, which is reproductive in function, and *trophochromatin*, which is vegetative in function. The hypothesis has not gained many adherents and is considered of doubtful value by eminent protozoölogists (Dobell, 1908).

METAZOA. If we consider the mature egg, either fertilized or parthenogenetic, as the starting point of the germ-cell cycle in the METAZOA, we may recognize seven or eight distinct periods as follows:

1. The segregation of the primordial germ cells; *i.e.*, the formation of one or more primordial germ cells during the segmentation of the egg;

2. Early multiplication of the primordial germ cells;

3. A long period of "rest" characterized by cessation of cell division, either active or passive change of position, separation of the germ cells into two groups which become the definitive germ glands, accompanied by the general growth of the embryo until the larval stage is almost attained;

4. Multiplication by mitosis of the primitive oögonia or spermatogonia to form a definite number (*Miastor* and perhaps others) or indefinite number (so far as we know) of oögonia or spermatogonia;

5. In some cases the differentiation of oögonia into nurse cells and ultimate oögonia, and the spermatogonia into Sertoli cells and ultimate spermatogonia;

6. The growth of the ultimate oögonia and sper-

matogonia to form primary oöcytes and primary spermatocytes;

7. Maturation;
8. Fertilization (if not parthenogenetic).

1. THE SEGREGATION OF THE PRIMORDIAL GERM CELLS. This phase of the germ-cell cycle is especially emphasized in this book (see Chapters III to VI) and need be referred to only casually here. The mature eggs of animals are organized both morphologically and physiologically; that is, differentiations have already taken place in their protoplasmic contents before they are ready to begin development. This organization determines what sort of divisions the egg will undergo during the cleavage stages. During cleavage certain parts of the cell contents become separated from other parts and thus the differentiated substances of the egg are localized in definite parts of the embryo. The contents of the cleavage cells likewise become differentiated as development proceeds, until finally the cells produced form two or three more or less definite germ layers. In some cases the egg always divides in the same way, and the history or "cell lineage" of the cells can be followed accurately, and the parts of the larva to which they give rise can be established. This is known as determinate cleavage in contrast to the indeterminate type in which there appears to be no relation between the cleavage cells and the structure of the egg or larva.

The degree of organization of the egg no doubt accounts for the differences in cleavage; those of the determinate type being more fully organized than those of the indeterminate type.

The period when the primordial germ cells are established is probably due in part to the state of organization of the egg when development begins, and it is not strange, therefore, that the primordial germ cell may be completely segregated in certain eggs as early as the four-cell stage; whereas in others germ cells have not been discovered until a late larval condition has been reached. An ever increasing number of species of animals is being added to those in which an early segregation of the germ cells has already been recorded. Nevertheless, there are certain zoölogists who still question the general occurrence of an early segregation of the germ cells, but more careful investigations will probably establish the fact of early segregation in species in which this has not yet been demonstrated.

2. EARLY MULTIPLICATION OF THE PRIMORDIAL GERM CELLS. The number of germ cells present at the time of their first appearance in the embryo varies in different species. There may be one, as in the majority of cases, for example the fly, *Miastor* (Fig. 17), the nematode, *Ascaris* (Fig. 51), the crustacean, *Cyclops* (Fig. 48), and the arrow worm, *Sagitta* (Fig. 54); or a number, as in chrysomelid beetles (Fig. 36), certain parasitic HYMENOPTERA (Fig. 44), and vertebrates (Fig. 6). As a rule the primordial germ cell or cells increase in number by mitosis soon after they are segregated, and then cease to divide for a considerable interval. For

example, in *Miastor* the single primordial germ cell produces eight; in the beetle *Calligrapha multipunctata* the original sixteen undergo two divisions resulting in sixty-four; and in the chick Swift (1914) has counted as many as eighty-two at this stage.

We shall see later that the primordial germ cells are often characterized by the presence of certain cytoplasmic inclusions (the keimbahn-determinants) which are absent from the other cells of the embryo. These inclusions appear to be equally divided between the daughter cells so that each of the eight or sixty-four, as the case may be, is provided with an equal amount of the keimbahn-determinants.

3. PERIOD OF "REST" AND MIGRATION. By rest here is really meant cessation of division. During this period the germ cells either actively migrate or are passively carried by surrounding tissues to the position the germ glands occupy in the larva. In species possessing two germ glands the germ cells separate to form two groups, with, at least in some cases, an equal number in each group. Thus in *Miastor* the number in each group is four (Fig. 22) and in *Calligrapha*, thirty-two (Fig. 37). There is evidence that an active migration of germ cells occurs both in vertebrates and invertebrates. Figure 6 shows the positions of the germ cells in four species of vertebrates during their change of position. That the germ cells at this time are actively migrating by ameboid movements is the general opinion of investigators, since frequently these cells are ameboid in shape and the distance between the place

of origin and the germinal ridge is too great to be traversed in any other way.

Professor B. M. Allen, who has made extensive studies of the germ cells of many species of verte-

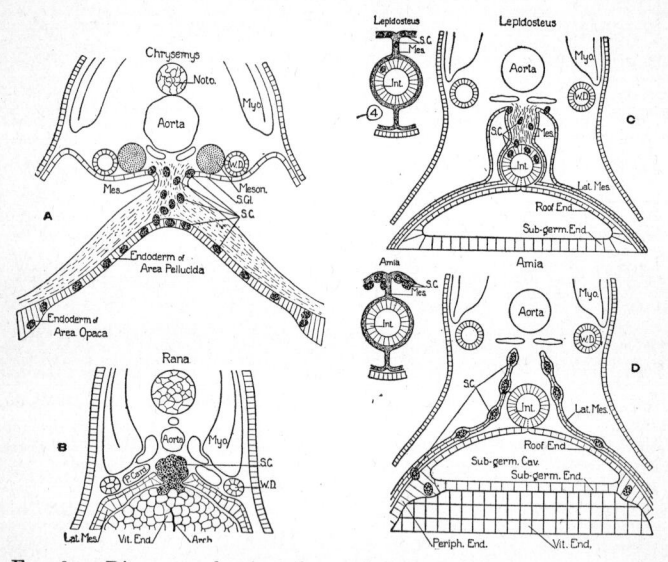

Fig. 6. — Diagrams showing the paths of migration in *A*, a turtle, *Chrysemys marginata*; *B*, a frog, *Rana pipiens*; *C*, a fish, *Lepidosteus osseus*, and *D*, the dog-fish, *Amia calva*. (*From Allen, 1911.*) *Arch* = archenteron; *Int.* = intestine; *Lat. Mes* = lateral plate of mesoderm; *Mes* = mesentery; *Meson* = mesonephros; *Myo* = myotome; *Noto* = notochord; *P. card* = post cardinal vein; *S.C* = sex-cells; *S.Gl* = sex gland; *Vit. End* = vitelline endoderm; *W.D* = Wolffian duct.

brates, makes the following statement regarding this phase of the germ-cell cycle:

"The sex-cells are migratory to a high degree. The path and time of their migration may vary greatly within a given group of animals, as illustrated by the case of *Amia* and *Lepidosteus*. While in the forms that I have studied they are first to be observed in the entoderm, I am quite open to conviction that in other forms they may migrate from this layer into the potential mesoderm before the two layers are separated, as shown by Wheeler in *Petromyzon*."

Swift (1914) has recently obtained evidence which seems to prove that not only do the germ cells of the chick migrate by ameboid movements but they enter the blood vessels and are distributed by the blood stream to all parts of the embryo and vascular area.

The migration of the germ cells has been noted in many invertebrates and has been fully described in chrysomelid beetles (Hegner, 1909*a*). In these insects the primordial germ cells are segregated at the posterior end of the egg at the time the blastoderm is formed (Fig. 36, *C*). The blastoderm is never completed just beneath them, but a canal, called the pole-cell canal, remains. Through this at a later embryonic stage the germ cells migrate by means of ameboid movements.

"As soon as the germ cells of *Calligrapha* have passed through the pole-cell canal, they lose their pronounced pseudopodia-like processes and become nearly spherical (Fig. 37, *E*); nevertheless, they undergo a decided change in position. They move away from the inner end of the pole-cell canal, and creep along between the yolk and the germ-band. Thus two groups are formed near the developing cœlomic sacs; each group probably contains an equal number of cells. The smallest number I have counted in one group at this time is thirty; the largest number, thirty-four. As there is some difficulty in obtaining an accurate count, it seems probable that the sixty-four germ cells are equally divided and that each germ gland receives thirty-two. Some of the germ cells migrate not only laterally along the germ gland but also back toward the posterior end of the egg, where we find them forming narrow strands in the last abdominal segments. From this stage on, the germ cells are not very active; they move closer to one another to form the compact germ glands. I was unable to determine whether the later movements of the germ cells are due to an active migration or to the tensions created by the growth of the surrounding tissues; the latter seems the more probable" (Hegner, 1909*a*, p. 280).

It is thus evident that during the blastoderm stage the germ cells of this beetle are actually *outside* of the egg. How well this illustrates the theory of primary cellular differentiation, that is, the differentiation of germ cells from somatic cells, since the two sorts are here completely separated, the former constituting a group in contact with but not connected with the somatic cells. Later, as the germinal continuity hypothesis demands, the germ cells migrate into the embryo, there to be nourished, transported, and protected by the body until they are ready to separate from the somatic cells, and thus to give rise to a new generation.

4. Period of Multiplication. Soon after the germ cells aggregate to form more or less rounded groups lying in the position of the definitive germ glands mitotic division is resumed. At about this time also, the sex of the individual can often be determined by the shape of the germ-gland. Then both the testes and the ovaries acquire envelopes of the follicular cells, and frequently testicular cysts and ovarian tubes or chambers develop. The question of the origin of the follicular cells is still unsettled, but the evidence in most cases seems to favor the view that they are mesodermal.

The multiplication of the germ cells by mitosis continues rapidly from this time on. In only one case, so far as I am aware, do we know the actual number of germ cells produced by the primordial germ cell; this is in *Miastor*, where typically sixty-four oögonia are formed (Fig. 26). As the germ cells multiply they become smaller in size and the substances present in the primordial germ cell become divided among a large number of progeny. Thus at the beginning of the growth period each germ gland contains many oögonia or spermatogonia, and each of these contains a small fraction of the material present in the primordial germ cell, plus whatever substances may have been assimilated during the period of multiplication.

5. The Origin of Nurse Cells and Sertoli Cells. Germ cells receive nourishment during the growth period in many ways, *e.g.*, from nurse cells, follicle cells, or directly from the blood. The origin

of the nurse cells and follicle cells is important since in a few cases the germ cells themselves are known to give rise to them. There is thus a second differentiation whereby somatic cells (follicle cells or nurse cells) become differentiated from germ cells (oögonia or spermatogonia). In some species, such as *Miastor*, we can prove without question that both the nurse cells and follicle cells are of mesodermal origin, and that the germ cells give rise only to germ cells. On the other hand, there are instances in both vertebrates and invertebrates of a common origin of germ cells and somatic cells from oögonia and spermatogonia. Perhaps the most striking examples are the differentiation of the nurse cells and ultimate oögonia in the water beetle, *Dytiscus*, and the differentiation of the Sertoli cells and ultimate spermatogonia in man. (See Chapter V.) Haecker (1912) distinguishes between a somato-germinative period and a true germinative period; the former is that during which the primordial germ cells are established and the latter that of the differentiation of nurse cells and ova.

6. THE GROWTH PERIOD. The last divisions of the oögonia and spermatogonia are followed by the growth of these cells. The extent of this growth depends, in the case of the female, upon whether or not the mature egg is to be supplied with an abundance of nutritive material. Nurse cells, follicle cells, and circulating fluids may all assist in the enlargement of the oögonia. If the eggs are small, sufficient nutriment is supplied by surrounding

liquids and no special nurse cells are required; but larger eggs either become surrounded by follicle cells which nourish them and with which they are often intimately connected by protoplasmic bridges, or special nurse cells are provided. In the primitive type of ovary, such as exists in most cœlenterates, any of the cells surrounding the oögonium may function as nurse cells and even neighboring oögonia are engulfed by the oögonium that is successful in the struggle for development. A more definite mechanism exists in higher organisms, where one or more cells become differentiated for the special purpose of supplying nutriment consisting of either their own substance or of material elaborated by them and then transferred to the egg. The egg of the annelid, *Ophryotrocha*, for example, is accompanied by a single nurse cell; that of *Myzostoma* is provided with two, one at either end; and the eggs of certain insects are more or less intimately connected with groups of cells in definite nurse chambers (Fig. 46).

The growth of an oögonium may be well illustrated by that of the potato beetle.

The general arrangement of the cells in the ovary of an adult beetle is shown in Fig. 7. The terminal chamber of the ovarian tubule contains three kinds of cells: (1) nurse cells ($n.c$), (2) young oöcytes ($y.o$) and growing oöcytes, and (3) epithelial cells. The nurse cells and oöcytes are both derived from the oögonia; the epithelial cells are of mesodermal origin.

The positions of the stages to be described are indicated in the diagram (Fig. 7) and the nuclear

38 GERM-CELL CYCLE IN ANIMALS

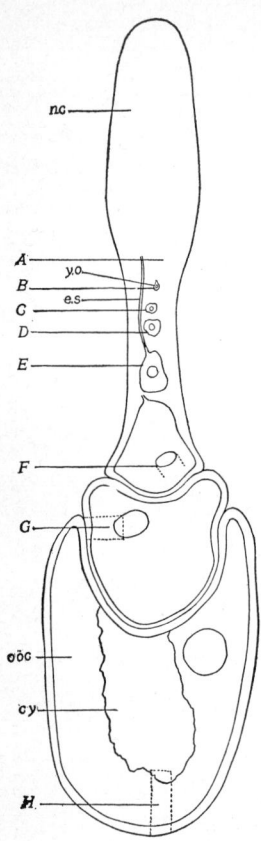

FIG. 7. — *Leptinotarsa decemlineata*. Diagram of an ovarian tubule showing various stages in the development of the oöcyte. The capital letters refer to the positions f cells shown in Fig. 8. cy = cytoplasm; es = egg string; $n.c$ = nurse chamber; $öoc$ = oöcyte; $y.o$ = young oöcyte.

and cytoplasmic structures are shown in Fig. 8. Two oöcytes and a neighboring epithelial cell from position A in Fig. 7 are shown in Fig. 8, A.

The nuclei of the oöcytes are large and contain a distinct spireme; the cytoplasm is small in amount and apparently homogeneous. After a short period of growth the oöcytes form a linear series in the ovarian tubule and become connected with the spaces between the nurse cells by means of egg strings (Fig. 7, $e.s$) through which the nutritive streams flow into the oöcytes. One of the youngest of these oöcytes is represented in Fig. 8, B (position B in Fig. 7). The nucleus is no larger than in those of the earlier stage; its chromatin forms a reticulum, and a distinct nucleolus is present. The cytoplasm, on the other hand, has trebled in amount and within it are embedded a number of spherical bodies

ACCOUNT OF THE GERM-CELL CYCLE 39

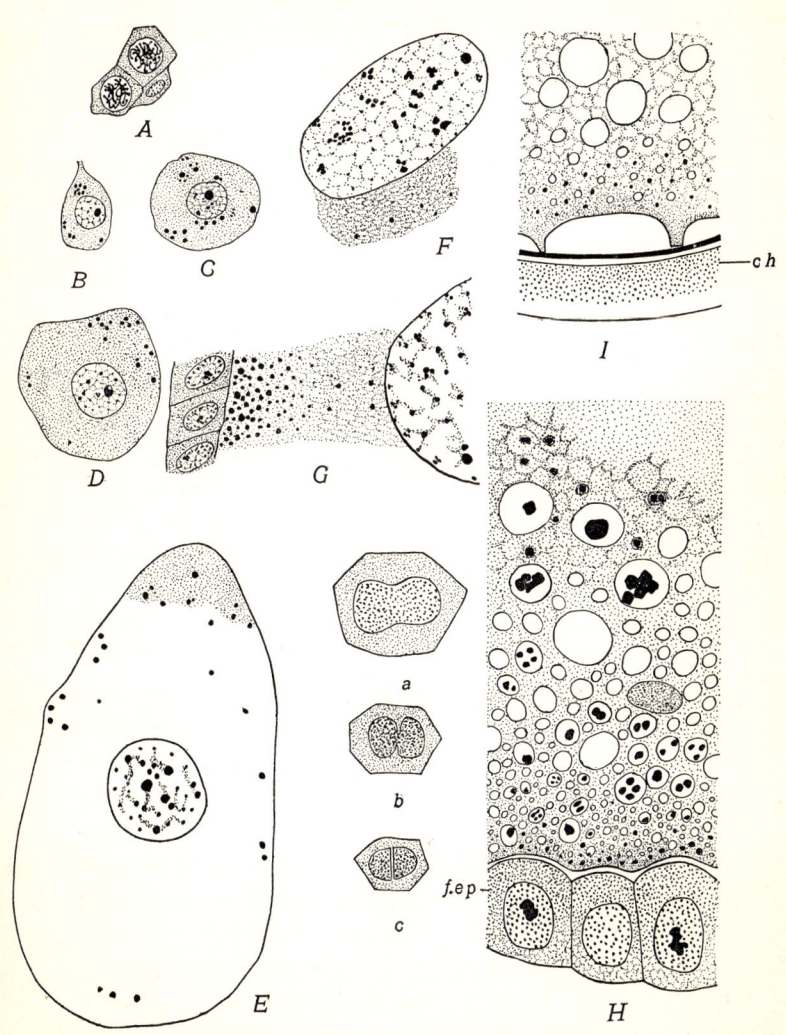

Fig. 8.—*Leptinotarsa decemlineata.* A–H, Stages in the growth of the oöcyte from positions indicated in Fig. 7. a–c = amitotic nuclear division of nurse cells. ch = chorion; f.ep = follicular epithelium.

which stain with crystal violet after Benda's method, and appear to be mitochondrial in nature. At a slightly later stage (Fig. 8, *C*; position *C* in Fig. 7) the nucleus is larger and contains several small spherical chromatic bodies besides the nucleolus. The cytoplasm has increased more rapidly in volume and a corresponding increase in the number of mitochondrial granules has also taken place. Further growth results in an increase in the volume of both nucleus and cytoplasm (Fig. 8, *D*; position *D* in Fig. 7), and a slight increase in the number of mitochondria. Whether these bodies developed de novo or by division of the preëxisting granules could not be determined.

In succeeding stages growth is very rapid. The cytoplasm (Fig. 8, *E*; position *E* in Fig. 7) still remains homogeneous except for the mitochondria, which increase slightly in size and become situated as a rule near the periphery. The nucleus at this time contains a large number of chromatin granules and a diffuse reticulum. Part of an older oöcyte is shown in Fig. 8, *F* (position *F* in Fig. 7); the cytoplasm has assumed a reticular appearance; the mitochondrial granules are present in greater numbers, and the nucleus is larger, oval in shape, and contains a distinct reticulum with many chromatin bodies of various sizes. A still older oöcyte (Fig. 8, *G*; position *G* in Fig. 7) is interesting particularly because of the rapid increase in the mitochondria and the localization of these near the periphery. From this stage on the character of the contents changes until, as shown in Fig. 7, the central part of the oöcyte consists of homogeneous cytoplasm (cy), and the outer region of the cytoplasm is crowded with granules and spherical bodies of various sizes. Apparently the mitochondria lying near the periphery (Fig. 8, H) increase in size, gradually losing their affinity for the crystal violet stain and swelling up until they constitute the large yolk globules so numerous in the mature egg. All stages in the evolution of these bodies are illustrated at this time as represented in Fig. 8, H. In the meantime material is brought into the egg through the egg string from the nurse cells, thus probably adding several sorts of granules to the contents of the oöcyte.

The growth period in the male germ-cell cycle is not so striking as in the female, since many spermatozoa of small size are produced, whereas only comparatively few large eggs develop. An increase in the size of the ultimate spermatogonia may occur, however, but the multiplication and growth periods are not nearly so distinct as in the case of the oögonia. In testes which are composed of cysts of spermatogonia there is evidence in some cases that all of the germ cells in a single cyst are descendants of a single spermatogonium. The proof for this seems certain in the potato beetle, where I have been able to follow the formation of the cysts by means of an uninterrupted series of stages (Hegner, 1914*a*).

7. MATURATION. Maturation or the ripening of the eggs and spermatozoa comprises a series of events which results in a reduction in the number

42 GERM-CELL CYCLE IN ANIMALS

of chromosomes and the amount of chromatin in the germ cells. Typically, both male and female germ cells divide twice during the process of matura-

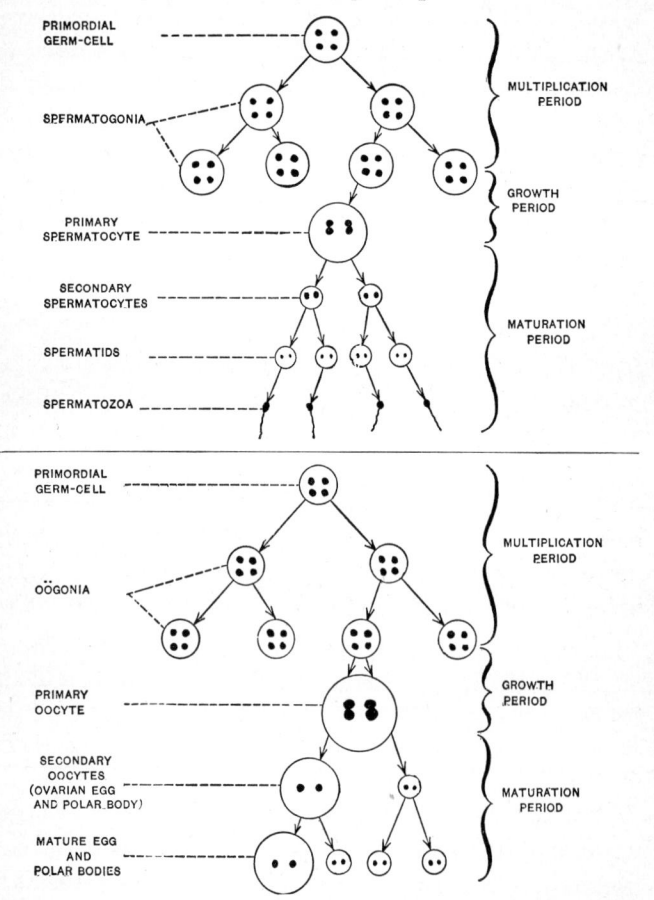

Fig. 9.— Diagrams illustrating (above) the stages of spermatogenesis and (below) of oögenesis. The primordial germ cell is represented as possessing four chromosomes.

tion, and as shown in Fig. 9 these divisions result in the production of four functional spermatozoa in the male, and one functional egg and three polar bodies (abortive eggs) in the female. This increase in the number of cells is not, however, the most important phase of the maturation process, since a large part of our knowledge of the physical basis of heredity has been derived from studies of the behavior of the chromatin at this time. This subject will be dealt with more fully in Chapter IX, and for the present only a brief account of events need be given.

The first thing to be noted is that the mitoses leading to the division of the germ cells during maturation differ from those of ordinary cell multiplication. The germ cells, when they are ready for the maturation divisions, are known as primary oöcytes and primary spermatocytes. The nuclei of these cells possess the complete or diploid number of chromosomes, characteristic of somatic cells; but after maturation the eggs and spermatozoa contain only one-half of the original diploid number, or the haploid number. These mitoses are consequently called reducing or meiotic. The details of these mitoses differ in male and female germ cells and in different species of animals.

During and at the close of the growth period in the male the chromatin granules form a spireme which condenses at one side of the nucleus, a condition known as synizesis. After a time the spireme again spreads throughout the nucleus, but is now divided into segments, the chromosomes, which are only haploid in number. The reduction from the diploid to the haploid number is brought about by the union of the chromosomes in pairs, a condition called synapsis. Each of the haploid chromosomes thus consists of two of the diploid chromosomes and is said to be bivalent. That one of the chromosomes of each pair is of maternal origin, *i.e.*, is a descendant of a chromosome present in the egg at the time of fertilization, and the other of paternal origin, *i.e.*, a descendant of one brought into the egg by the spermatozoön, seems to be well established. The final act of fertilization, therefore, occurs at this point in the germ-cell cycle — an act of much greater significance than that of the union of the egg and spermatozoön. Furthermore, there is considerable evidence that the chromosomes differ one from another and that in synapsis corresponding (homologous) chromosomes unite. The importance of such a union from a theoretical standpoint will be discussed later.

The nuclei now prepare for the two maturation mitoses. In many nematodes, annelids, and arthropods these are characterized by the formation of tetrads. Divisions of this sort may be illustrated as in Fig. 10. The diploid number of chromosomes is for convenience supposed to be four, as in the spermatogonium *A*. During the spermatogonial divisions these divide as in *B*, so that each daughter cell receives the diploid number, four. After synapsis, however, each of the haploid chromosomes of the

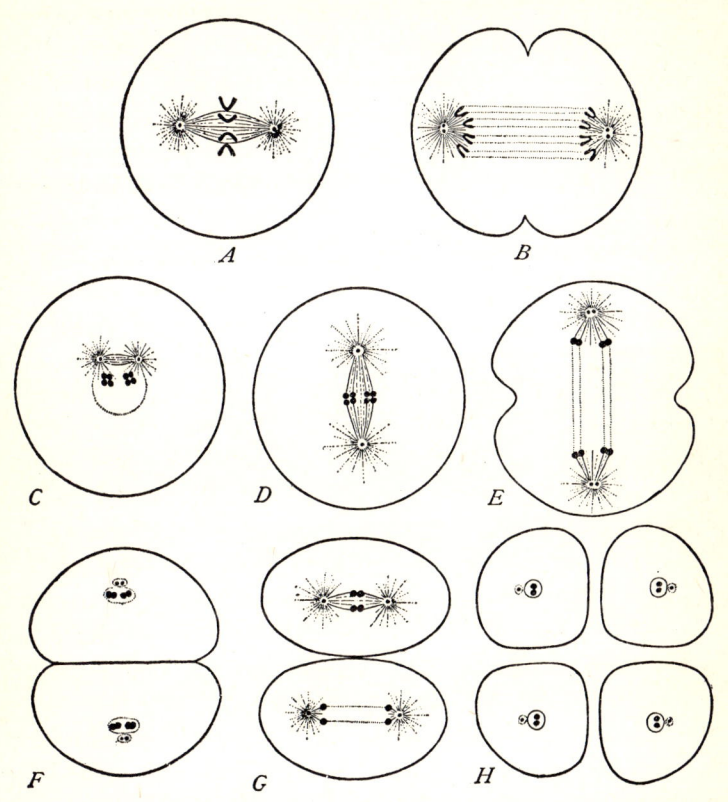

Fig. 10. — Diagrams showing the essential facts of reduction in the male. The somatic number of chromosomes is supposed to be four. *A, B*, division of the spermatogonia, showing the full number (four) of chromosomes. *C*, primary spermatocyte preparing for division; the chromatin forms two tetrads. *D, E, F*, first division to form two secondary spermatocytes, each of which receives two dyads. *G, H*, division of the two secondary spermatocytes to form four spermatids. Each of the latter receives two single chromosomes and a centrosome which passes into the middle piece of the spermatozoön. (*After Wilson.*)

primary spermatocyte is seen to be divided into four parts, thus forming in this case two tetrads (*C*). During the division of the primary spermatocyte, as shown in *D*, *E*, and *F*, half of each tetrad, or two dyads, passes to each daughter cell. The division of the daughter cells, which are known as secondary spermatocytes (*G H*), results in the separation of the two parts of each dyad so that each of the four spermatids (*H*) receives one member of each original tetrad or two monads. Thus the chromosomes (monads) of the spermatids (*H*) are already formed in the primary spermatocytes (*C*) by two divisions; whereas the nuclear and cell divisions do not occur until later. The spermatids (*H*), which proceed to metamorphose into spermatozoa, possess, therefore, only two chromosomes, *i.e.*, one-half of the number present in the spermatogonia (*A*) and somatic cells.

Tetrad formation does not occur in most animals; but usually the members of the bivalent chromosomes become separated on the first maturation spindle, the pairs appearing *U*-, *V*-, or ring-shaped, as in Fig. 62. Each secondary spermatocyte receives one-half of each haploid, bivalent chromosome. The second maturation mitosis then ensues, during which each daughter cell is provided with one-half of each chromosome as in ordinary mitotic division. Because of the peculiar behavior of the chromosomes the first division is often called the heterotype, whereas the second is known as the homotype division. The final results are the same whether tetrads are formed or not, each spermatid containing the haploid number of chromosomes.

The maturation of the egg differs in no very important respects from the process as it has been described in the male cells. Tetrads may or may not be formed according to the species, and the mature egg and polar bodies each contain the haploid number of chromosomes. Two phases of the maturation of the egg may be referred to here: (1) when the nucleus of the primary oöcyte prepares for division a considerable amount of chromatin separates from the chromosomes and is lost in the cytoplasm. The size of the chromosomes is thus diminished, but no entire chromosomes are lost. (2) The cellular divisions are very unequal, the polar bodies being very small as compared with the rest of the egg. The chromatin content of the polar bodies, however, is equal to that of the much larger egg. In the male all of the four spermatids are functional, but in the female only the egg survives, the polar bodies degenerating. As a rule two polar bodies are produced, but in certain cases of parthenogenesis (rotifers, CLADOCERA, OSTRACODA, and aphids) only one is formed. Rarely the first polar body divides into two.

8. FERTILIZATION. Eggs that develop parthenogenetically are ready to begin a new germ-cell cycle as soon as they become mature; but the eggs of the majority of species must be fertilized before they are able to develop. Fertilization may be defined as the fusion of an egg with a spermatozoön and the resulting processes of rearrangement of the egg

contents which result in the formation of a uninuclear cell, the zygote. As a rule one spermatozoön only enters the egg (monospermy); but in a few species (certain insects, selachians, tailed amphibians, reptiles, and birds) many spermatozoa may normally fuse with the egg (physiological polyspermy). The spermatozoön, which consists usually of three rather distinct parts, the head, the middle piece, and tail, may become entirely embedded within the egg substance, or the tail may be left outside, or, in exceptional cases, only the head succeeds in entering.

The union of the egg and spermatozoön may occur before, during, or after the polar body formation (Fig. 11). If the spermatozoön enters before the maturation of the egg is completed (*A*), its head transforms into a nucleus equal in size to that of the egg (*C*); the middle piece dissolves, giving rise to a centrosome which inaugurates the formation of a spindle with asters (*B*); and the tailpiece apparently takes no active part in the fertilization processes. The middle piece also does not seem to be necessary for the formation of the centrosomes and asters. The nucleus of the spermatozoön and that of the mature egg approach each other and come into contact between the asters (*C*). Then the nuclear walls dissolve; a spireme which segments into the haploid number of chromosomes is produced by each nucleus, and the first cleavage spindle of the developing egg results. This spindle bears the haploid number of chromosomes from the spermatozoön and a like number from the egg nucleus

ACCOUNT OF THE GERM-CELL CYCLE 49

and thus the diploid or somatic number of chromosomes is regained.

When the spermatozoön enters an egg which has completed polar-body formation, the head does not

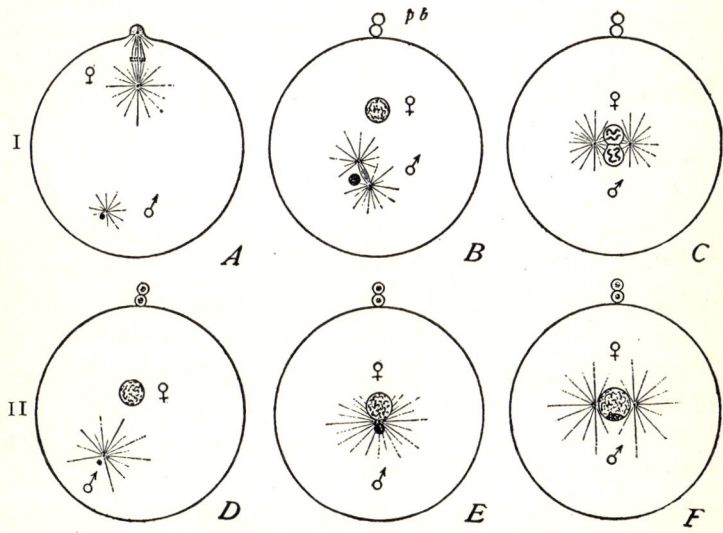

Fig. 11.— Diagrams of two principal types of fertilization. I. Polar bodies formed after the entrance of the spermatozoa (annelids, mollusks, flat-worms). II. Polar bodies formed before entrance (echinoderms).

A, sperm-nucleus and centrosome at ♂; first polar body forming at ♀. *B*, polar bodies formed; approach of the nuclei. *C*, union of the nuclei. *D*, approach of the nuclei. *E*, union of the nuclei. *F*, cleavage-nucleus. (*After Wilson*.)

have time to transform into a nucleus as large as the egg nucleus, but nevertheless fuses with the latter (Fig. 11, *D*, *E*, *F*). Although the two nuclei are very unequal in size, they possess an equal amount of chromatin and furnish an equal number of chromosomes to the first cleavage spindle.

As already indicated, perhaps the most essential phase in the fertilization process does not occur until the homologous maternal and paternal chromosomes unite during synapsis, when the germ cells of the new individual become mature. The immediate results of fertilization are: (1) the inauguration of the development of the egg, (2) the increase of the chromosomes from the haploid to the diploid (somatic) number, and (3) the union of hereditary substances from, as a rule, two individuals.

This completes the last stage in the germ-cell cycle of animals. Many extremely important and interesting phases of the subject have had to be omitted from the account. Certain of these will be more fully discussed in succeeding chapters, especially those concerned with the early history of the germ cells during embryological development, but for the details of the nutrition, growth, maturation, and fertilization of the germ cells, the reader must be referred to other sources (Wilson, 1900; Jenkinson, 1913; Kellicott, 1913).

CHAPTER III

THE GERM-CELL CYCLE IN THE PÆDOGENETIC FLY, MIASTOR

Thus far in only one genus of animals has the history of the germ cells from one generation to the next been followed in detail through the entire cycle. This is a genus of flies, *Miastor*, of the family Cecidomyidæ. One species, *Miastor metraloas*, occurs in Europe and has there been studied especially by Leuckart (1865), Metschnikoff (1865, 1866), and Kahle (1908), and the only other species that has been investigated is *M. americana* (Hegner, 1912, 1914a).

Pædogenesis in *Miastor* was discovered by Wagner in 1862, and was confirmed by Meinert in 1864. In 1865 the first investigations of its embryological development were published by Leuckart and Metschnikoff. These were the earliest accounts of the keimbahn in any animals. Only a glance at Metschnikoff's report is necessary to convince one of the favorableness of *Miastor* as material for germ-cell studies. The primordial germ cell is shown to be established at a very early period in the cleavage of the egg, and the descendants of the primordial germ cell are quite easily distinguishable from other cells in the body even in *in toto* preparations. In spite of the work of the above named investigators there were many who were not convinced that pædogenesis occurs in the genus, and the larvæ which were known to develop within the bodies of other larvæ were considered by these skeptics as parasites. However, the results of Kahle's (1908) studies, which have been decisively confirmed (Hegner, 1912, 1914a), have finally settled the question in favor of pædogenesis.

Previous to 1910 no specimens of the genus *Miastor* had been recognized in this country, but on Oct. 5 of that year, Dr. E. P. Felt found them in great abundance, living in the partially decayed inner bark and in the sapwood of a chestnut rail. With material supplied by Dr. Felt, the writer has been able to follow the entire keimbahn in these insects. Pædogenetic reproduction normally occurs during the spring, summer, and autumn, multiplication being arrested during the cold winter months. This method of reproduction is interrupted in midsummer by the appearance of male and female adults.

The larva of *Miastor* possesses two ovaries, one on either side of the body in the tenth or eleventh segment. Each ovary (Fig. 12) consists of typically thirty-two oöcytes (*oöc.n*); these are inclosed in a cellular envelope (*en*). Associated with each oöcyte is a group of mesoderm cells which function as nurse cells (*n.c.*) and together with the oöcyte are surrounded by a follicular epithelium (*f.ep*). The nurse cells furnish nutrition to the growing oöcytes,

THE PÆDOGENETIC FLY, MIASTOR 53

gradually becoming reduced as the oöcytes increase in size. Finally the oöcyte (and accompanying nurse cells), still surrounded by the follicular epithelium,

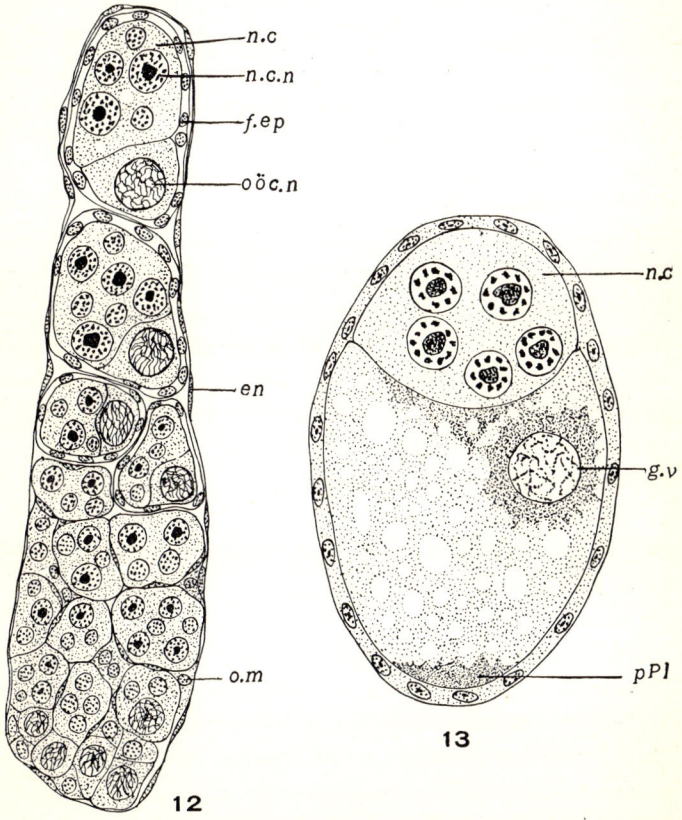

Fig. 12. — *Miastor americana*. Longitudinal section through an ovary. *en* = envelop; *f.ep* = follicular epithelium; *n.c* = nurse chamber; *n.c.n* = nurse-cell nucleus; *o.m* = mesoderm; *oöc.n* = oöcyte nucleus.

Fig. 13. — *Miastor americana*. Longitudinal section through a nearly full-grown oöcyte. *g.v* = germinal vesicle; *n.c* = nurse chamber; *pPl* = pole-plasm.

becomes separated from the rest of the ovary and is forced by the movements of the larva into some other part of its body. Here it continues its growth and development at the expense of the tissues of the mother-larva. Not all of the oöcytes (thirty-two in each ovary) complete their development, since usually only from five to seventeen young are produced by a single mother-larva. Those oöcytes that do not perish pass through the stages described in the following paragraphs.

Figure 13 represents the condition of an oöcyte just before the initiation of the maturation processes. The nucleus, or germinal vesicle ($g.v.$), is eccentrically placed and nearer the anterior than the posterior end of the cell. The nurse chamber has greatly decreased in volume.

The contents of the oöcyte are not homogeneous, but several distinct regions can be distinguished. Near the nurse chamber is a body of cytoplasm evidently elaborated by the nurse cells, and at the posterior end is an accumulation which we may call the pole-plasm (pPl) and which is of particular interest since it is intimately associated with the formation of the primordial germ cell.

The maturation division occurs soon after the stage just described has been attained. The germinal vesicle, which lies near the periphery of the oöcyte, breaks down, and the chromatin contained within it becomes aggregated into about twenty chromosomes. As a result of the maturation division (Fig. 14) a polar body ($p.b$) and the female pronucleus (*f.n*) are produced. The nucleus of the polar body divides by mitosis and the two nuclei thus formed

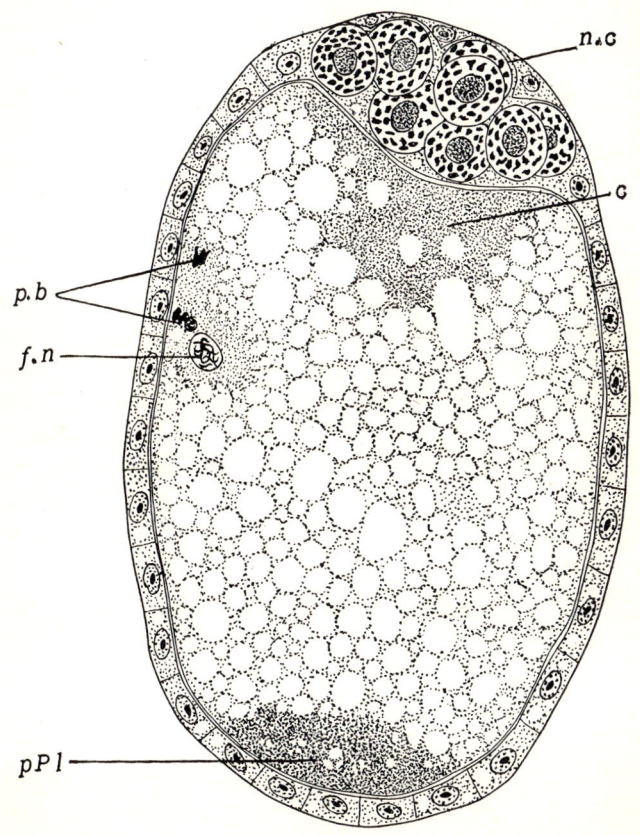

Fig. 14. — *Miastor americana*. Longitudinal section through mature egg. *c* = cytoplasm; *f.n* = female nucleus; *n.c* = nurse chamber; *p.b* = polar bodies; *pPl* = pole-plasm.

remain within the egg substance near the periphery for a considerable period (Fig. 14), but finally disintegrate and disappear, apparently without performing any function. As in most other animals, these polar bodies may be considered abortive eggs. The female pronucleus moves into the central anterior part of the egg where it becomes embedded in the cytoplasmic mass near the nurse chamber. It may now be designated as the cleavage nucleus, since the eggs of *Miastor* develop without fertilization and hence no male pronucleus is present to unite with it. The cleavage divisions take place by mitosis, and, as in most of the ARTHROPODA, the early cleavage nuclei are not separated by cell walls, but simply move apart after each successive division. The egg during this period is thus a syncytium within which the limits of the cells are difficult to define.

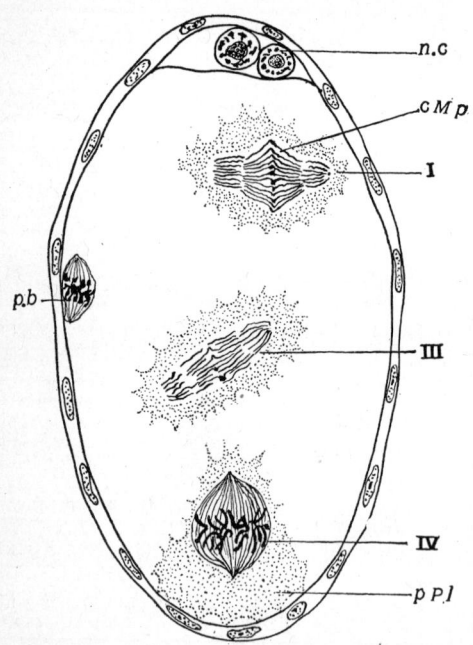

FIG. 15. — *Miastor metraloas*. Three of the four division figures (I, III, IV) of the four- to eight-cell stage represented. cMp = chromosome middle plate; $n.c$ = nurse chamber; $p.b$ = polar body; pPl = pole-plasm. (*From Kahle, 1908*.)

THE PÆDOGENETIC FLY, MIASTOR

The nuclei present at the four-cell stage occupy rather definite positions and may be numbered for convenience by the Roman numerals I, II, III, and IV, as indicated in Fig. 15. The division from the four- to the eight-cell stage is a very important one, since it is at this time that the primordial

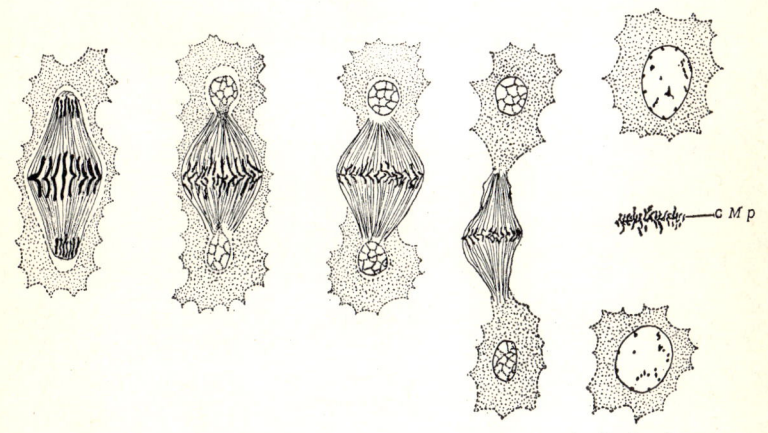

Fig. 16. — *Miastor metraloas*. Stages in the chromatin-diminution process. (*From Kahle, 1908.*)

germ cell is established. Each of the four nuclei divides by mitosis, but nuclei I, II, and III undergo a chromatin-diminution process during which a large part of their chromatin remains in the cytoplasm when the daughter nuclei reform. The details of such a process are indicated in Fig. 16. Nucleus IV, on the other hand, divides as usual (Fig. 15) and each daughter nucleus receives one-half of its chromatin. One of these daughter nuclei becomes embedded in that peculiar mass of cytoplasm at the posterior end which we have called the pole-plasm, and apparently all of the pole-plasm, together with this

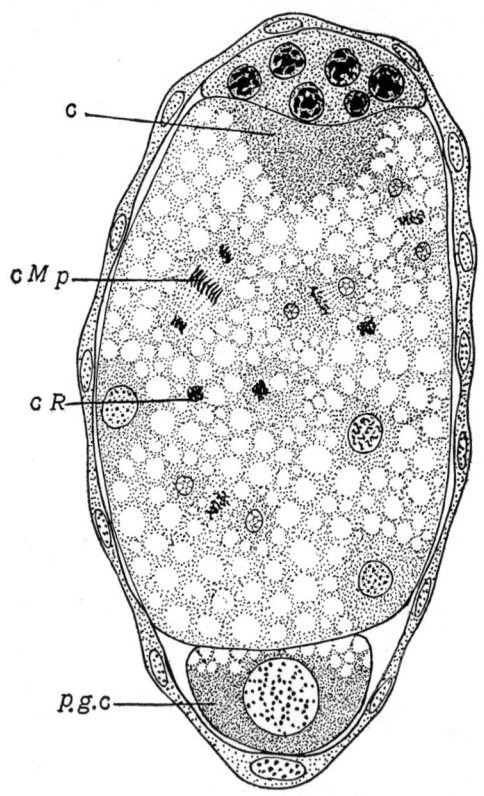

FIG. 17.—*Miastor americana*. Longitudinal section of egg with one germ cell (*p.g.c.*) and nuclei undergoing chromatin-diminution process. *c* = cytoplasm; *c M p* = chromosome middle plate; *c R* = chromatin remains.

nucleus, is then cut off from the egg (Fig. 17). This cell, as has been conclusively proven by studies of later stages, is the primordial germ cell. At this time, then, the egg consists of one primordial germ cell provided with a nucleus with an undiminished amount of chromatin, and a syncytium containing seven nuclei of which the sister nucleus of the primordial germ cell contains a complete supply of chromatin, whereas the other six nuclei have lost part of this chromatin material. Reference to the diagram on page 65 will assist in making more clear this stage and the stages yet to be described.

The next developmental process is the mitotic division of the seven nuclei in the syncytium thus producing a fifteen-cell stage (Fig. 17). The sister nucleus of that of the primordial germ cell now undergoes a chromatin-diminution process and the other six nuclei in the syncytium pass through a second chromatin-diminution process. As a result every nucleus in the egg has lost a part of its chromatin except that of the primordial germ cell which still contains a complete amount. The further history of the somatic nuclei does not differ essentially from that of the somatic nuclei in other insects. They increase in number by mitosis, migrate to the periphery, and there are cut off by cell walls forming a single layer of cells over the entire surface except where interrupted at the posterior end by the primordial germ cells. Next, a thickening of the cells occurs on the ventral surface, thus forming the ventral plate. From this plate most of the embryo arises; it lengthens until the anterior or cephalic end almost reaches the anterior end of the egg, and until the posterior or tail end has been pushed around for a considerable distance on the dorsal surface. A broadening and a shortening of this germ-band then takes place so that the posterior end of the embryo coincides with the posterior end of the egg and the edges of the embryo grow laterally around the egg until they meet in the median dorsal line. Meanwhile various changes have taken place within the embryo, among which is the formation of the germ glands or ovaries.

Returning now to a consideration of the germ cells, we shall see that it is possible to trace the descendants of the primordial germ cell with comparative ease. This cell divides by mitosis, forming two oögonia approximately equal in size (Fig. 18). These two then produce four oögonia of the second order (Fig. 19), and these in turn increase by mitosis, forming eight oögonia of the third order (Fig. 20). When this stage is reached a period sets in during which the oögonia do not divide, but are apparently passively carried about by the somatic tissues as shown in Fig. 21, where they occupy a position near the end of the tail fold.

One of the most satisfactory conditions in the keimbahn of *Miastor* is the comparatively large size and peculiar structure of the primordial germ cells leaving in the mind of the observer no doubt as to the identity of the cells concerned. Throughout the entire embryonic development of this insect the germ cells are considerably larger than any of the somatic cells. The nuclei are correspondingly

THE PÆDOGENETIC FLY, MIASTOR

large and are characterized by the possession of a number of spherical chromatin granules which are evenly scattered about in the nuclear sap.

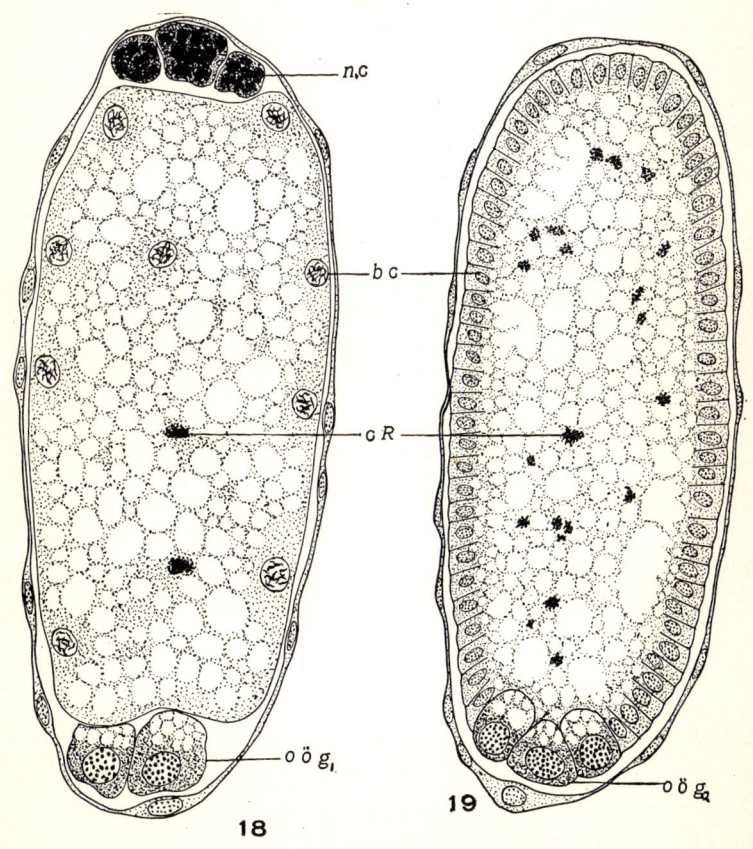

Fig. 18. — *Miastor americana*. Longitudinal section through an egg with two oögonia ($oög_1$). bc = blastoderm nucleus; cR = chromatin remains.

Fig. 19. — *Miastor americana*. Longitudinal section through an egg with four oögonia ($oög_2$).

Even under the lower powers of the compound microscope the germ cells stand out with great distinctness and could not possibly be confused with any other cells in the embryo.

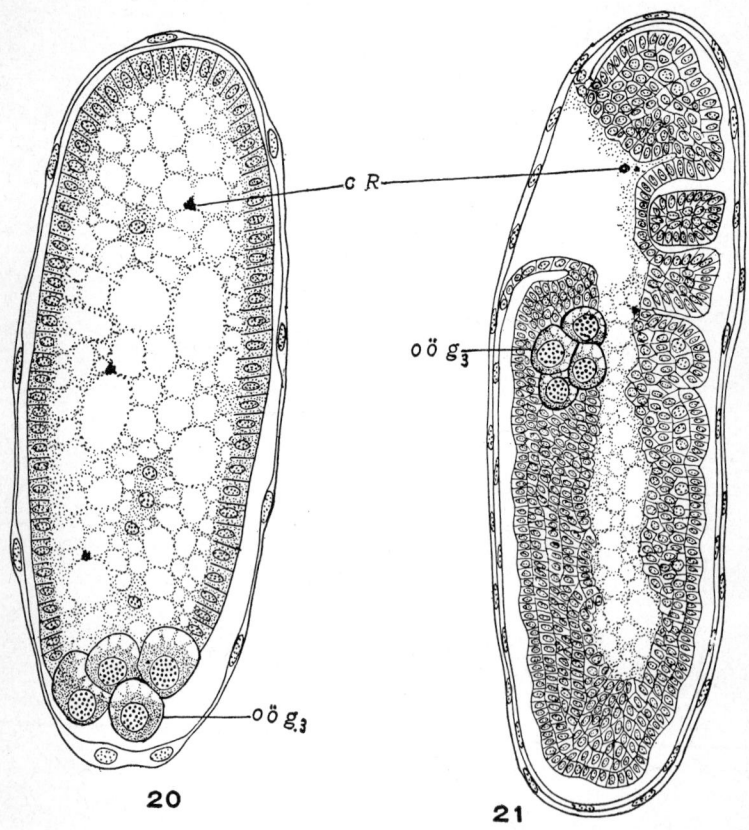

FIG. 20.—*Miastor americana*. Longitudinal section through an egg with eight oögonia ($oög_3$). cR = chromatin remains.

FIG. 21.—*Miastor americana*. Sagittal section through embryo showing oögonia ($oög_3$) near end of tail fold.

During the shortening and broadening of the germ band the group of eight oögonia of the third order becomes separated into two rows of four each — one row on either side of the body in the region of the eleventh segment (Fig. 22). Each group of four oögonia then becomes surrounded by a layer of mesoderm cells and forms a more or less spherical body which may now be called an ovary (Fig. 23). Soon after this occurs, the oögonia begin to divide again (Fig. 23, *a*) and by successive mitoses there are formed oögonia of the fourth, fifth (Fig. 24), and sixth orders. This completes the number of oögonia, which is typically thirty-two in each ovary, and provides us with the only case thus far on record where the number of oögonial divisions during the multiplication period in the history of the germ cells is known (Fig. 26).

There are then six of these oögonial divisions between the formation of the single primordial germ cell and the production of the complete number of oögonia in the two ovaries. Some of the oögonia of the fifth order may be prevented from dividing, in which case of course there are less than thirty-two germ cells in each ovary. And not all of the oögonia in the ovary succeed in developing into oöcytes and larvæ, since a struggle for supremacy takes place among the germ cells resulting in the survival of only a few offspring, as may be determined by the fact, already referred to, that one larva gives rise as a rule to only from five to seventeen daughter larvæ. Each oögonium that succeeds in developing becomes

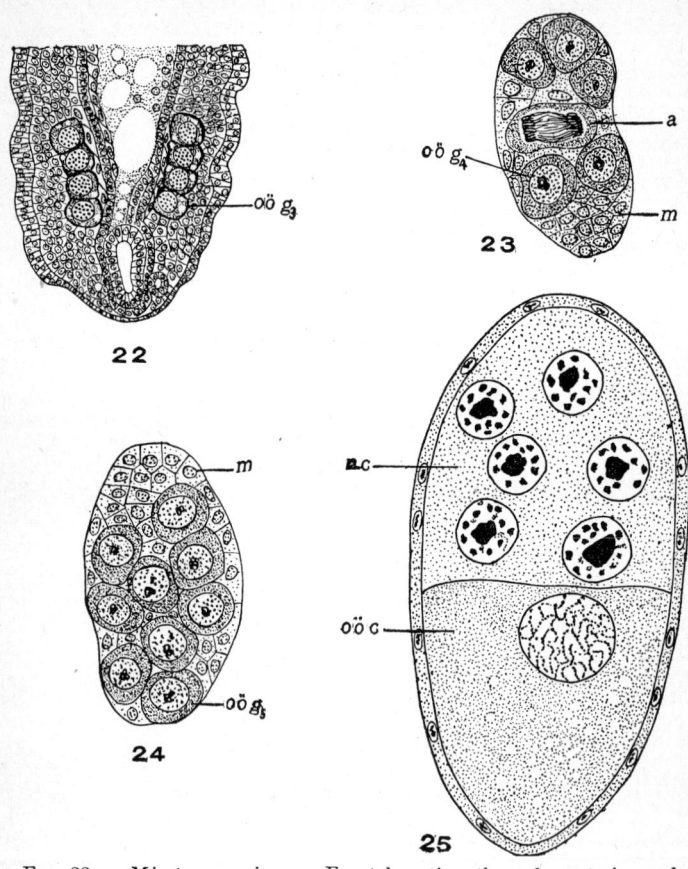

FIG. 22.— *Miastor americana.* Frontal section through posterior end of embryo showing oögonia ($oög_3$) forming two rows of four each.
FIG. 23.— *Miastor americana.* Ovary containing sixteen oögonia ($oög_4$), one dividing by mitosis (a). m = mesoderm.
FIG. 24.— *Miastor americana.* Ovary containing thirty-two oögonia ($oög_5$). m = mesoderm.
FIG. 25.— *Miastor americana.* Young oöcyte ($oöc$) with nurse cells ($n.c$).

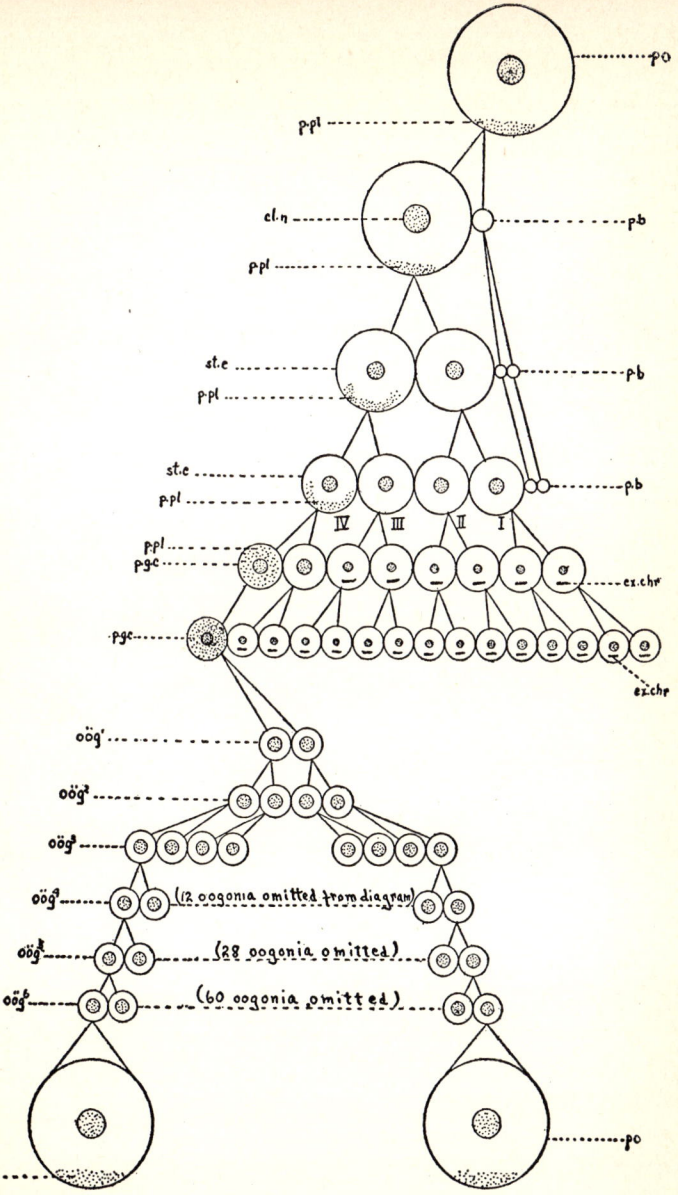

FIG. 26. — *Miastor americana.* Diagram illustrating origin and history of germ cells from one generation to the next. *cl.n* = cleavage nucleus; *ex.chr* = extruded chromatin; *oög* = oögonia; *p.b* = polar body; *p.g.c* = primordial germ cell; *p.o* = primary oöcyte; *p.pl* = polar plasm. *st.c* = stem cell. (65)

provided with a group of about twenty-four mesoderm cells which form a syncytium at the anterior end and may be called nurse cells (Fig. 25, *n.c*), since they furnish food material to the oöcyte. Another group of mesoderm cells forms a cellular layer about the oöcyte and nurse cells, and thus constitutes a follicular epithelium. At this stage the oöcytes break away from the ovary and become distributed in various parts of the body of the mother-larva.

Several facts regarding the germ-cell cycle of *Miastor* deserve special emphasis: (1) There is no stage in the entire keimbahn when the germ cells cannot be distinguished without the least difficulty; (2) the number of oögonial divisions has been definitely established, and so it is no longer necessary to make the general statement that the germ cells pass through n divisions during the period of multiplication, since here n is undoubtedly six; (3) the descendants of the primordial germ cell are only germ cells, *i.e.*, the primordial germ cell does not give rise to both oögonia and nurse cells as seems to be the case in most other insects; (4) chromatin-diminution processes take place during the mitotic divisions of the nuclei from the four- to the eight-cell stage and form the eight- to the fifteen-cell stage of such a nature that all of the cells in the embryo finally are deprived of part of their chromatin with the exception of the primordial germ cell which retains the complete amount of this substance; (5) the primordial germ cell is established at the eight-cell stage and is the first complete cell formed in

THE PÆDOGENETIC FLY, MIASTOR

embryonic development; and (6) the contents of the primordial germ cell consist of the nucleus with undiminished chromatin and of all of the pole-plasm and apparently no other part of the egg substance.

The fact that only the primordial germ cell receives a complete amount of chromatin is of particular interest, since a similar condition has long been known in the case of *Ascaris* as we shall see later. It may also be noted in this place that the cytoplasmic substance in the primordial germ cell may be recognized as the pole-plasm in the growing oöcyte. Attempts have been made to determine the origin of this pole-plasm, but so far without success. It may be distinguished from the rest of the egg contents by its position at the posterior end and because of its affinity for certain dyes. It appears shortly before the maturation division is initiated, but no transition stages have been discovered — it has been either present or entirely absent in the preparations thus far studied. If we consider the history of this substance from the formation of the primordial germ cell to the growth period of the oöcytes produced by this primordial germ cell, we may conclude that at the time the multiplication period ends the pole-plasm has become equally distributed among the sixty-four oögonia. Then ensues the growth period during which the pole-plasm cannot be distinguished. Later, however, just before maturation, pole-plasm substance reappears which is equal in amount to that contained in the primordial germ cell of the preceding generation or to that contained in all of the sixty-four oögonia which descended from that primordial germ cell. That is, the pole-plasm of the oöcyte under discussion has in some way increased until its mass is sixty-four times as great as that of the oögonium before the growth period began. How this increase has taken place can only be conjectured. The pole-plasm in the oögonium may have produced new material of its own kind either by the division of its constituent particles or by the influence of its presence. In any case a localization of this substance occurs at the posterior end of the egg just before maturation. Therefore, although we can follow the germ cells in *Miastor* throughout their entire cycle without difficulty, there are certain problems, such as the history of the pole-plasm during the growth period of the oöcytes, which still remain unsolved.

CHAPTER IV

THE SEGREGATION OF THE GERM CELLS IN PORIFERA, CŒLENTERATA, AND VERTEBRATA

THE history of the germ cells has not been seriously investigated in a number of groups of animals, but, as will be demonstrated in Chapters V and VI, there are many species belonging to widely separated groups in the animal series in which the germ-cell cycle is almost as well known as in *Miastor*. On the other hand, the three phyla to be discussed in this chapter have been carefully studied for many years, but an early segregation of germ cells has not yet been established in them to the satisfaction of a majority of investigators. It seems strange because of the uncertainty of the morphological continuity of the germ cells in these animals that one of these groups, the CŒLENTERATA, should have furnished the material upon which Weismann based his elaboration of the germ-plasm theory.

1. PORIFERA

Sponges reproduce asexually by budding and by the formation of gemmules, and sexually by means of ova and spermatozoa. Budding occurs in almost all sponges. In most cases the buds remain attached to the parent (continuous budding); but in some species the buds become free (discontinuous budding).

Gemmules are groups of cells (statocytes) which occur at certain times of the year in the bodies of fresh-water sponges and in many marine species. These gemmules acquire a resistant covering and serve to preserve the race during the winter in the north or the dry season in the south. The peculiar "budding" observed in *Tethya* by Désö (1879, 1880) may be a sort of gemmule formation (see p. 76).

The eggs and spermatozoa are situated in the middle layer (so-called mesoderm) and in most cases seem to become ripe at different times in the same sponge. Fertilization is apparently similar to this process in other METAZOA. The fertilized ovum is holoblastic; the free-swimming ciliated larva becomes fixed, and then metamorphoses into a young sponge.

The body wall of the sponge consists of two distinct layers, an outer dermal layer and an inner gastral layer, and an intermediate jelly-like stratum containing ameboid wandering cells. The various sorts of cells in these layers are indicated in the table on page 71 (from Minchin, 1900, p. 62).

The reproductive cells lie in the jelly-like middle layer, but all of the cells in this layer are not reproductive.

The origin of the archeocytes from which the reproductive cells arise can easily be pointed out in the comparatively simple development of *Clathrina blanca* (Minchin, 1900). In this species a ciliated

TABLE OF THE VARIOUS CLASSES OF CELLS IN SPONGES

Dermal Layer	I. Epithelial stratum	1. Pinacocytes (epithelial cells)
		2. Myocytes (contractile cells)
		3. Gland cells
	II. Porocytes	4. Spongoblasts
		5. Pore cells
		6. Scleroblasts
	III. Skeletogenous stratum	7. Collencytes (stellate cells)
		8. Desmacytes (fiber cells)
		9. Cystencytes (bladder cells)
Gastral Layer	IV. Gastral epithelium	10. Choanocytes (collar cells)
Archæocytes (primordial cells)	V. Amebocytes (wandering cells)	11. Phagocytes (ingestive cells)
		12. Trophocytes (nutritive cells)
		13. Thesocytes (storage cells)
	VI. Tokocytes (reproductive cells)	14. Statocytes (gemmule cells)
		15. Gonocytes (sexual cells)

blastula-like larva is formed (Fig. 27, *A*). At the posterior pole two blastomeres (posterior granular cells, *p.g.c.*) remain undifferentiated; they are much larger than the other cells, are granular, and possess vesicular nuclei. The larva becomes fixed by the anterior pole, and during the metamorphosis that then takes place, the two posterior granular cells, the archeocytes, multiply rapidly, forming a large number of minute cells which resemble certain leucocytes. These are known as amebocytes. By the fourth day the amebocytes become separated into wandering cells or their derivatives and reproductive cells or tokocytes as indicated in the table.

The primordial archeocytes do not always occur in the Clathrinidæ as in *Clathrina blanca*. In some

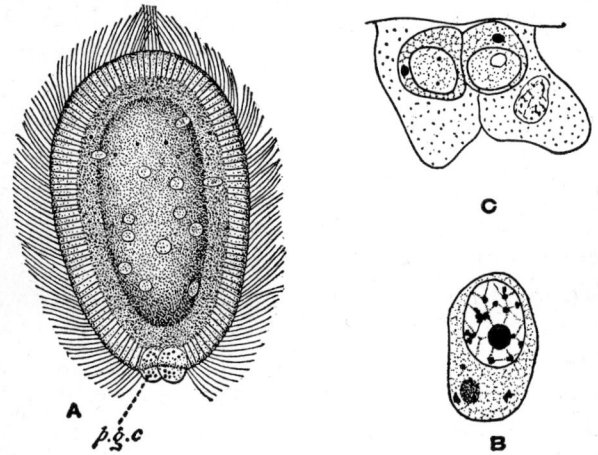

FIG. 27. — *A. Clathrina blanca.* Blastula stage showing posterior granular cells (*p.g.c.*). (*From Minchin, 1900.*) *B.* Oögonium of a sponge containing inclusions in the cytoplasm. (*From Jörgensen, 1909.*) *C.* Two oögonia in the ectoderm of *Hydra fusca*, each with a cytoplasmic inclusion. (*From Downing, 1909.*)

species there is only one; in others four or more appear; and sometimes they are entirely absent. This last condition results from the formation of amebocytes before the fixation of the larva. In many other sponges the archeocytes migrate in at the posterior pole and partially or entirely fill up the segmentation cavity. Comparatively little is known about the embryology of Hexactinellida and

Demospongiæ, and few observations have been made upon their archeocytes. These archeocytes are of the greatest importance since they give rise to the amebocytes and tokocytes (reproductive cells). According to Weltner (1907) both amebocytes and tokocytes are only physiological states of one and the same kind of cell. Many authors have emphasized the importance of the amebocytes, such as Görich (1904), who maintains that this class of cells gives rise not only to the gonocytes, statocytes, and trophocytes, but also to certain pinacocytes. Weltner (1907) goes further than this when he states from studies upon the fresh-water sponge that the sponge could not exist without amebocytes.

The earlier investigators almost invariably considered the germ cells as mesodermal in origin. Lieberkühn (1856) discovered the eggs in *Spongilla* and later (1859) in *Sycandra raphanus*. Sponge eggs were also observed by Kölliker (1864). Haeckel (1872) thought that the eggs were derived from the flagellated cells of the gastral epithelium. Schulze (1875), on the contrary, maintains that they lie deep in the so-called mesoderm; and Fiedler (1888) concludes that in *Spongilla* only certain cells of the middle layer may become germ cells.

Maas (1893) distinguished two sorts of cells in the middle layer; one characterized by uniform, fine-granuled cytoplasm and an oval nucleus containing a very fine net-work of chromatin; the other filled with coarse-granuled cytoplasm and a spherical nucleus containing a deeply staining nucleolus and chromatin aggregated into large masses. Only from the latter do the sex cells arise. These two kinds of cells could be distinguished in larval stages and the early separation of germ cells from somatic cells was pointed out. Maas, however, does not insist that there is here a demonstrated continuity of germ cells, since the cells which become sex-cells are separated from the egg by a long series of generations.

The recent investigations of Jörgensen (1910) on *Sycon raphanus* and *S. setosa* have added considerably to our knowledge of the origin, structure, and early history of the germ cells of sponges. Jörgensen does not agree with Maas (1893) regarding the early segregation of the germ cells from somatic cells, but finds no particular difference between so-called mesoderm cells and wandering or egg cells. It is worthy of note, however, that the youngest recognizable oögonia were found to contain several distinct bodies in their cytoplasm (Fig. 27, *B*).

The method of formation of the gemmules has engaged the attention of many investigators, but several important points concerning it are still in doubt. Gemmule formation is of particular interest since the cells (amebocytes), which by most authorities are said to give rise to the germ cells, are also considered the cells which form the reproductive portion of the gemmules. At least four views have been held concerning the origin of the gemmule cells: (1) Carter (1849) believed that the gemmule is derived from a single cell, the "ovi-bearing cell";

(2) Goette (1886) maintains that the gemmule consists of cells from several germ layers; (3) Carter believed at one time that the gemmule was made up of only one kind of cell; and (4) several authors (Marshall, 1884; Wierzejski, 1886; Zykoff, 1892; Weltner, 1892) believe that a number of cells belonging to several classes are concerned in the origin of the gemmule.

Evans (1900) has described in detail the formation and structure of the gemmules of *Ephydatia blembingia*. In this species the first sign of the formation of a gemmule is the presence of "single cells or groups of cells scattered about chiefly in the dermal membrane; the strands of tissue which support the dermal membrane; and in the tissues situated immediately below the subdermal cavity" (p. 89). No mitotic figures were discovered in these cells and consequently the reproductive part of the gemmule is probably not derived from one mother-cell. These cells wander "through the dermal membrane, and strands of tissue which support the membrane, and become aggregated in groups situated either deep in the tissues of the sponge or even in the strands of tissue above mentioned."

Whether the reproductive cells of the gemmule arise from a single cell by proliferation or represent an aggregation without a common origin is still unsettled, but the latter view is held by most investigators. If they do arise from a single cell, as H. V. Wilson (1902) admits is a possibility, the gemmule formation may be considered a kind of parthenogenesis. If, on the other hand, the reproductive cells of the gemmule are of multiple origin, they may either be looked upon as true germ cells which form a group physiologically equivalent to the morula stage in the development of an egg, or as a collection of regenerative cells capable of producing a new individual.

In this connection should be mentioned the budding of *Tethya* (Désö, 1879–1880) which develops from a group of amebocytes (Maas, 1910) and the gemmules of *Tedania* and *Esperella* (Wilson, 1902) and of hexactinellids (Ijima) which become ciliated larvæ. Wilson has shown " that silicious sponges, when kept in confinement under proper conditions degenerate in such a manner that while the bulk of the sponge dies, the cells in certain regions become aggregated to form lumps of undifferentiated tissue. Such lumps or plasmodial masses, which may be exceedingly abundant, are often of a rounded shape resembling gemmules, more especially the simpler gemmules of marine sponges (*Chalina*, *e.g.*), and were shown to possess in at least one form (*Stylotella*) full regenerative power. When isolated they grow and differentiate, producing perfect sponges " (1907, p. 295). These "lumps of undifferentiated tissue" have also been noted by F. E. Schulze (1904) and recognized as probably reproductive; they have been named by this author, "sorites," and have been called by several authors "artificial gemmules." The process involved in their formation is termed "regressive differentiation." The undifferentiated tissue of which they are composed, undoubtedly consists largely, if not entirely, of amebocytes (Weltner, 1907). These amebocytes are, however, of heterogeneous origin (Maas, 1910), since some of them represent transformed pore cells, whereas the rest are wandering cells.

Even more interesting than these reproductive bodies are the artificial plasmodia produced by Wilson (1907, 1911) in *Microciona*, *Lissodendoryx*, and *Stylotella* and by Müller (1911) in the Spongillidæ. The method and results from a study of *Microciona* as stated by Wilson (1911) are briefly as follows. Branched specimens are cut up and strained into a dish of water through fine bolting cloth. The cells, which are dissociated in this way, "settle down on the bottom of the dish like a fine sediment." Three classes of cells are present: (1) "the most conspicuous and abundant" are unspecialized granular "ameboid cells of the sponge parenchyma (amœbocytes)"; (2) "a great abundance of partially transformed collar cells"; and (3) "more or less spheroidal cells ranging from the size of the granular cells down to much smaller ones."

"Fusion of the granular cells begins immediately and in a few minutes' time most of these have united to form conglomerate masses which at the surface display both blunt and elongated pseudopodia. These masses (plasmodia) soon begin to incorporate the neighboring collar and hyaline cells." "The small conglomerate masses . . . early begin to fuse with one another," and if the tissue is strewn sparsely over a slide, in the course of a week it will be found that the slide is covered with a thin incrusting sponge provided with pores, oscula, canals, and flagellated chambers." Many, at the end of two months, had "developed reproductive bodies (eggs or asexual embryos?) . . ." Whether these reproductive bodies arose from eggs or masses of cells was not determined. "When the plasmodia have metamorphosed and the canals and chambers have developed, the skeleton makes its appearance."

Experiments with *Lissodendoryx* and *Stylotella* were not quite so successful, but plasmodial masses were formed in every case. Further experiments proved that "when the dissociated cells of these two species [*Microciona* and *Lissodendoryx*] are intermingled, they do not fuse with one another, but fusion goes on between the cells and cell masses of one and the same species." A similar result was obtained by intermingling dissociated cells of *Microciona* and *Stylotella*.

DISCUSSION AND SUMMARY. The foregoing account of the origin of the germ cells in sponges shows conclusively that these cells arise in the so-called mesoderm from wandering cells (amebocytes) and that amebocytes are descended from archæocytes which may be distinguished in certain cases very early in embryological development (Fig. 27, *A*, *p.g.c*). Oögonia and spermatogonia have not been recognized by most investigators except in the adult, but Maas (1893) has observed them in the planula. Jörgensen (1910), who has made the most careful study of the development of the oögonia, states that the youngest recognizable oögonia lie in the mesoderm, and his figure (Fig. 27, *B*) shows that they may be distinguished from neighboring cells by certain characteristics, among which is the presence of a darkly staining inclusion. In the adult sponge the amebocytes from which the oögonia and spermatogonia arise occur in the middle layer of all regions of the body, but, as pointed out by Korschelt and Heider (1902), the oögonia and spermatogonia may develop in only certain definite regions (*Plakina monolopha*), or in groups (*Aphysilla violacea*) which contain a more or less definite number of cells and occupy a similar position in each individual (*Euspongia*). Such an aggregation is the most primitive form of ovary.

Some of the amebocytes of the sponge are undoubtedly germ cells (tokocytes) and are able to develop into oögonia or spermatogonia, or to form aggregations (gemmules, " artificial gemmules," " sorites," etc.) which can "regenerate" an entire sponge, but whether the amebocytes that produce oögonia and spermatogonia are the same as the reproductive cells of the gemmules, the regenerative cells of the " artificial gemmules," and amebocytes which form the buds in *Tethya* is still uncertain. It seems probable that they are all alike potentially but develop differently because of the effects of different environmental factors. The distribution of amebocytes with reproductive powers throughout the entire sponge-body accounts for the great regenerative ability of these animals and must also account for the development of plasmodia formed by dissociated cells (Wilson, 1911; Müller, 1911) into adult sponges with all specific characteristics including reproductive bodies.

It therefore seems possible that there may exist in the sponges a continuity of the germ-plasm and that the germ-cell material is distributed among thousands of cells (tokocytes, see Table, p. 71) which are derived from archæocytes, and that under proper conditions these tokocytes may produce oögonia or spermatogonia, or may aggregate to form gemmules or regenerative bodies. This wide distribution of the germ cells is what might be expected in such lowly organized animals. Figure 28 shows the probable history of the germ cells in the PORIFERA from one generation to the next.

2. CŒLENTERATA

The origin of the germ cells in the CŒLENTERATA has been a much debated subject among zoölogists for three-quarters of a century. As early as 1843 van Beneden undertook to determine the germ layer from which the germ cells arise and concluded that the ova originate in the entoderm and that the spermatozoa come from the ectoderm. F. E. Schulze (1871) claims that in *Cordylophora* both the ova and spermatozoa are of ectodermal origin. Kleinenberg (1872), working on *Hydra*, announced that the germ cells are interstitial in origin and, since the interstitial cells arise from the ectoderm,

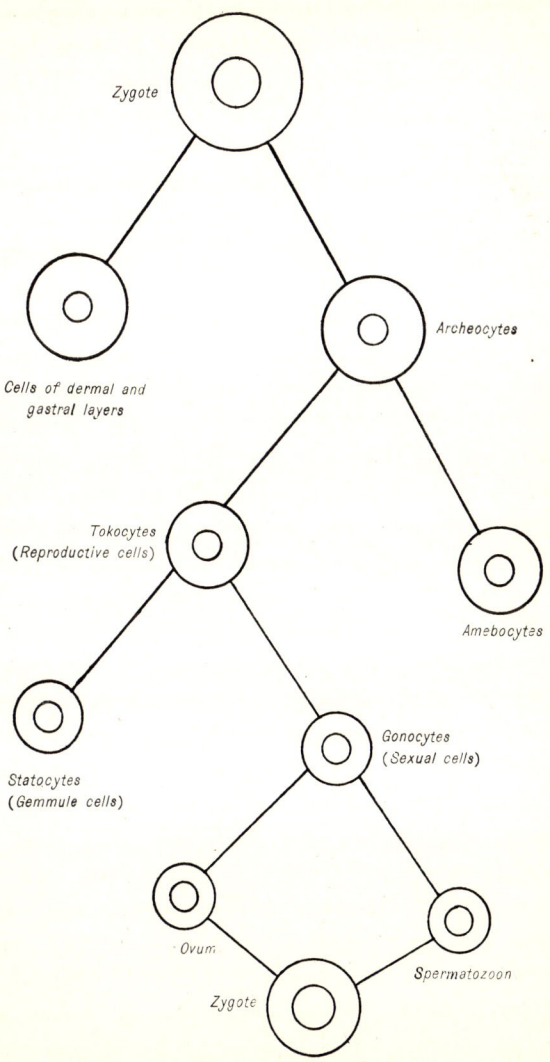

FIG. 28. — Diagram illustrating the probable history of the germ cells in sponges from one generation to the next.

are therefore also ectodermal. Van Beneden (1874), from investigations on *Hydractinia, Clava,* and Campanularidæ, confirms his earlier results and again maintains that the ova arise in the entoderm. The brothers Hertwig (1878) decided that the germ cells of Hydromedusæ arise from the ectoderm and those of the Scyphomedusæ and Anthozoa from the entoderm. In a second paper, Kleinenberg (1881) reports the ova of *Eudendrium* as of ectodermal origin. Varenne (1882) maintains that both the ova and the spermatozoa of half a dozen species examined arise from entoderm cells of the young blastostyle before the appearance of medusa buds. The results of Weismann's extended studies were published in a monograph (1883), and later (1884) a brief general account appeared.

From this time until the present day almost every year has witnessed one or more contributions to the subject of the origin of the germ cells in cœlenterates, and a perusal of this mass of literature shows that the problem is not yet solved.

Hydra. The fresh-water polyp, *Hydra*, has been employed for germ-cell investigations more often than any other cœlenterate, and a number of detailed papers have appeared within the past ten years upon this genus. Among the earlier workers who actually saw the egg should be mentioned Trembley (1744), Rösel V. Rosenhoff (1755), Ehrenberg (1836) and Leydig (1848). The processes involved in oögeneses were not clearly determined, however, until Kleinenberg's classic investigations in 1872, upon which most of the accounts in our zoölogical textbooks are still based. Kleinenberg's researches were followed by those of Korotneff (1883), Nussbaum (1887), Schneider (1890), and Brauer (1891). Investigations of the germ cells of *Hydra* then almost ceased until 1904, when another period of activity in this field began and papers quickly followed one another (Guenther, 1904; Downing, 1905; Hadzi, 1906; Hertwig, R., 1906; Tannreuther, 1908, 1909; Downing, 1909; and Wager, 1909). The following account is based chiefly upon the researches of Downing (1905, 1908, 1909), Tannreuther (1908, 1909), and Wager (1909).

The origin of the male germ cells has been carefully investigated by Downing (1905) and Tannreuther (1909). Previous to Downing's researches all investigators, beginning with Kleinenberg (1872), considered the sex cells as interstitial in origin. Downing, however, believes that germ cells and interstitial cells may be distinct. The sex cells, according to this investigator, are distinguished "by their very large nuclei, extremely granular, and often by the presence of a Nebenkern" (Fig. 27, *C*). "The characters of the sex cells . . . seem constant, and my conclusion would be that at some stage of the embryonic development certain cells are stamped with these characters and that they and their progeny form the sex cells distinct throughout the life of the individual . . . the germ-plasm is then continuous in *Hydra*" (p. 413). This tentative opinion is expressed with more certainty in a later paper (Downing, 1909), since the "distinctive character of the germ cell is more marked in the ovary than in the spermary" (p. 311). Tannreuther (1909), on the other hand, claims that the male germ cells are interstitial in origin, and "the progenitors of the spermatozoa have no special characters by which they can be recognized as germ cells."

The origin of the eggs of *Hydra* is better known than that of the male germ cells. The ova have by most investigators been considered modified interstitial cells. Downing (1908, 1909) disagrees in several respects with the results of Tannreuther and Wager. His most important difference is regarding the question of the origin of the ova directly from interstitial cells or from definite propagative cells that are set aside for reproductive purposes at some stage in the animal's embryonic development. He believes "that in the adult *Hydra* the oögonia (and spermatogonia) are distinctly differentiated as a self-propagating tissue" (p. 310). Wager (1909), on the contrary, claims that it is impossible to prove that eggs do not arise from ordinary interstitial cells; whereas Tannreuther (1909) finds that the primitive ova can be distinguished from interstitial cells "by their large nucleus, nucleolus, and abundance of chromatin, even before the growth of the ovary begins" (p. 205), especially during the breeding season, and admits that "If these sex cells could be distinguished during the budding season as well, it would at least suggest specificity of the germ cells" (p. 205).

By far the most important question arising from a study of the origin of the germ cells of *Hydra* is whether these cells arise from ordinary interstitial cells, as is claimed by most investigators, or whether they originate from cells that are set aside for reproductive purposes at some stage of development, as Downing maintains. If the latter be true, "the germ-plasm is then continuous in *Hydra*" (Downing, 1905, p. 413).

Wager (1909) thinks the presence of special propagation cells to be "extremely improbable" and Tannreuther (1909) does not believe the known facts warrant the view that there is continuity of the germ-plasm in *Hydra*. This is, of course, a matter that may never be decided definitely, and at least not until some method of distinguishing the primordial germ cells, if these be present, from ordinary interstitial and other cells, has been found. Furthermore, if the germ-plasm is continuous, primordial germ cells must be present in buds, in adults at all times of the year, and in pieces of tissue that are capable of regenerating sexually reproductive adults. That such primordial germ cells exist seems to me to be quite possible.

HYDROZOA. Many HYDROZOA besides *Hydra* have furnished material for germ-cell studies. Thus Weismann (1883) reported upon about forty species belonging to a number of different families. The results of the researches of the various investigators do not agree in many instances. In order to indicate the variety of the opinions expressed, the data regarding the germ cells in the following genera is considered below: (1) *Eudendrium*, (2) *Hydractinia*, (3) *Pennaria*, and (4) *Clava*.

EUDENDRIUM. Five species of this genus have been investigated. In *E. racemosum*, according to Weismann (1883), the ova arise in the ectoderm and the male germ cells originate either from entoderm cells or from ectoderm cells that later migrate into the entoderm. Ischikawa (1887) asserts that the germ cells arise in the ectoderm and migrate into the entoderm, and Hargitt (1904*a*) found ova in both the ectoderm and entoderm, but, since those in the entoderm were always the smaller, he concludes that they may have wandered into that layer from the ectoderm, though such a migration was not observed.

In *E. capillare* Hargitt found ova in the entoderm except in one case where they occurred in the ectoderm. This author also reports the female germ cells of *E. tenue* and *E. racemosum* from the entoderm only. The ova of the EUDENDRIDÆ when first distinguishable "are slightly larger than the ordinary cells of the surrounding tissue, and differ also in shape, being generally ovoid or spherical and with comparatively conspicuous nuclei. . . . Growth at this period would seem to take place *in situ*, through the direct nutritive activity of the surrounding tissue cells. . . . As growth continues, the ova become more or less amœboid, migrating toward the gonophore region, where they seem to aggregate in considerable numbers, the presence of which may act as a stimulus from which results the formation of the gonophore" (Hargitt, 1904 a, pp. 261-262).

HYDRACTINIA has been investigated by van Beneden (1874), Weismann (1883), Bunting (1894), and Smallwood (1909). Weismann considered the ectoderm of the blastostyle to be the probable place of origin of the germ cells in this genus. Bunting (1894) was unable to trace the ova to this layer, although she found them to be quite abundant in the entoderm of the blastostyle, even before the gonophore appeared. According to this author the ova apparently arise in the entoderm of the blastostyle, and "reach maturity on the outside wall of the spadix, lying between the endoderm and the inner layer of the bell nucleus. The spermatozoa arise from the inner layer of the bell nucleus; we see that they are, therefore, ectodermal in origin" (p. 228).

These results are not confirmed by the researches of Smallwood (1909), who finds that the eggs arise in the entoderm in any region of the polyp, at the base, the side of the polyp, or in the gonophore. They may be distinguished from other entoderm cells by the larger size of the nucleus.

In *Pennaria cavolini* the germ cells arise in the ectoderm, according to Weismann (1883), and this conclusion is confirmed for the ova by Hargitt (1904b). In *P. tiarella* the germ cells are likewise of ectodermal origin (Smallwood, 1899, Hargitt, for the ova, 1904b). The eggs of this species arise in the ectoderm of the manubrium and grow by engulfing other primitive ova. Only six or eight, rarely more, of the eggs survive.

In *Clava*, according to van Beneden (1874), the ova arise in the entoderm. Weismann (1883) was not able to determine whether they originated in the entoderm or migrated into that layer from the ectoderm, but he was certain that the male germ cells were ectodermal. This conclusion regarding the male germ cells was confirmed by Thallowitz (1885). Harm (1902) was able to trace the primitive germ cells back to a very early stage, and could distinguish them in even young hydranths. The oöcytes differed from the remaining ectoderm cells in the possession of a larger amount of cytoplasm, a larger nucleus with a big nucleolus, and an ameboid shape.

Hargitt (1906), working on *Clava leptostyla*, comes to conclusions different from those of Harm on *C. squamata*. He says "that eggs probably never arise in the ectoderm but always in the entoderm of the peduncle of the gonophore, or in that of the polyp very near the base of the gonophore. . . . *Clava*, like other Hydroids, has its breeding season, during which the germ cells are extremely abundant, and at other times these cells are either entirely absent or very scarce" (p. 208). Concerning the early origin of germ cells Hargitt says, "it may not be impossible that 'Urkeimzellen' should perhaps exist in undifferentiated stages, still the probability is so extremely remote as to render doubtful to a degree any but the most thoroughly substantial claims" (p. 209).

One more Hydrozoön may be mentioned — *Gonothyræa loveni* — since Wulfert (1902) traced the germ cells of this species back to the planula stage where they arise from the interstitial cells of the ectoderm and later undergo characteristic migrations.

Our knowledge of the origin of the germ cells in other cœlenterates is very fragmentary and even less decisive than that of the Hydrozoa. For this reason a consideration of the subject is omitted here.

Discussion. As in the Porifera we are here confronted with the question whether or not there is continuity of the germ-plasm in the Cœlenterata. There is sufficient evidence for the belief that the cells which develop into germ cells are not derived from the ectoderm or the entoderm but belong to a special sort of propagative cells which are scattered about among the other cells throughout the body and which give rise to ova or spermatozoa under certain environmental conditions differing in the different species. This conclusion is based partly upon the results of Downing (1905, 1908, 1909), who still holds, as stated in his published papers, that there is continuity of the germ-plasm in *Hydra*; and upon the fact that germ cells have been recognized in the young hydranths of *Clava* (Harm, 1902) and in the planula of *Gonothyræa* (Wulfert, 1902). It seems certain that more careful studies of the early stages of cœlenterates with special regard to the origin of the germ cells and with the use of many and varied stains would result in the discovery

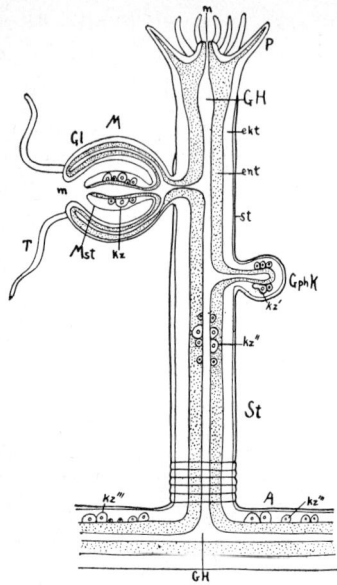

Fig. 29. — Diagram to illustrate the phylogenetic shifting back of the origins of the germ cells in medusoids and hydroids. A composite picture. *A*, branch of a polyp-colony; *P*, polyp-head with mouth (*m*) and tentacles; *St*, stalk of the polyp; *M*, medusoid-bud with the bell (*Gl*); *T*, marginal tentacle; *m*, mouth; *Mst*, manubrium; *GphK*, a gonophore-bud; *GH*, gastric cavity; *ekt*, ectoderm; *ent*, endoderm; *st*, supporting lamella. The germ cells (*kz*) arise in the medusoid in the ectoderm of the manubrium — first phyletic stage — where they also attain maturity. In the gonophore-bud (*GphK*) they arise in the ectoderm (*kz′*), or further down in the stalk of the polyp at *kz″* — third phyletic stage — or in the ectoderm of the branch from which the polyp has arisen, at *kz‴* — fourth phyletic stage of the shunting of the originative area of the germ cells. In the last two cases the germ cells migrate until they reach their primitive place of origination in the medusoid, or in the corresponding layer of the medusoid gonophore, as may be more clearly seen in Fig. 30. (*After Weismann, 1904.*)

of these cells in younger embryos than yet recorded, and might even disclose characteristics which would enable us to trace the keimbahn in some species back into the early cleavage stages.

In discussing the germ cells of cœlenterates, it is necessary to refer to the work of Weismann who has added so much to our knowledge of this subject. Weismann's position may best be presented in his own words (*The Evolution Theory*, Vol. I, pp. 413–415, 1904).

"In the hydroid polyps and their medusoids the germ-cells always arise in the ectoderm; in species which produce sexual medusoids by budding, the germ cells arise in the ectoderm of the manubrium of these medusoids (Fig. 29, M, kz). But in many species these sexual stages have degenerated in the course of phylogeny into so-called gonophores, that is, to medusoids which still exhibit more or less complete bells, but neither mouth (m) nor marginal tentacles (T), and which no longer break away from the colony to swim freely about, to feed independently, and to produce and ripen germ-cells. The degeneration of the 'gonophores' often goes even farther; in many the medusoid bell is represented only by a thin layer of cells, and in some even this token of descent from medusoid ancestry is absent, and they are mere single-layered closed brood-sacs (Fig. 30, Gph).

"The adherence of the sexual animal to the hydroid colony has, however, made a more rapid ripening of the germ-cells possible, and nature has taken advantage of this possibility in all cases known to me, for the germ-cells no longer arise in the manubrium of the mature degenerate medusoid, that is, of the gonophore, but *earlier*, before the bud which becomes a gonophore possesses a manubrium. The birthplace of the germ-cells is thus shifted back from the manubrium of the medusoid to the young gonophore-bud (Fig. 29, M, kz). The same thing occurs in species in which the medusoids are liberated, but live only for a short time, for instance, in the genus

GERM-CELL CYCLE IN ANIMALS

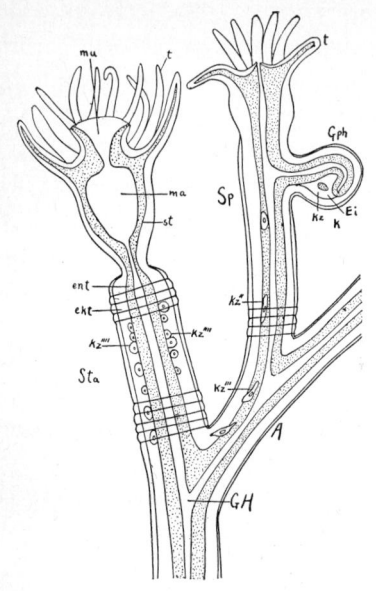

Fig. 30.— Diagram to illustrate the migration of the germ cells in hydromedusæ from their remotely shunted place of origin to their primitive place of origin in the gonophore, in which they attain to maturity. The state of affairs in Eudendrium is taken as the basis of the diagram. *mu*, mouth; *ma*, gut-cavity; *t*, tentacle; *Sta*, stem; *A*, a branch of the polyp-colony; *SP*, lateral polyp; *Gph*, a medusoid-bud completely degenerated into a mere gonophore; *Ei*, ovum; *GH*, gastric cavity; *st*, supporting lamella. The originative area of the germ cells lies in the stem of the principal polyp at kz'''', whence the germ cells first migrate into the endoderm of the branch (*A*) at kz''', creeping within which they reach kz'' in the lateral polyp (blastostyle), finally reaching the gonophore (*kz*) and passing again into the ectoderm. (*After Weismann, 1904.*)

Podocoryne. Although perfect medusoids are formed, these have their germ-cells fully developed at the time of their liberation from the hydroid colony. But in species in which the medusoid-buds have really degenerated and are no longer liberated, the birthplace of the germ-cells is shifted *even farther back*, and in the first place into the stalk (*St, kz''*) of the polyp from the gonophore-buds. This is the case in the genus *Hydractinia*. In the further course of the process the birthplace of the germ-cells has shifted as far back as to the branch from which the polyp has grown out (Fig. 29, *A, kz'''*); and finally, in the cases in which the medusoid has degenerated to a mere brood-sac (Fig. 30, *Gph*), even to the generation of polyps immediately before, that is, into the polyp-stem from which the branch arises that bears the polyps producing the gonophore-bud (Fig. 30, *kz'''*). Then we find the birthplace of the germ-cells *still* further back (Fig. 30, *kz''''*), for the egg and sperm cells arise in the stem of the principal polyps (the main stem of the colony). The advantage of this arrangement is easily seen, for the principal polyp is present earlier than those of the secondary branches, and these again earlier than the polyp which bears the sexual buds, and this, finally, earlier than the sexual bud which it bears. Thus this shunting backwards of the birthplace of the germ-cells means an earlier origin of the primordium (*Anlage*) of the germ-cells, and consequently an earlier maturing of these.

"But none of these germ-cells come to maturity in the birthplace to which they have been shifted, for they migrate independently from it to the place at which they primitively arose, namely, into the manubrium of the medusoid, which is still present even when great degeneration has occurred, or even — in the most extreme cases of degeneration — into the ectoderm of the brood-sac. This is the case in the genus *Eudendrium*, of which Fig. 30 gives a diagrammatic representation.

"The most interesting feature of this migration of

the germ-cells is that the cells invariably arise in the ectoderm (kz''''), then pierce through the supporting lamella (st) into the endoderm (kz'''), and then creep along it to their maturing-place. Once there, they break through again to the outer layer of cells, the ectoderm (kz), and come to maturity (Ei). That they make their way through the endoderm is probably to be explained by the fact that they are there in direct proximity to the food-stream which flows through the colony (GH = gastric cavity), and they are thus more richly nourished there than in the ectoderm. But, although this is the case, they never arise in the endoderm; in no single case is the birthplace of the germ-cells to be found in the endoderm, but always in the ectoderm, no matter how far back it may have been shunted. Even when the germ-cells migrate through the endoderm, their first recognizable appearance is invariably in the ectoderm, as, for instance, in *Podocoryne* and *Hydractinia*. The course of affairs is thus exactly what it would necessarily be if our supposition were correct, that only definite cell-generations — in this case the ectoderm-cells — contain the complete germ-plasm. If the endoderm-cells also contained germ-plasm it would be hard to understand why the germ-cells never arise from them, since their situation offers much better conditions for their further development than that of the ectoderm-cells. It would also be hard to understand why such a circuitous route was chosen as that exhibited by the migration of the young germ-cells into the endoderm. Something must be lacking in the endoderm that is necessary to make a cell into a germ-cell: that something is the germ-plasm."

Several important contributions have appeared within recent years which seem to deprive Weismann's contentions of much of their importance. For example, Goette (1907) has found that the germ cells of many HYDROMEDUSÆ may arise in the entoderm or in the ectoderm, and that in *Clava multicornis* the germ cells are transformed half-entoderm cells. After a long series of studies on cœlenterate development C. W. Hargitt (1911) has attacked Weismann's position in the following words: "That there is any such region as may be designated a 'Keimzone' or 'Keimstätte' may be at once dismissed as absolutely without warrant as a general proposition. Furthermore, that the germ cells have their origin in the ectoderm alone in hydromedusæ may be similarly denied and dismissed as unworthy of further inquiry or doubt. And still further, I am thoroughly convinced that the still more recent controversy as to the hypothesis of the 'germ-plasm,' if not as clearly a delusion as the preceding, is yet without the slightest support from the ontogeny of the group under review.

"It is a matter of easy demonstration that in many species of hydroids the egg may be followed in every detail from its origin as an ectoderm or an entoderm or interstitial cell through its gradual differentiation and growth to maturation, as a distinct individual cell, without the slightest tendency to multiplication."

"It is passing strange that he should ignore the body of facts concerned in regeneration, and among them the reproductive organs. And it is still more strange that in support of this he should cite in detail the HYDROZOA as illustrating and supporting the hypothesis, ignoring the well-known facts that among these are abounding evidences which afford insuperable objections to just these assumptions. The present author has, in many cases, shown that gonads may be as readily regenerated by hydroids and medusæ as any other organs; and that not for once or twice, but repeatedly in the same specimen, and that *de novo* and *in situ;* not the slightest evidence being distinguishable that any migration through preëxisting 'germ-tracks' occurred. The assumption that in these animals the gonads have 'been shifted backwards in the course of phylogenetic evolution, that is, have been moved nearer to the starting point of development' seems so at variance with known facts as to be difficult to appreciate or respect."

Professor Hargitt finally concludes with the following sentence: "I believe the foregoing facts must suffice to show that, both as to origin, differentiation, and growth, the germ-cells of the HYDROZOA, so far from sustaining the doctrine of the germ-plasm, afford the strongest and most direct evidence to the contrary."

G. T. Hargitt (1913) has also discovered facts regarding the history of the germ cells in cœlenterates which are decidedly opposed to Weismann's views. He finds that "The egg cells of *Campanularia flexuosa* arise in the entoderm of the pedicel of the gonophore, by the transformation of a single epithelial cell, or from the basal half of a divided cell, the distal half of which remains an epithelial cell and retains its epithelial functions. Therefore the egg cells have come from differentiated body-cells (so-called) and there is no differentiation of the germ-plasm in the sense that germ-cells are early differentiated and set aside and do not participate in the body functions. Any cell of the entoderm of *Campanularia flexuosa* may become an egg cell if it is in the position of the developing gonophore" (p. 411).

In spite of these attacks upon the germ-plasm theory as applied to cœlenterates, the possibility and even probability of such a condition seems to the writer to exist, and he is inclined to accept Downing's position in the matter. Weismann's views must, however, be modified, since the germ cells are not ectoderm cells, as he claims, nor do they belong to any germ layer. They are, according to the view adopted here, set aside as a separate class of cells at some stage during early development, are scattered about among the cells of the ectoderm or entoderm, depending upon the species, or lie in the mesoglea. We know that external conditions may stimulate reproductive activity in certain cœlenterates (Frischholz, 1909) and consequently the development of germ cells, and we must conclude that these germ cells are present at all times in a more or less dormant condition, just as they are in more complex animals. Furthermore, the germ cells must be widely scattered, as has been shown by Harm (1902) in the young hydranths of *Clava*, by Wulfert (1902) in the planula of *Gonothyræa*, and by Smallwood (1909) in the polyp of *Hydractinia*. This wide distribution of primitive germ cells accounts for the reproductive powers of regenerated pieces of hydroids.

3. VERTEBRATA

Efforts have been made by many investigators to trace the keimbahn in vertebrates, but thus far no method has yet been devised which will enable us to distinguish germ cells from other cells in the early embryonic stages. That we shall be able to recognize germ cells in still earlier stages of development than has yet been accomplished seems certain, and the recent contributions of Rubaschkin (1910), Tschaschkin (1910), von Berenberg-Gossler (1912a) and Swift (1914) have already made considerable advances by the use of some of the more modern cytological methods. Three principal theories have been advanced regarding the origin of the germ cells in vertebrates, and these will be briefly stated before the histories of the germ cells in special cases are discussed.

The *germinal epithelium theory* was advanced by Waldeyer in 1870. At that time nothing was known regarding the migration of germ cells during the embryonic development of vertebrates, and it is not strange that he should have come to the conclusion that the primordial ova arise from the epithelial cells of the genital ridge among which they were observed. Although this theory was accepted by most embryologists, it has gradually been abandoned until now it has very few supporters.

The *gonotome theory* resulted from the studies of Rückert (1888) and Van Wijhe (1889). The germ cells appeared to these investigators to arise in a part of the segmental mesoblast of the embryo to which the latter applied the term 'gonotome.' From the gonotome they become embedded in the peritoneum. Thus the same cells are recognized as germ cells by the adherents of both theories, but a difference exists regarding their origin.

The *theory of early segregation* has become the most prevalent view of the origin of the germ cells of vertebrates, although there are many who still hold one of the other hypotheses. According to this theory the germ cells are set aside during the early embryonic stages before definite germ layers are formed, and they later arrive at the germinal ridge either by their own migration or by changes in the position of the tissues during development. The germinal epithelium theories have little if any evidence in their favor, since no one has actually observed a transformation of peritoneal or mesoblast cells into germ cells. On the other hand, there is an abundance of proof that these cells migrate from some distance into the position of the sex glands.

According to Dustin (1907), Firket (1914) and

several others there are two methods of origin, and primary and secondary sex cells are produced. The former are probably derived from the blastomeres; whereas the secondary sex cells are entirely independent and arise from the cœlomic epithelium.

The first statement of the theory of early segregation was made by Nussbaum (1880), who studied the history of the germ cells in the trout. Following Nussbaum, Eigenmann (1892, 1896) contributed to the support of the theory by his investigations on the viviparous teleost, *Cymatogaster*. This proved to be excellent material for such studies and led Eigenmann to the conclusion that the germ cells are set aside in this fish during the early cleavage stages of the egg, probably at the thirty-two cell stage. In other cases it has been impossible to trace the germ cells back to such an early embryonic condition, but nevertheless the evidence has been almost uniformly in favor of early segregation. Some of those who have advocated such an early origin of germ cells are Wheeler (1900) in the lamprey, Beard (1900, 1902) in *Raja* and *Pristiurus*, Nussbaum (1901) in the chick, Woods (1902) in *Acanthais*, Allen (1906, 1907, 1909, 1911) in *Chrysemys*, *Rana*, *Amia*, and *Lepidosteus*, Rubaschkin (1907, 1909, 1910, 1912) in the chick, cat, rabbit, and guinea-pig, Kuschakewitsch (1908) in *Rana*, Jarvis (1908) in *Phrynosoma*, Tschaschkin (1910) in the chick, von Berenberg-Gossler (1912) in the chick, Schapitz (1912) in *Amblystoma*, Fuss (1912) in the pig and man, and Swift (1914) in the chick. This is by no means a complete list but indicates the range of forms studied and the current interest in this subject.

Some of the characteristics by means of which germ cells can be distinguished in vertebrate embryos are as follows: (1) the presence of yolk, (2) an ameboid shape, (3) large size, and (4) slight staining capacity. By sectioning embryos of various ages the changes in position of the germ cells can be followed with considerable accuracy. Most investigators agree that the movement of the germ cells from the tissues where first observed to the genital ridge is caused by ameboid activities of the cells themselves and by changes in the position of the organs of the embryo. The paths of migration of four vertebrates, a turtle, *Chrysemys*, a frog, *Rana*, the gar pike, *Lepidosteus*, and the fresh-water dogfish, *Amia*, are shown in Fig. 6. For example:

"In Lepidosteus the sex-cells [Fig. 6, *3*, *Sl*] first seen in the ventral and lateral portions of the gut-entoderm [*Int*] migrate to occupy a position in the dorsal portion of it, from which they pass dorsally into the loose mesenchyme that forms the substance of the developing mesentery [*Mes*]. As the mesentery becomes more narrow and compact, owing to the increase in size of the body cavity, the sex cells migrate to its dorsal portion and laterally to the sex-gland anlagen (Fig. 6, *4*, *Sc*). Roughly speaking, one-half of the total number of sex-cells reach the sex-gland anlagen, the remainder being distributed between the intestinal entoderm, the mesodermal layers of the intestine, the mesentery, and the tissues at and dorsal to the root of the intestine" (Allen, 1911, p. 32).

Of the more recent investigations, facts discovered by Dodds (1910), Rubaschkin (1910, 1912), Tschaschkin (1910), von Berenberg-Gossler (1912), and Swift (1914) are especially worthy of mention. Dodds (1910) found that in the teleost, *Lophius*, the germ cells in the embryos cannot be definitely distinguished previous to the appearance in their cytoplasm of a body which stains like a plasmosome (Fig. 31, *A*). Germ cells are undoubtedly segregated before this period, but they exhibited no characteristics with the methods employed which rendered them distinguishable. Dodds believes that this cytoplasmic body is extruded plasmosome material, probably part of one of the two plasmosomes possessed by many of the cells at this period.

Rubaschkin, in 1910, announced the results obtained with the eggs of the guinea-pig by certain methods designed to bring into view the chondriosomes. He shows that the chondriosomes of the undifferentiated cells are granular, and that as differentiation proceeds, these granules unite to form chains and threads (Fig. 31, *B*). The sex cells, however, retain the chondriosomes in their primitive granular form, and remain in an undifferentiated condition situated in the posterior part of the embryo among the entoderm cells. Tschaschkin (1910), in the same year, came to a similar conclusion from studies made with chick embryos. Rubaschkin (1912) has also extended his investigations on guinea-

PORIFERA, CŒLENTERATA, VERTEBRATA

pig embryos. The accompanying diagram (Fig. 32) shows the fertilized egg and the early cleavage cells all alike (in black); some of their descendants become differentiated into the somatic cells of the germ

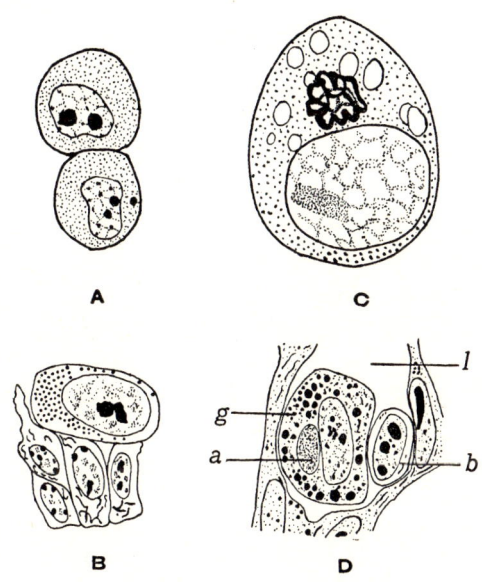

FIG. 31. — Germ cells of vertebrates. *A*. From embryo of the teleost, *Lophius*, with plasmosome (?) extruded into cytoplasm. (*From Dodds, 1910.*) *B*. One germ cell and four somatic cells from a guinea-pig embryo. (*From Rubaschkin, 1912.*) *C*. Germ cell of chick showing " Netzapparat." (*From von Berenberg-Gossler, 1912.*) *D*. Primordial germ cell (*g*) and blood cell (*b*) in lumen of blood vessel (*l*) of a nineteen somite chick embryo. *a* = attraction-sphere. (*From Swift, 1914.*)

layers (circles), but others (in black) remain in a primitive condition and are recognizable as the primordial germ cells; these remain at rest for a considerable period, but finally multiply and become part of the germinal epithelium (*g.ep*).

104   GERM–CELL CYCLE IN ANIMALS

Von Berenberg-Gossler (1912) considers the "Netzapparat" in the primitive germ cells of the chick of particular importance (Fig. 31, *C*), comparing it with the "wurstförmige Körper" described by Hasper

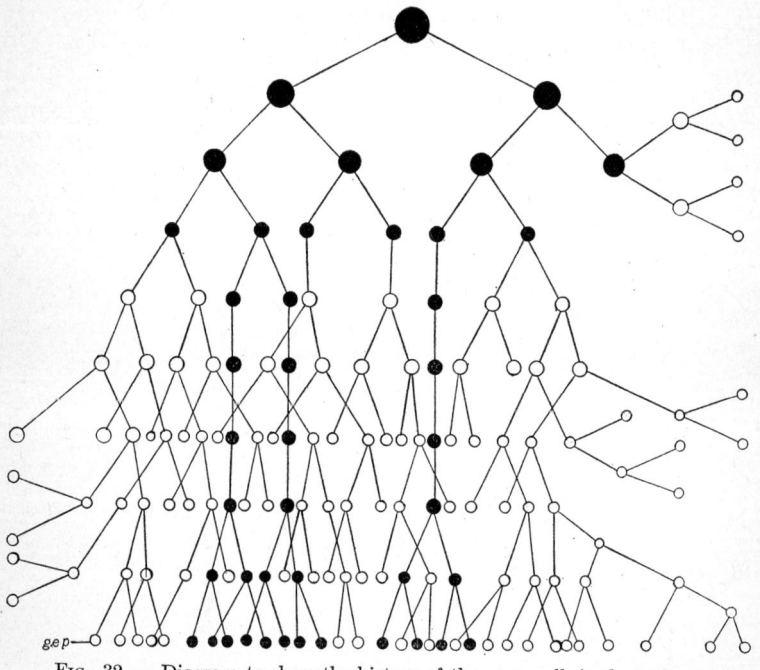

Fig. 32. — Diagram to show the history of the germ cells in the embryo of the guinea-pig.   *g.ep* = germinal epithelium.   (*From Rubaschkin, 1912.*)

(1911) in *Chironomus* (p. 108, Fig. 33). The appearance of this structure in "Keimbahnzellen" is thought to be due to the long period during which these cells do not divide. Duesberg (1912), however, after an exhaustive review of the literature on this structure concludes that it is not a special cell organ but an artifact. Kulesch (1914), on the contrary, finds it to be a constant organ in the eggs of the cat, dog, and guinea-pig.

The evidence of a continuous germ-cell cycle in the vertebrates is more convincing than in the sponges and cœlenterates, and leads us to predict that it will not be long before the gap still existing during which germ cells cannot be recognized will be filled in to the satisfaction of the majority of investigators.

CHAPTER V

THE SEGREGATION OF THE GERM CELLS IN THE ARTHROPODA

1. THE KEIMBAHN IN THE INSECTS

THE insects have furnished a very large proportion of the data upon which many of our biological conceptions are now based, and they are becoming more and more popular for studies of the physical basis of heredity, and for purposes of animal breeding. It was in insects (*Miastor*) that the early segregation of the germ cells in animals was first definitely established. The accessory chromosome was discovered in insects by Henking in 1891, and our knowledge of the chromosomes, which has increased so remarkably within the past fifteen years, is due principally to the study of oögenesis and spermatogenesis in insects. In this chapter the chromosomes will only be considered incidentally, a more detailed account being deferred until later (Chapter IX). The *early history of the germ cells* in insect development has not been slighted, for there are many reports based on this subject alone and still more data hidden away in contributions on general embryology. It will be necessary here to select from this abundance of material those reports that give us the clearest pictures of the keimbahnen. As

GERM CELLS IN THE ARTHROPODA

usual, certain species or groups of species have proven more favorable than others for germ-cell studies, especially those belonging to the orders DIPTERA, COLEOPTERA, and HYMENOPTERA.

DIPTERA. Robin, in 1862, described what he called "globules polaries" at one end of the nearly transparent eggs of the crane fly, *Tipulides culiciformes*, and the following year Weismann (1863) reported the formation of similar cells, the "Polzellen" at the posterior end of the eggs of the midge, *Chironomus nigroviridis*, and the blow fly, *Calliphora (Musca) vomitoria*. It remained for Leuckart (1865) and Metchnikoff (1865, 1866), however, to identify the pole cells (in *Miastor*) as primordial germ cells; their results were confirmed for *Chironomus* by Grimm (1870) and Balbiani (1882, 1885).

Pole cells have also been described among the DIPTERA, in *Musca* by Kowalevsky (1886), Voeltzkow (1889), and Escherich (1900); in *Calliphora* by Graber (1889) and Noack (1901); in *Chironomus* by Ritter (1890) and Hasper (1911); in *Lucilia* by Escherich (1900); in *Miastor* by Kahle (1908) and Hegner (1912, 1914a), and in *Compsilura* by Hegner (1914a).

Four genera of flies will serve to illustrate the methods of germ-cell segregation in this order: (1) *Chironomus* (Ritter, 1890; Hasper, 1911), (2) *Calliphora* (Noack, 1901), (3) *Miastor* (Kahle, 1908; Hegner, 1912, 1914a), and (4) *Compsilura* (Hegner, 1914a). Since *Miastor* has been discussed in detail in Chapter III it will be only briefly referred to here.

We owe the first accurate account of the germ cells in *Chironomus* to Ritter (1890), who, by means of the section method, showed that the "yolk granules" described by Weismann (1863) in the pole cells are derived from a disc-shaped mass of substance situated near the posterior end of the egg and termed by him the "Keimwulst." Hasper (1911) was able to confirm this discovery, to add other interesting facts, and to correct several of Ritter's errors. The "Keimwulst" of Ritter is called by Hasper the "Keimbahnplasma."

Ritter advanced the idea that the cleavage nucleus of *Chironomus* divides within the "Keimwulst" and that here the first cleavage division occurs, one daughter nucleus remaining in the "Keimwulst" and becoming the center of the primordial germ cell, the other giving rise to somatic nuclei. This is probably the basis for Weismann's (1904) statement regarding his conception of the germ-plasm that, "If we could assume that the ovum, just beginning to develop, divides at its first cleavage into two cells, one of which gives rise to the whole body (soma) and the other only to the germ-cells lying in this body, the matter would be theoretically simple. . . . As yet, however, only one group of animals is known to behave demonstrably in this manner, the Diptera among insects. . . ." There is, however, nothing in the literature to warrant the above statement, since Ritter's hypothesis has been disproved by Hasper.

According to Hasper one of the cleavage nuclei

at the four cell stage becomes separated from the rest of the egg, together with all of the Keimbahnplasma as the primordial germ cell (Fig. 33 *B*, *p.g.c.*). The Keimbahnplasma is apparently equally divided between the daughter cells when the primordial germ cell divides. Later the nuclei of the germ cells increase in number without an accompanying division of the cell, thus producing binucleated cells (Fig. 33, *C*). The history of the pole cells during embryonic development will be more fully described in the COLEOPTERA, since in the beetles the Keimbahn is much more distinct. The origin and nature of the Keimbahnplasma was not determined by Hasper, but it was found to persist in certain cases even until the larval stage was reached (Fig. 33, *D*).

In *Calliphora* Noack (1901) described a dark granular disc at the posterior end of the egg (Fig. 34) which he termed the "Dotterplatte" and which, like the pole-plasm of *Miastor* and the Keimbahnplasma of *Chironomus* takes part in the formation of the primordial germ cells. The eggs of the parasitic fly, *Compsilura concinnata*, were also found by the writer (Hegner, 1914*a*) to possess a granular pole-disc, thus adding one more species to the list of DIPTERA in which such a structure exists.

COLEOPTERA. The origin of the germ cells in beetles and their subsequent history are well known only in certain species of the family CHRYSOMELIDÆ of the genera *Calligrapha* and *Leptinotarsa*. The contributions of Wheeler (1889), Lecaillon (1898),

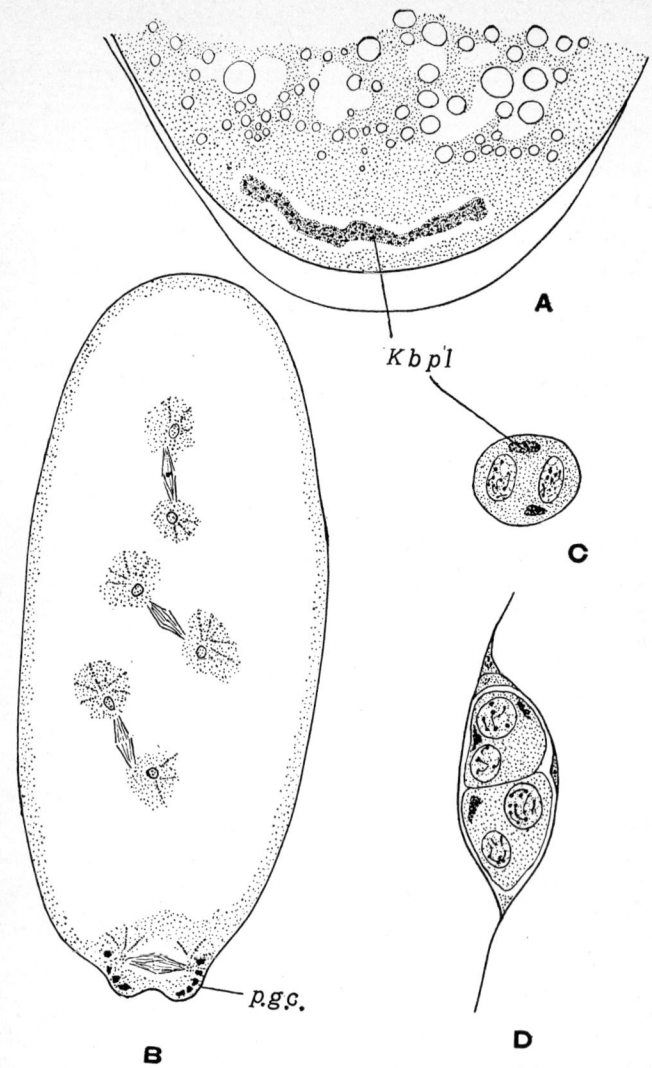

Fig. 33.—*Chironomus*. *A.* Longitudinal section through the posterior end of a freshly laid egg. *B.* Longitudinal section through egg during division of first four cleavage nuclei; at posterior end the primordial germ cell is just being formed. *C.* One of primordial germ cells containing two nuclei and remains of "Keimbahnplasma." *D.* Germ gland of the larva in which remains of "Keimbahnplasma" still appear. *Kbpl* = "Keimbahnplasma"; *p.g.c.* = primordial germ cell. (*From Hasper, 1911.*)

Hegner (1908, 1909*a*, 1909*b*, 1911*a*, 1911*b*, 1914*a*), and Wieman (1910*a*, 1910*b*) will be referred to in the following paragraphs.

Wheeler (1889) figured several primordial germ cells in an egg of *Leptinotarsa* with a segmented germ band and suspected their true nature, but did not discover them in earlier stages. Lecaillon (1898) described the pole-cells in several chrysomelid beetles, but did not make out any of the details concerning their origin, structure, and migrations.

Within the last seven years the writer has devoted a considerable portion of his time to morphological and experimental studies of the eggs of beetles, particularly *Calligrapha bigsbyana*, *C. multipunctata*, *C. lunata*, and *Leptinotarsa decemlineata*. The eggs of these species are peculiarly favorable for study, since they are definitely oriented in the body of the mother and various surfaces can be recognized in the newly laid egg: they can be placed under the most severe

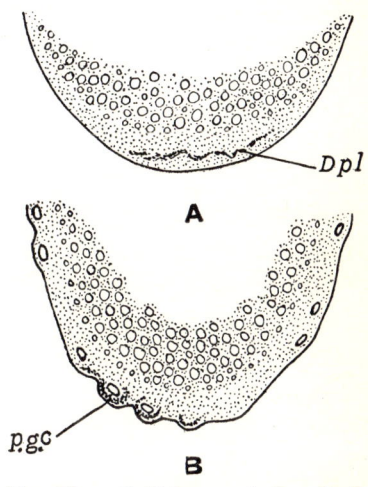

FIG. 34. — *Calliphora*. A. Longitudinal section through posterior end of freshly laid egg, showing "Dotterplatte (*Dpl*). B. Longitudinal section through posterior end of egg at time of blastoderm formation, showing protrusion of primordial germ cells (*p.g.c.*). (*From Noack, 1901.*)

experimental conditions without killing them or stopping their progressive development; and they can be killed, fixed, sectioned, and stained with comparative ease. Furthermore, the eggs of these beetles possess a well-defined pole-disc, and the primordial germ cells which arise even before the blastoderm is formed are easily distinguishable from the somatic cells and thus can be traced from the time of their appearance until they become mature eggs and spermatozoa.

The ova of insects have long been considered among the most highly organized of all animal eggs. That they are definitely oriented while still within the ovary was expressed by Hallez (1886) in his "Law of the Orientation of Insect Embryos" as follows: "The cell possesses the same orientation as the maternal organism that produces it; it has a cephalic pole and a caudal pole, a right side and a left side, a dorsal surface and a ventral surface; and these different surfaces of the egg-cell coincide to the corresponding surfaces of the embryo." The orientation of an ovarian egg is indicated in Fig. 35, and here also is shown the position and surfaces of the egg at the time of deposition. When the egg is laid the beetle clings to the under surface of a leaf, and with a drop of viscid substance from the accessory glands of the reproductive organs, fastens the egg by its posterior end (p) to the leaf; then with the tip of the abdomen the egg is pushed back through the arc indicated by the dotted line. It is a simple matter to determine the various surfaces of eggs

GERM CELLS IN THE ARTHROPODA

laid in this manner. Gravity apparently has no influence upon the development, since eggs in a state of nature occupy all positions with respect to this factor without becoming altered in any way. Only one case has come to the writer's attention of an influence of gravity in insect development — the eggs of the water beetle, *Hydrophilus atterimus*,

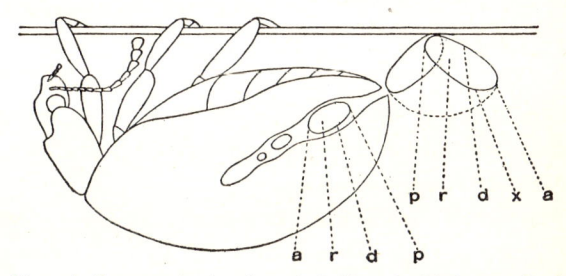

Fig. 35. — A diagramatic drawing of *Calligrapha bigsbyana* clinging to the under side of a willow leaf and showing the orientation of the egg in the ovarian tubule and after deposition. a = anterior; d = dorsal; p = posterior; r = right side; x = place where egg was marked with India ink as means of orientation after removal from leaf.

according to Megusar (1906), develop abnormally if the cocoon in which they are laid is inverted.

The events that precede the establishment of the primordial germ cells in chrysomelid beetles may be described briefly as follows: The egg, when laid (Fig. 36, A), consists of a large central mass of yolk globules (y), among which are very fine strands of cytoplasm; a thin peripheral layer of cytoplasm, the "keimhautblastem" of Weismann ($khbl$), a delicate vitelline membrane ($v.m.$), a chitinous shell, the chorion, and a nucleus consisting of the egg nucleus

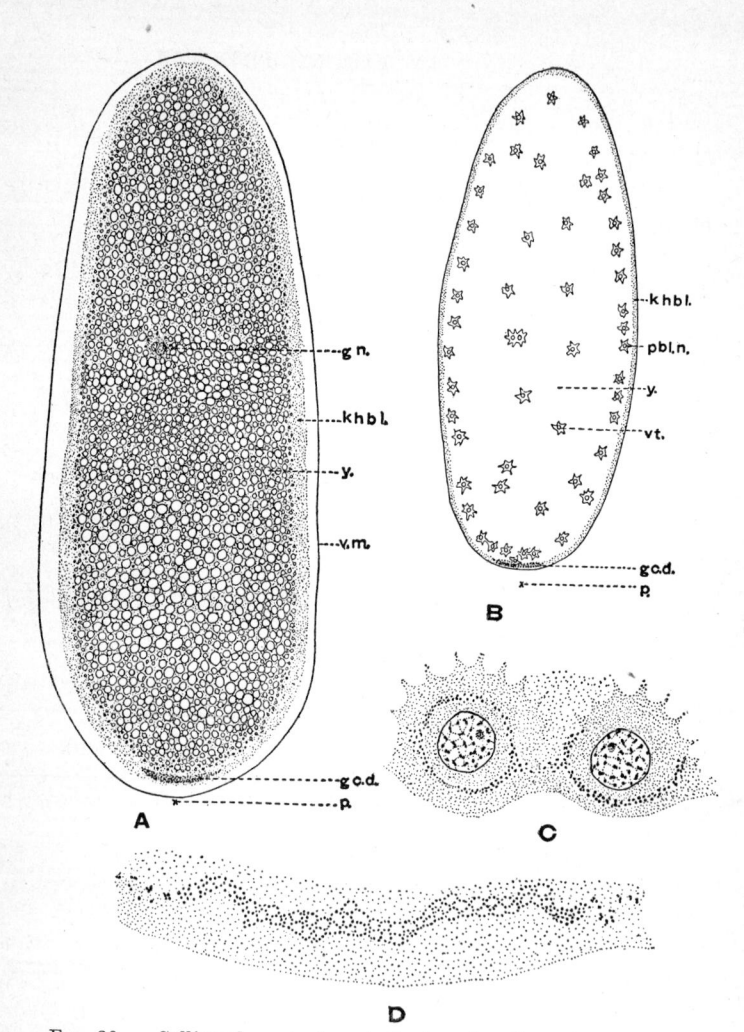

Fig. 36.—*Calligrapha.* *A.* Longitudinal section through an egg of *C. bigsbyana* four hours after deposition. *B.* Longitudinal section through an egg of *C. bigsbyana* 14 hours after deposition. *C.* Two germ cells just protruding from posterior end of egg of *C. multipunctata.* *D.* The pole-disc in an egg of *C. multipunctata.* *g.c.d.* = pole-disc; *g.n.* = germ nuclei fusing; *khbl* = keimhautblastem; *p.* = posterior end of egg; *p.bl.n.* = preblastodermic nuclei; *v.m.* = vitelline membrane; *vt.* = vitellophags; *y.* = yolk. (114)

and a sperm nucleus combined (*g.n*). Frequently the two polar bodies have not yet been produced when the egg is laid and thus many stages may be encountered in the newly laid eggs. Polyspermy is a normal condition in insects and several spermatozoa are often observed among the yolk globules. The keimhautblastem is not homogeneous throughout, for at the posterior end there is embedded in it a disc-shaped mass of darkly staining granules which I have called the pole-disc (*g.c.d.*) and which resembles the pole-plasm of *Miastor*, the "Keimwulst" or "Keimbahnplasma" of *Chironomus* and the "Dotterplatte" of *Calliphora*.

The cleavage nucleus divides by mitosis; the daughter nuclei separate slightly, and divide; and this process is continued until nuclei, each surrounded by a small mass of cytoplasm, are scattered more or less regularly throughout the egg. Then a division of the nuclei into two groups occurs; those of one group migrate to the periphery, fuse with the peripheral layer of cytoplasm, and are cut off by cell walls, thus forming the blastoderm; whereas the other nuclei, the vitellophags, remain behind among the yolk globules which it is their function to dissolve. The blastoderm consists of a single layer of cells, except at the posterior end where its formation has been interrupted by the process resulting in the establishment of the primordial germ cells.

The primordial germ cells are formed in the following manner. The cleavage nuclei at the posterior end of the egg that encounter the pole disc granules behave differently from those at other points, since they do not remain to form part of the blastoderm but continue to migrate until they have become entirely separated from the rest of the egg. During this process each of the sixteen nuclei that act in this way becomes surrounded by a halo of granules — part of the pole-disc. Then cell walls appear and sixteen primordial germ cells result. These form a group at the posterior end, each member of which divides twice, thus producing sixty-four germ cells in all. During these divisions, which are mitotic, the pole-disc granules appear to be equally distributed between the daughter cells (Fig. 37, *B*). A rest period then occurs, as far as cellular multiplication is concerned, during which a ventral plate, which later grows into the germ band, develops on the ventral surface of the egg. As in *Miastor* the germ-band pushes around on the dorsal surface and the group of sixty-four germ cells is carried along with it. In the meantime the germ cells begin to migrate from the amniotic cavity in which they lie through a sort of canal at the bottom of a groove in the germ-band and thus make their way inside of the embryo (Fig. 37, *F*). That the germ cells actually migrate and are not simply forced about by the surrounding tissues seems certain since they are ameboid in shape and pseudopodia extend out in the direction of their movement (Fig. 37, *F*).

After penetrating into the embryo the germ cells become separated into two groups. It was difficult to count the number in each group, but many

GERM CELLS IN THE ARTHROPODA 117

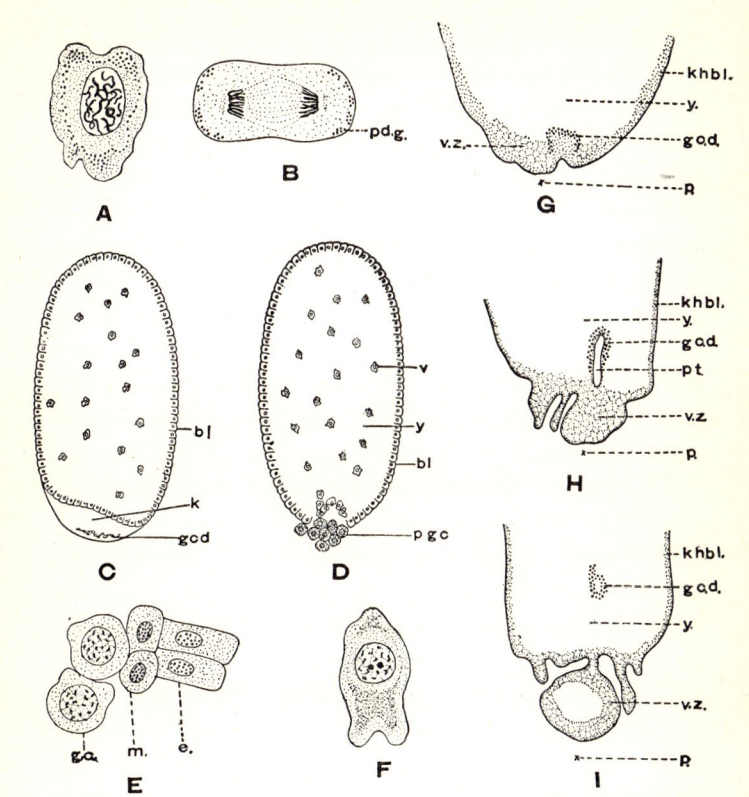

Fig. 37.—*Calligrapha*. *A.* A germ cell of *C. multipunctata* shortly after being cut off from the egg. *B.* Division of a primordial germ cell. *C.* Longitudinal section through egg of *C. bigsbyana* at blastoderm stage; the posterior end was killed with a hot needle just after deposition. *D.* Longitudinal section through uninjured egg at same stage. *E.* Two ectoderm cells (*e*), two mesoderm cells (*m*), and two germ cells (*g.c.*) from an egg three days old. *F.* Germ cell during migration into the embryo (three days old). *G.H.I.* Longitudinal sections through eggs centrifuged for one hour, two hours, and four hours respectively. *bl* = blastoderm; *g.c.d.* = granules of pole-disc; *k* = killed portion of egg; *khbl.* = keimhautblastem; *p.* = posterior; *pgc* = primordial germ cells; *v* = vitellophags; *v.z.* = vesicular zone; *y.* = yolk.

attempts seem to justify the conclusion that the division is equal or approximately equal, that is, each group contains about thirty-two germ cells. These groups acquire a covering of mesoderm cells, are carried by the somatic tissues to a position near the dorsal surface on either side of the body in the last two abdominal segments, and thus become germ glands situated in their definite positions. Some time before the larval stage is reached, the sex of the embryo can be determined by the shape of the germ glands; those of the male become dumbbell shape, whereas the female organs retain the earlier pear shape and begin to acquire terminal filaments.

It is interesting to note that much time and effort have been wasted by those who have attempted to influence the sex of caterpillars by over-feeding or starving. Kellogg (1907), for example, "discovered," after an unsuccessful attempt to change the sex of silk worms by this means, that these caterpillars already possess germ glands which are differentiated as male or female. If he, and others who have undertaken similar experiments, had examined the literature on the origin of the germ cells in insects, they would have found that as long ago as 1815, Herold published results of investigations on *Papilio brassica* and other species of LEPIDOPTERA which proved that the sex of the larva is already determined before it hatches from the egg. A similar condition was reported in *Bombyx pini* by Suckow (1828), in *Zeuzera œsculi* by Bessels (1867), and in *Pieris brassica* by Brandt (1878).

There now ensues a period of activity during which a large number of ovarian tubules develop in the female and testicular follicles appear in the male. A number of much debated problems exist regarding the cellular elements within the ovaries and testes of insects — problems which are of considerable importance in any discussion of the germ-cell cycle. Put in the form of questions, two of these are with respect to the ovary: (1) Do the nurse cells originate from the oögonia, thus becoming abortive eggs, or are they of mesodermal parentage? (2) Does amitotic nuclear division occur in nurse cells and oögonia?

The answers to these questions differ according to the species of insects studied, and, as usual, the observations and interpretations of different investigators do not always agree. They can be answered with certainty in the case of *Miastor*. All of the oögonia in this form are direct descendants of the primordial germ cell; the nurse cells are of mesodermal origin; and amitotic division occurs neither in the nurse cells nor in the oögonia. The situation is quite different in chrysomelid beetles. The nurse cells in the ovaries of the potato beetle all seem to be of germ-cell origin. That the nurse cells which are derived from oögonia are abortive eggs is the general opinion of zoölogists. Convincing evidence for this view has recently been provided by De Winter (1913) from studies of the apterous insect, *Podura aquatica*. In this species the proportion of eggs and nurse cells which develop from the oöcytes is about one to ten. The oöcytes that become eggs are those that chance to lie at the periphery of the ovary and hence are in a position to derive abundant nutrition from the blood. The oöcytes that fail to become eggs are not, according to De Winter, "vitellogénes" but true abortive eggs, representing a more primitive stage than the nurse cells of other insects which have acquired, secondarily, a nutritive function.

On the other hand, Govaerts (1913) argues strongly in favor of the view that the oögonia divide differentially, the daughter cells becoming true germ cells (the ultimate oögonia) and true somatic cells (the nurse cells). He bases his position upon the conditions existing in the ovaries of certain beetles of the genera *Carabus* and *Cicindela*, and upon the discoveries of Giardina (1901), Debaisieux (1909), and Günthert (1910) in *Dytiscus marginalis*. Giardina established for *Dytiscus* the fact that the mitoses which result in the formation of nurse cells are differential, as theoretically postulated by Paulcke (1900). During the four divisions preceding the formation of the oöcyte a single oögonium gives rise to one oöcyte and fifteen nurse cells (Fig. 38). A differentiation takes place in the chromatin of the oögonial nucleus, one half consisting of a condensed mass, the other half of large granules which correspond to the forty chromosomes of the oögonium (Fig. 38, *A*). During mitosis the chromosomes become arranged as an equatorial plate, and the chromatic mass forms a ring about it — the "anello

GERM CELLS IN THE ARTHROPODA 121

cromatico" (*B*). This ring passes intact to one of the daughter cells (*C*), whereas the chromosomes are

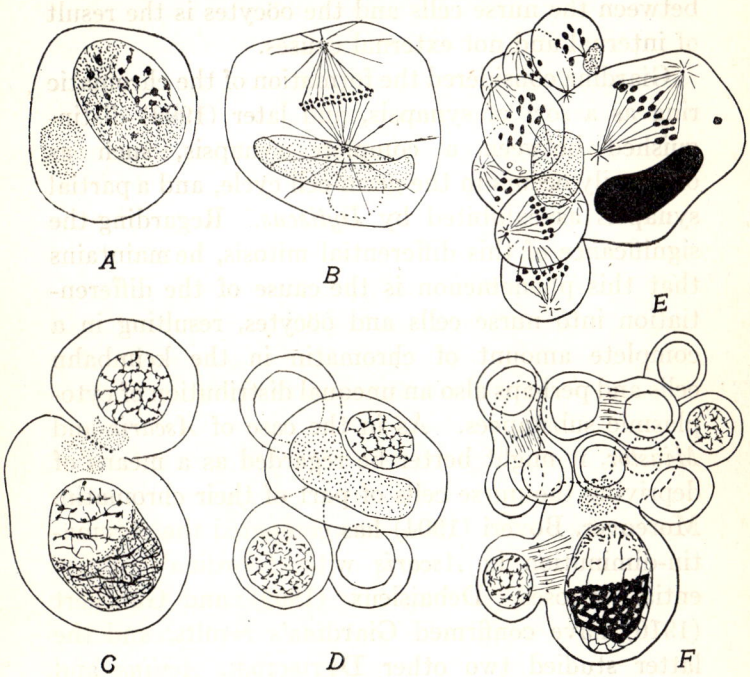

Fig. 38. — Differentiation of nurse cells and oöcytes in *Dytiscus marginalis*. *A*. Oögonium with chromatin of nucleus separating into two parts. *B*. Metaphase of oögonial mitosis; the "anello cromatico" is situated at the lower end of spindle. *C*. Two-cell stage; the lower cell with nucleus containing two sorts of chromatin. *D*. Four-cell stage; "anello cromatico" in one cell. *E*. Eight-cell stage; cells ready to divide. *F*. Sixteen-cell stage; one large cell (oöcyte) with chromatin from the "anello cromatico," and fifteen nurse cells. (*A–D, F, from Giardina, 1901; E, from Debaiseaux, 1909.*)

equally divided. During the succeeding mitoses similar differential divisions occur resulting in one oöcyte containing the chromatic ring (Fig. 38, *F*) and fifteen nurse cells lacking this nuclear substance. Thus as Paulcke's theory demands, the difference between the nurse cells and the oöcytes is the result of internal and not external causes.

Giardina considered the formation of the chromatic ring as a sort of synapsis, and later (1902) distinguished between a complete synapsis, such as ordinarily occurs in the germ-cell cycle, and a partial synapsis as exhibited by *Dytiscus*. Regarding the significance of this differential mitosis, he maintains that this phenomenon is the cause of the differentiation into nurse cells and oöcytes, resulting in a complete amount of chromatin in the keimbahn cells and perhaps also an unequal distribution of cytoplasmic substances. As in the case of *Ascaris* and *Miastor*, it might better be regarded as a means of depriving the nurse cells of part of their chromatin. Moreover, Boveri (1904) has compared the chromatin-diminution in *Ascaris* with Giardina's differential mitoses. Debaisieux (1909) and Günthert (1910) have confirmed Giardina's results, and the latter studied two other Dytiscidæ, *Acilius* and *Colymbetes*, which also exhibit differential mitoses similar except in certain details. Günthert found that the chromatic ring is composed of fine granules which may split off from the surface of the chromosomes (compare with *Ascaris* and *Miastor*) and stain like cytoplasm. He interprets this as "Zerfallsprodukte" of the chromosomes. Debaisieux, on the other hand, claims that this cast-out nuclear material is nucleolar rather than chromatic in nature.

It seems highly probable that the "anello cromatico" of Giardina consists of chromatin, and Goldschmidt (1904) and others do not hesitate to class it as an example of a "Chromidialapparat." Furthermore it is apparently the result of a chromatin-diminution, as Boveri (1904) maintains, differing from the similar process in *Ascaris* and *Miastor* in details but not in the ultimate result. Finally, the discovery of this peculiar body in *Dytiscus* adds one more argument to the hypothesis that the chromatin content of the germ cells differs from that of the somatic cells quantitatively, at least in some cases, and perhaps also qualitatively.

Many are the bodies that have been homologized with the "anello cromatico" of *Dytiscus*. Buchner (1909) claims that the nucleolar-like structure in the oögonia and young oöcytes of *Gryllus* is homologous to both accessory chromosomes of the spermatogenesis and to this chromatin ring in *Dytiscus*. This "accessorische Körper" passes intact into one half of the oöcytes where it disintegrates into granules of a "tropische Natur." Foot and Strobell (1911) have also compared it with the chromatin nucleolus in the oögonia of *Protenor* with which it has certain characteristics in common, but no such differential divisions occur as in *Dytiscus*.

Govaerts (1913) was unable to find anything resembling the chromatic ring of Giardina, and concludes that the formation of a chromatic mass differentiating the oöcytes and the nurse cells is unique in the DYTISCIDÆ. His investigations demonstrate that this phenomenon does not occur in all insects and that we must seek some larger cause than the unequal distribution of chromatic elements.

If no differential divisions are present, as in *Dytiscus*, what is the cause of the formation of oöcytes and nurse cells? Govaerts decides that since the ultimate oögonium possesses a definite polarity marked by the localization of the "residu fusorial," and the two kinds of daughter cells arise from opposite ends of the mother cell, the cause of the differentiation resides in the polarization of the oögonium. He does not, however, account for this "polarité pre-differentielle."

Haecker (1912) has described in *Cyclops* and *Diaptomus* a three-cell stage in the development of the gonad which is brought about by the delayed division of one of the germ cells of the two-cell stage, and concludes that as in *Dytiscus* there must be an internal difference in the cells to account for this condition.

Wieman (1910b) has followed the history of the oögonia in *Leptinotarsa signaticollis* through the larval and adult stages, but was unable to find any evidence that the nuclei inaugurate differentiation as in *Dytiscus*. He concludes that "the process seems to be the result of several distinct cell elements which operate together as a whole" (p. 148) and that the semi-fluid matrix which results from the liquefaction of cells at the base of the terminal chamber may exert a "specific effect on those germ cells coming under its influence, enabling them to develop into ova, while the more distant germ cells become nurse cells" (p. 147). My observations agree with those of Wieman; no definite relations nor nuclear evidence were discovered during the differentiation of the oögonia into oöcytes and nurse cells. The data available do not suggest any method of differentiation not already proposed, and still leave the question whether the nurse cells should be regarded as abortive germ cells or true somatic cells one of personal opinion.

A study of cyst formation in the testis of the potato beetle has revealed what seems to be a series of events in the male germ-cell cycle parallel to that in the females of *Dytiscus*, *Carabus*, and *Cicindela*, during which the nurse cells are produced. There are in *Leptinotarsa* two pairs of testes, one on either side of the body. Each testis consists of a large number of follicles radiating out from near the center. Figure 39 is a diagram of a longitudinal section made from the testis of an old larva. At the lower end is attached the sperm duct (*s.d*) which is connected with a cavity (*c*) within the testis. Just above this cavity is a region containing degenerating cells; above this region is a mass of spermatogonia (*sg*) not yet within cysts; and this mass is capped by a small group of epithelial cells (*t.c*). The major part of the testis is composed of radiating follicles containing cysts of spermatogonia, spermatocytes, or spermatozoa (*cy*).

In that region of the testis surrounding and underlying the terminal cap (Fig. 39, *t. c*) there are a large number of spermatogonia not yet contained in cysts. All stages in cyst formation may be observed here not only in larval testes but also in those of pupæ and adults. The youngest spermatogonia are those lying near the terminal cap. Figure 40, *A* shows a few cells of the terminal cap (*t.c*), some of the neighboring spermatogonia (*spg*), and several of the epithelial cells (*ep*) that are scattered about among the spermatogonia. Cysts are formed toward the edge of the spermatogonial mass away from the terminal cap, and Fig. 40, *A* to *G* represent certain of the stages observed. The spermatogonia divide apparently exclusively by mitosis. A well-developed spindle is formed and this persists after the cell wall has separated the two daughter cells. The spindle fibers which are at first perfectly distinct (Fig. 40, *B*) unite into a compact strand (Fig. 40, *C*) which stains dense black in iron hæmatoxylin after fixation in Carnoy's fluid. In many cases it was impossible to distinguish an intervening cell wall

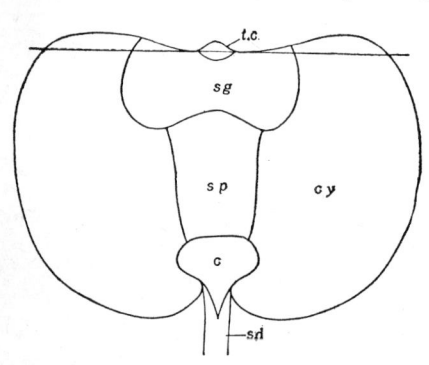

FIG. 39.—*Leptinotarsa decemlineata*. Longitudinal section through testis of full-grown larva. *c* = cavity; *cy* = region of cysts; *s.d* = sperm duct; *sg* = region of spermatogonia; *sp* = region of spermatozoa; *t.c* = terminal cap.

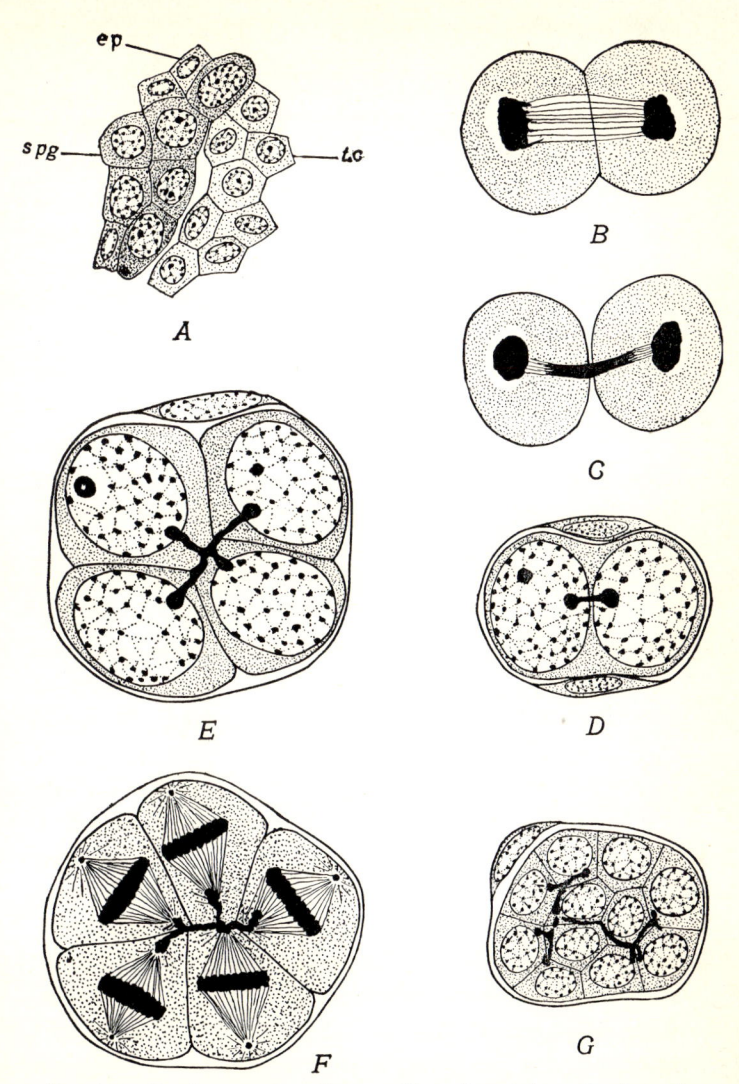

Fig. 40.—*Leptinotarsa decemlineata*. Stages in cyst formation in testis. *A*. Spermatogonia (*spg*), cells of terminal cap (*t.c*), and epithelial cells (*ep*). *B*. Mitotic division of spermatogonium. *C*. Later stage in same process. *D*. Binucleate spermatogonial cell within epithelial envelope. *E*. Four spermatogonia connected by spindle remains. *F*. Spermatogonia from cyst containing eight cells. *G*. Section through cyst containing thirty-two spermatogonia. (127)

between the daughter nuclei (Fig. 40, *D*). In either case, however, the spindle remains persist, forming a basic staining strand with enlarged ends connecting the two nuclei. Since at this time and in all later stages the two or more spermatogonia may be found surrounded by an envelope of epithelial cells, it seems certain that, as Wieman (1910*b*) maintains, the spermatozoa in a single cyst are derived from a single spermatogonium.

A cyst containing four spermatogonia is represented in Fig. 40, *E*. Here again appear the strongly basic staining spindle remains connecting the nuclei. These black strands persist until the succeeding mitotic division occurs as Fig. 40, *F*, which was drawn from a section of a cyst containing eight spermatogonia, shows. Spindle remains are still evident in later stages, as in Fig. 40, *G*, which represents a cyst containing thirty-two spermatogonia, but were not observed in cysts containing more than sixty-four cells.

Many investigators have figured spermatogonial divisions which result in rosette-like groups of cells similar to that represented in Fig. 40, *F*. Apparently, however, the spindle remains, if present, did not possess such a strong affinity for basic stains. Furthermore, only those of my preparations that were fixed in Carnoy's fluid and stained in iron hæmotoxylin exhibited these black strands. Similar spindle remains have been observed in *Dytiscus*, especially by Günthert (1910), and *Carabus* (Govaerts, 1913), during the differentiation of nurse

GERM CELLS IN THE ARTHROPODA

cells and oöcytes from oögonia, and there can be little doubt but that the process of cyst formation in the male as described above is similar to the differential divisions in the female.

Thus the discovery of these distinct spindle remains in the spermatogonial divisions enables us to homologize one more period in the cycle of the male germ cells with a corresponding period in the cycle of the female germ cells.

According to this view the ultimate spermatogonium passes through a certain number of divisions — probably five or six — which correspond to the differential divisions so clearly exhibited by the ultimate oögonia of *Dytiscus*. Just as in the maturation processes, however, where only one female cell but all of the male cells are functional, so these earlier divisions result in the female in the production of a single oöcyte and a number of nurse cells which may be considered abortive eggs, whereas in the male every daughter cell is functional. The limited period of division in the cycle of the male germ cells in man (Montgomery, 1911; von Winiwarter, 1912) is also similar to those in *Dytiscus* and *Leptinotarsa*. The Sertoli cells are intimately connected with the germ cells in the mammalian testis and probably perform three functions: (1) they nourish the spermatocytes; (2) they provide the spermatic fluid; and (3) they exert some chemicotactic stimulus which serves to orient the spermatozoa into bundles. The origin of the Sertoli cells has been for many years in doubt. Many investigators

K

claim that they arise from cells other than germ cells; these writers have been called by Waldeyer (1906) "dualists." An equal number of authorities believe that both Sertoli cells and spermatogonia

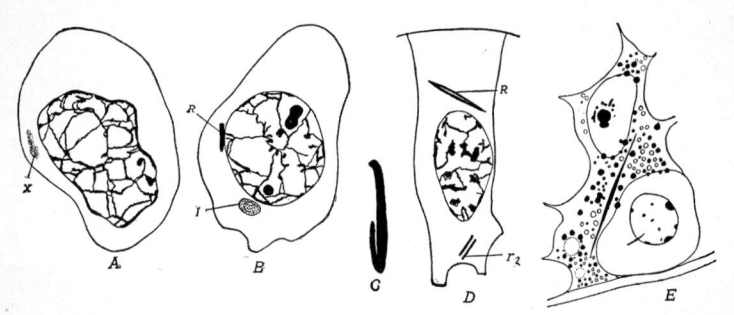

Fig. 41. — Stages in the formation of the Sertoli cell in man. *A*. Spermatogonium containing granular inclusion (*X*) from which "Sertoli cell determinant" *may* arise. *B*. Antepenultimate spermatogonium showing rod (*R*) and idiozome (*I*). *C*. Division of rod. *D*. A Sertoli cell containing a divided rod (*R*) and two rodlets (r_2). *E*. Sertoli cell with crystalloid of Charcot and lipoid granules; at lower right corner a spermatogonium with crystalloid of Lubarsch. (*A–D, from Montgomery, 1911; E, from von Winiwarter, 1912.*)

originate from primordial germ cells; these are the "monists."

The researches of Montgomery and von Winiwarter have decided the question, at least so far as man is concerned, in favor of the monists. Montgomery's results are diagrammatically shown in Fig. 42. Of thirty antepenultimate spermatogonia examined, twenty-three contained each a rod-shaped structure (Fig. 41, *B*, *R*) and it seems probable that this peculiar body, which is identified by von Winiwarter with the "cristalloide de Lubarsch" (Lubarsch, 1896), is present in every cell of this

GERM CELLS IN THE ARTHROPODA

generation. This rod is considered by Montgomery to be of cytoplasmic origin and is termed by him a "Sertoli cell determinant." During the division

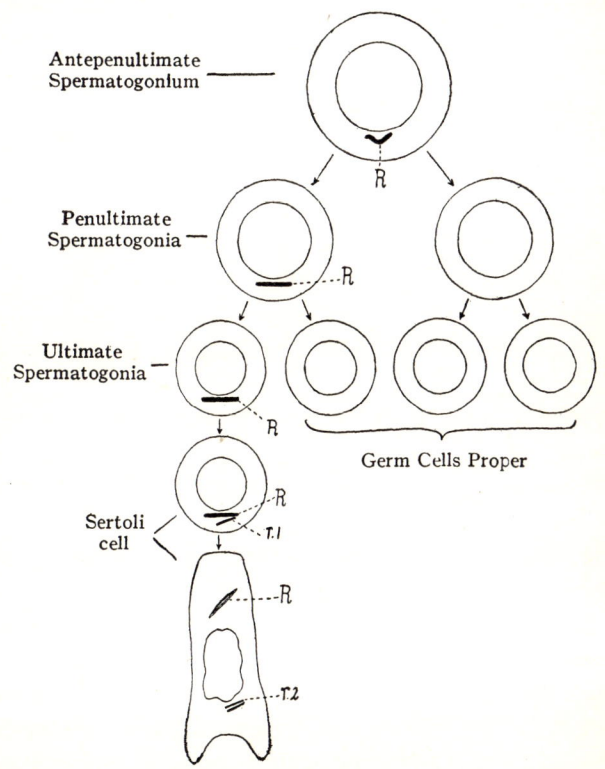

Fig. 42. — Diagram illustrating the differentiation of the Sertoli cell in man. (*From Montgomery, 1911.*)

of the antepenultimate spermatogonia the rod passes undivided into one of the daughter cells; thus one-half of the penultimate spermatogonia possess a rod, the other half do not. Of the forty-nine penultimate spermatogonia examined, twenty-four exhibited a rod and twenty-five did not. This result has been confirmed by von Winiwarter. When the rod-containing penultimate spermatogonia divide, there is a similar segregation of the rod in one of the daughter cells, hence only one-fourth of the cells resulting from the divisions of the antepenultimate spermatogonia possess a rod. Of one hundred and forty-two cells of this generation studied by Montgomery, twenty-five were found with a rod and one hundred and seventeen without. That this ratio is less than one to three (1 : 3) is explained by the fact that some of the spermatogonia with rods may already have become Sertoli cells. The further history of the rod in the Sertoli cell is as follows: A primary rodlet is produced by a splitting of the rod (Fig. 41, *C*) after which the rod either disappears at once or else persists for a time, in which case it may split longitudinally as shown in Fig. 41, *D*. However, in four-fifths of the cells examined (one hundred in number) the large rod disappeared before the growth of the Sertoli cell had begun. Each primary rodlet splits longitudinally into two approximately equal parts, called secondary rodlets (Fig. 41, *D*, r_2), which persist until the end of the cycle of the Sertoli cell.

Neither Montgomery nor von Winiwarter were able to determine the origin of the rod. They do not consider it mitochondrial in nature, although it may arise from granules lying in the cytoplasm.

Montgomery found in one cell a mass of granules from which the rod may have developed (Fig. 41, *A*, *X*), and von Winiwarter noted that the rod had a granular appearance in the earliest stages he examined. It is also perfectly distinct from the iozome (see Fig. 41, *B*, *I*) and is apparently not directly derived from the nucleus. Von Winiwarter is not so certain as Montgomery regarding the history of the spermatogonia, the "cristalloide de Lubarsche," and the "bâtonnets accessoires," as he calls the rodlets. He was unable to decide regarding the number of spermatogonial divisions and believes it to be indeterminate. He finds, contrary to Montgomery, the rod persisting in fully developed Sertoli cells, and considers the fragmentation or fission of the rod to form the primary rodlets as doubtful. Further investigations with more favorable material are very desirable, but notwithstanding certain differences of opinion between the two writers whose results have been briefly stated above, it seems certain that Sertoli cells and germ cells are both derived from primordial germ cells, and that the Sertoli cells differ from the ultimate spermatogonia in the possession of a peculiar rod probably of cytoplasmic origin. Montgomery considers this a sort of secondary somatic differentiation (the Sertoli cells representing the soma of the testis); the first somatic differentiation occurring when the tissue cells become differentiated from the germ cells in the embryo.

AMITOSIS. Wilson (1900) defines amitosis as "mass-division of the nuclear substance without the formation of chromosomes and amphiaster" (p. 437) and concludes from a review of the literature up to the year 1900 "that in the vast majority of cases amitosis is a secondary process which does not fall in the generative series of cell-divisions" (p. 119). During the past ten years interest in direct nuclear division has been maintained principally because of the claims of certain investigators that germ cells may multiply in this way and still give rise to functional eggs or spermatozoa.

During amitosis the chromatin remains scattered within the nucleus and does not form a spireme nor chromosomes, and therefore its individual elements, the chromatin granules, do not divide. As a result of this *mass*-division there can be no accurate segregation of chromatin granules in the daughter nuclei as is demanded by the theory that the nucleus, and particularly the chromatin, contains the determiners of hereditary characteristics. Furthermore, nuclear division without the formation of chromosomes obviously condemns the hypothesis of the genetic continuity of the chromosomes, and hence seriously interferes with current ideas regarding the significance of the accessory chromosomes in the determination of sex. Among the animals in whose germ cells amitosis has been reported are certain AMPHIBIA, cœlenterates, cestodes, and insects.

AMPHIBIA. Vom Rath (1891, 1893), Meves (1891, 1895), and McGregor (1899) have recorded amitosis in the germ cells of AMPHIBIA. Meves claims that the spermatogonia of *Salamandra* divide amitotically in the autumn but return to the mitotic method in the spring, later giving rise to functional spermatogonia. Vom Rath finds amitosis but contends that the cells that divide in this way do not become spermatozoa but are degenerating, being used as nutritive material by the other spermatogonia. The amitotic divisions described by McGregor (1899) in *Amphiuma* differ in certain respects from those of both Meves and vom Rath. In this species the primary spermatogonia divide by amitosis; their products later divide by mitosis and produce functional spermatozoa. Our knowledge concerning amitosis in the spermatogonia of AMPHIBIA is therefore in an unsatisfactory state, although the observations of Meves and McGregor argue strongly in favor of this method.

CŒLENTERATA. While no direct nuclear divisions were recorded by Hargitt (1906) in the germ cells of *Clava leptostyla* the absence of mitotic figures in the early cleavage stages of the egg led him to the conclusion that the "nuclear activity differs greatly from the oridinary forms of mitosis, and appears to involve direct or amitotic division" (p. 229). If this were true, the germ cells which are derived from these cleavage cells must be descended from cells which once divided amitotically. This case of supposed amitosis has been cleared up by the subsequent studies of Beckwith (1909), who collected material of *Clava* very early in the morning and found typical mitotic divisions during the maturation and early cleavage of the egg and no evidence of amitosis.

CESTODA. Child concluded (1904) from a study of the cestode, *Moniezia expansa*, that this method of cell division occurs in the antecedents of both the eggs and the spermatozoa. This writer has published a series of papers upon this subject using *Moniezia expansa* and *Moniezia planissima* for his material (1904, 1906, 1907, 1910, 1911), and his principal conclusion is that in these species the division of the cells destined to become eggs and spermatozoa is predominantly amitotic. Mitotic division also occurs but comparatively rarely. Cells which have divided amitotically then divide mitotically during maturation and form typical ova.

The nature of the nuclear division in the cestodes was later investigated by Richards (1909, 1911) who studied the female sex organs of the same species employed by Child as well as material obtained from *Tænia serrata*. Richards finds that mitosis unquestionably occurs in the young germ cells but was unable to demonstrate amitosis. Richards claims that amitosis cannot be demonstrated except by the observation of the process in the living material and the subsequent study of this material by cytological methods. Child (1911) agrees with Richards that amitosis cannot be demonstrated in fixed material but nevertheless concludes after an examination of Richards' preparations "that direct division plays an important part in the developmental cycle of *Moniezia*, in the germ cells as well as in the soma" (Child, 1911, p. 295).

Finally Harman (1913) was unable to find any

evidence of amitotic divisions in the sex cells of either *Tænia teniæformis* or *Moniezia* and concludes that the conditions that suggest amitosis can just as well or better be explained by mitosis. Experiments with living cells of *Tænia* were without results, since the cells did not divide when placed in Ringer's solution, although they continued to live outside the body of the host for forty-eight hours. Morse (1911) likewise failed to observe divisions in living cells of *Calliobothrium* and *Crossobothrium* which were kept in the plasma of the host. That the observation of amitosis in living cells is possible seems certain since Holmes (1913) has recorded an actual increase in the number of epithelial cells from the embryos and young tadpoles of several Amphibia that were cultivated in lymph, and has noted various stages of amitotic nuclear division, although no convincing evidence was obtained that this was followed by cell division.

INSECTA. In the HEMIPTERA amitosis was described by Preusse (1895) in the ovarian cells of *Nepa cinerea* and similar conditions were reported by Gross (1901) in insects of the same order. Gross, however, claims that the cells which divide amitotically do not produce ova but are degenerating or secretory.

Foot and Strobell (1911) described in ovaries of the bug, *Protenor*, the amitotic division of certain cells which later produce ova. There is, however, considerable difference of opinion among investigators as to the origin of the ova from the various regions of the insect ovary and, since Payne (1912) has shown that in *Gelastocoris* the cells that apparently multiply amitotically do not produce ova, it seems safe to conclude that in *Protenor* the ova are not descended from cells that divide amitotically.

Amitotic division of germ cells followed by mitotic division has been described by Wieman (1910*b*, 1910*c*) in the ovaries and testes as well as in the nurse

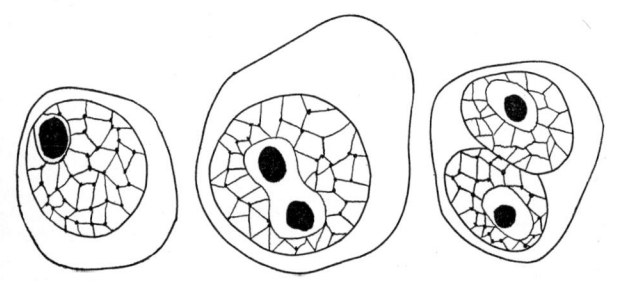

Fig. 43. — Stages in amitosis in spermatogonium of *Leptinotarsa signaticollis*. (*From Wieman, 1910.*)

cells of a chrysomelid beetle, *Leptinotarsa signaticollis*. Germ cells in both ovary and testis taken from full-grown larvæ were found in stages of division recognized by Wieman as amitotic (Fig. 43). It was difficult to demonstrate actual division of the cytoplasm, but that such a division really occurs was inferred because binucleated cells apparently gave rise to spermatocytes with single nuclei. Rapid cell division is assumed by Wieman to account for amitosis. This is brought about by fluctuations in the nutritive supply or, in the case of the testis, by the rapid proliferation of cells during the formation of cysts.

I have studied my preparations of chrysomelid beetles carefully with the aim of detecting amitotic division and have observed what appears to be direct nuclear division among the nurse cells, but could not demonstrate with certainty this kind of division among the oögonia, or spermatogonia. Three stages in the direct division of nurse cell nuclei in *Leptinotarsa decemlineata* are shown in Fig. 8, *a–c*. Oögonia and spermatogonia, however, do not exhibit such clearly defined stages and after examining my preparations and several slides kindly sent me by Doctor Wieman I am forced to conclude that amitosis has not been demonstrated. It is true that frequently dumb-bell shaped nucleoli occur in certain of the nuclei and frequently two nucleoli are present at opposite ends. Also two nuclei may be surrounded by a single cell wall, but no stages were present which could not be attributed as well or better to mitotic phenomena.

CONCLUSION. From the evidence at present available we must conclude that amitotic division of the germ cells has not been demonstrated, and that not until such a process is actually observed in living cells will any other conclusion be possible.

There are still two questions regarding the germ-cell cycle in beetles that we shall attempt to answer; (1) Does a chromatin-diminution process occur such as has been described in *Miastor* and *Ascaris?* and (2) Is the segregation of the germ cells controlled by the nuclei or by the cytoplasm?

The fact that part of each chromosome is cast out

into the cytoplasm in all except the "stem-cell" during the early cleavage of *Ascaris* is well known (see p. 174, Fig. 51). A similar process was described by Kahle (1908) in *Miastor metraloas* and confirmed by me (Hegner, 1912, 1914a) in *Miastor americana* (see p. 57, Fig. 16). This chromatin-diminution process results in the formation of a single primordial germ cell containing the complete amount of chromatin and a number of somatic cells with a reduced amount of chromatin. The origin of the germ cells has been carefully studied in a number of forms which in other respects resemble *Ascaris* and *Miastor*, but in none of them has such a process been discovered. Hasper (1911) was unable to establish it for *Chironomus* which is very similar to *Miastor* in early development, nor has such a phenomenon been found in *Sagitta* (Elpatiewsky, 1909, 1910; Stevens, 1910b; Buchner, 1910a, 1910b) and the copepods (Haecker, 1897; Amma, 1911) and CLADOCERA (Kühn, 1911, 1913) which undergo total cleavage and are in certain other respects similar to *Ascaris*.

The nuclear divisions in the eggs of chrysomelid beetles have been examined by the writer with considerable care, but nothing resembling a diminution process was found. Furthermore, there are no evidences of chromatin bodies in the cytoplasm or yolk as in *Ascaris* (Fig. 51) and *Miastor* (Fig. 18, cR), where the cast-out chromatin does not disintegrate immediately, but can be distinguished for a considerable period during early embryonic development. It seems necessary to conclude therefore that in chrysomelid eggs both germ cells and somatic cells possess the full amount of chromatin or else the elimination of this substance takes place in some other way.

THE DIFFERENTIATION OF THE NUCLEI OF THE BLASTODERM CELLS, PRIMORDIAL GERM CELLS, AND VITELLOPHAGS. The conclusion that no chromatin-diminution process occurs during the early cleavage divisions in the eggs of chrysomelid beetles necessitates the search for some other method of differentiation among the cleavage nuclei. The insect egg is particularly advantageous for testing Roux's hypothesis of qualitative nuclear division, since we have here the production of an enormous number of nuclei before any cell walls are formed, and an egg that is remarkably definitely organized, as indicated by my experiments (Hegner, 1909*b*, 1911*a*), before the blastoderm is formed.

I have been unable to find any differences in the nuclei before they fuse with the keimhautblastem, but as soon as this does occur, a gradual change takes place, and at the time when the blastoderm is completed three sorts of nuclei are distinguishable: (1) The nuclei of the primordial germ cells (Fig. 36, *C*) are larger than the others and contain comparatively few spherical chromatin granules evenly distributed. The cytoplasm of these cells is distinguishable from that of all other cells because of the presence of granules from pole-disc. (2) The nuclei of the blastoderm cells are small and completely filled with large spherical chromatin granules.

(3) The nuclei of the vitellophags resemble the early cleavage nuclei; they are midway between the other two kinds in size, and their chromatin is in a more diffuse condition.

Whether these three kinds of nuclei were all potentially alike before their differentiation is an important question. Visibly they are all similar until they become localized in definite regions of the egg, and associated with particular cytoplasmic elements. One cannot help but conclude that they were all potentially alike and that their differentiation was brought about through the influence of the cytoplasm in which they happened to become embedded. The writer has shown (Hegner, 1911*a*) that if the posterior end of a freshly laid egg of *Leptinotarsa decemlineata* is killed with a hot needle, thus preventing the pole-disc granules and surrounding cytoplasm from taking part in development, no primordial germ cells will be produced. A large series of similar experiments have also proved that at the time of deposition, "The areas of the peripheral layer of cytoplasm (Fig. 36 *khbl.*) are already set aside for the production of particular parts of the embryo, and if the areas are killed, the parts of the embryo to which they were destined to give rise will not appear. Likewise, areas of the blastoderm are destined to produce certain particular parts of the embryo" (Hegner, 1911*a*, p. 251). What becomes of the nuclei that are prevented from entering the injured region of the egg? No evidence has been discovered to indicate that they disintegrate, so they probably take part in development after becoming associated with some other part of the egg. If these nuclei were qualitatively different they should produce germ cells and other varieties of cells in whatever region they chance to reach. It is evident that they are not potentially different and that their "prospective potency" and "prospective significance" do not coincide. The cytoplasm is, therefore, the controlling factor at this stage in the germ-cell cycle, although cytoplasmic differentiations are for the most part invisible and probably the result of nuclear activity during earlier stages.

HYMENOPTERA. A number of papers have appeared which contain references to the germ glands of HYMENOPTERA (Hegner, 1909, pp. 245–248). The most important of these from the standpoint of the present discussion are: (1) Silvestri (1906, 1908) and Hegner (1914*b*) on some parasitic species, and (2) Petrunkewitsch (1901, 1903), Nachtsheim (1913), and others on the honey-bee.

In an endeavor to test the "Dzierzon theory," that the eggs which produce drone bees are normally unfertilized, Petrunkewitsch (1901–1903) discovered some usual maturation divisions. In "drone eggs" the first polar body passes through an equatorial division, each of its daughter nuclei containing one-half of the somatic number of chromosomes. The inner one of these daughter nuclei fuses with the second polar body, which also contains one-half of the somatic number of chromosomes; the resultant nucleus with sixteen chromosomes, the "Richtungskopulationskern" passes through three divisions, giving rise to eight "doppelkernige Zellen." After the blastoderm is completed, the products of these eight cells lie in the middle line near the dorsal surface of the egg, where the formation of the amnion begins; the nuclei of these cells are small, and lie embedded in dark staining cytoplasm. Later they are found just beneath the dorsal surface near the point of union of the amnion with the head-fold of the embryonic rudiment. They are next located between the epithelium of the mid-intestine and the ectoderm; from here they migrate into the cœlomic cavities, and finally, at the time of hatching, form a "wellenartigen" strand, the germ-gland, extending through the third, fourth, fifth, and sixth abdominal segments. The fertilized eggs of the bee were also examined by Petrunkewitsch, but no "Richtungskopulationskern" was discovered. In these eggs the genital glands arise from mesoderm cells. Doubt was immediately cast on these results, although Weismann (1904, p. 336) vouched for their accuracy. Thus Wheeler (1904) says, "Even in his first paper there is no satisfactory evidence to show that the cells regarded as derivatives of the polar bodies in the figures on plate 4 are really such, and not dividing cleavage cells or possibly vitellophags. . . . When we take up the second paper we wonder how anybody could regard the figures there presented as even an adumbration of proof that the testes of the drone are developed from the polar bodies." Dickel (1904) could find no connection between the polar bodies and the cells Petrunkewitsch claims originate from the " Richtungskopulationskern," but considers these " Dotterzellen." Nachtsheim (1913) agrees with Dickel, that these are yolk cells and have no relation to the polar bodies. He also finds these cells in both fertilized and unfertilized eggs, not as Petrunkewitsch states only in the latter.

The investigations of Silvestri (1906, 1908) on parasitic Hymenoptera are of particular interest, since in both the polyembryonic species and those whose eggs produce a single individual, the keimbahn-determinant is considered by him to represent a plasmosome which escapes from the germinal vesicle. Silvestri (1906, 1908) has described the embryonic development of both monembryonic and polyembryonic hymenopterous parasites. Of the former *Encyrtus aphidivorus* and *Oöphthora semblidis* were studied; in both species the series of events were found to be similar. The egg at the time of deposition is elongated and irregularly oval in shape (Fig. 44, *A*); it contains a germinal vesicle (*A*) in the anterior region and a deeply staining body near the posterior end which is called by Silvestri the "nucleolo" (*N*) and is stated to be derived from the nucleolus of the oöcyte nucleus. The eggs may develop parthenogenetically or after fertilization; the unfertilized eggs produce males, whereas the fertilized eggs develop into females. In either case two polar bodies are produced; these disintegrate later. The cleavage nucleus produces by a series of divisions a number of nuclei which migrate to the periphery, as is the rule in insect development. The "nucleolo" remains during this cleavage period unchanged near the posterior end (Fig. 44, *B*); then, when cell walls appear, it becomes distributed among several of the cells thus formed. These multiply less rapidly than the other embryonic cells and are the only cells that give rise to the germ cells in the adult. It is thus obvious that there is here an early segregation of germ cells and that these germ cells differ from the somatic cells in the possession of part of the disintegrated "nucleolo."

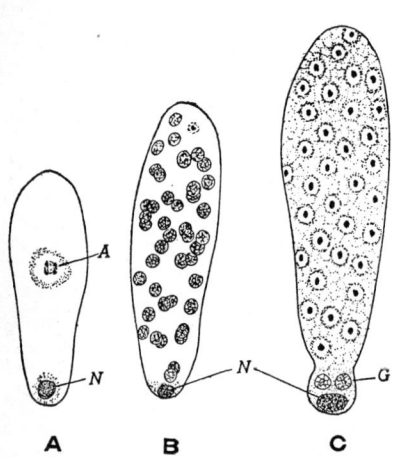

FIG. 44.—*Oöphthora*. *A*. Egg with germinal vesicle (*A*) and "Nucleolo" (*N*). *B*. Egg containing many cleavage nuclei. *C*. Formation of primordial germ cells (*G*) at posterior end of an egg. (*From Silvestri, 1908.*)

The polyembryonic species described by Silvestri are *Copidosoma* (*Litomastix*) *truncatellus* and *Ageniaspis* (*Encyrtus*) *fuscicollis*. The eggs of these species when laid are vase-shaped (Fig. 45), the posterior end corresponding to the base of the vase. Here also a germinal vesicle and "nucleolo" are present, the latter almost always near the posterior end. Parthenogenetic eggs were found to produce males,

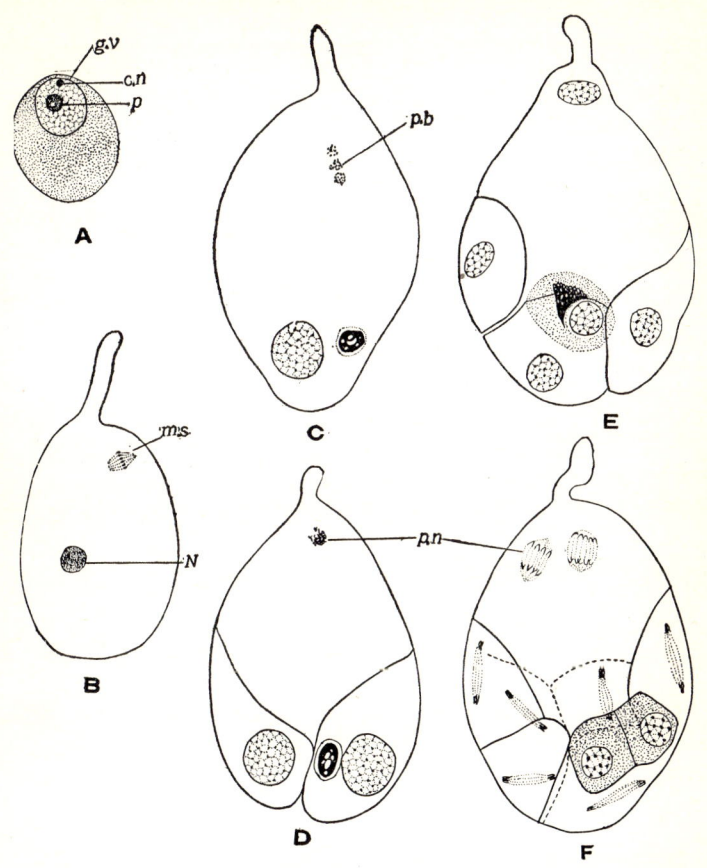

FIG. 45.—*Copidosoma (Litomastix) truncatellus.* *A.* Oöcyte showing germinal vesicle (*g.v*) containing a chromatin-nucleolus (*c.n*) and a plasmosome (*p*). *B.* Egg a few minutes after deposition showing first maturation spindle (*m.s*) and "Nucleolo" (*N*). *C.* Egg about one hour after deposition, showing three polar bodies (*p.b*), the first cleavage nucleus and the "Nucleolo." *D.* Egg in two-cell stage, about one and one-half hours old. *p.n* = polar nucleus. *E.* Four-cell stage. *F.* Egg about four and one-half hours old showing two polar nuclei dividing, two embryonic cells containing nucleolar substance, and six embryonic cells (dividing) without nucleolar substance. (*From Silvestri, 1906.*) (147)

whereas fertilized eggs give rise to females. First and second polar bodies are formed and the first divides, thus making three in all. The events of early cleavage are the same whether the nucleus consists of the female pronucleus only or of the female and male pronuclei fused. Unlike the eggs of monembryonic species, the cleavage nuclei here become separated from one another by cell walls and the "nucleolo" from the very beginning is segregated at each division in a single cleavage cell (Fig. 45, *D*). This cell divides more slowly than the others; the "nucleolo" gradually becomes vacuolated, breaks down, and finally is evenly scattered throughout the entire cytoplasm. Just before the sixteen-cell stage is reached the cell containing the disintegrated "nucleolo" divides and the two daughter cells are provided with equal amounts of its substance (Fig. 45, *F*). Silvestri was only able to trace the cells containing the remains of the "nucleolo" until four of these were present. Nevertheless, he concludes that these and these alone give rise to the germ cells. This conclusion seems well founded when the history of this "nucleolo" is compared with that of similar bodies (keimbahn-determinants) in the eggs of certain other animals.

Two regions develop in the eggs of these polyembryonic HYMENOPTERA: (1) an anterior or polar region containing the polar bodies, and (2) the posterior embryonic region. The latter again becomes differentiated into two regions: (1) an anterior "massa germinigera," which gives rise to normal larvæ, and (2) a posterior "massa monembrionale," which produces the so-called asexual larvæ. These lack reproductive, respiratory, circulatory, and excretory systems. They are supposed to develop from cell masses which do not contain descendants of the cell with "nucleolar" material, and to serve the purpose of tearing apart the organs of the host, thus making it available as food for the normal larvæ. The "massa monembrionale," according to this view, consists entirely of somatic cells, whereas the "massa germinigera" possesses both somatic and germ cells. Doubts have been expressed regarding the development of the asexual larvæ, and Silvestri's results need confirmation. There seems to be no doubt that the "nucleolo" is a keimbahn-determinant in both monembryonic and polyembryonic HYMENOPTERA, but its identification as the nucleolus from the oöcyte nucleus did not seem to the writer to be well established. Its history was, therefore, studied by the writer (Hegner, 1914b) during the growth period of the eggs, with the following results.

My material consisted of a brood of females belonging to the polyembryonic species *Copidosoma gelechiæ*. As in most other insects, the two ovaries of *Copidosoma* consist of rows of oöcytes in various stages of growth — the oldest and largest near the posterior end, and the youngest and smallest at the opposite pole. Before the oögonia enter the growth period (Fig. 46, *A*, *o*) each becomes surrounded by a follicular epithelium (*fe*) and is provided with a group of nurse cells (*nc*) which likewise are enclosed

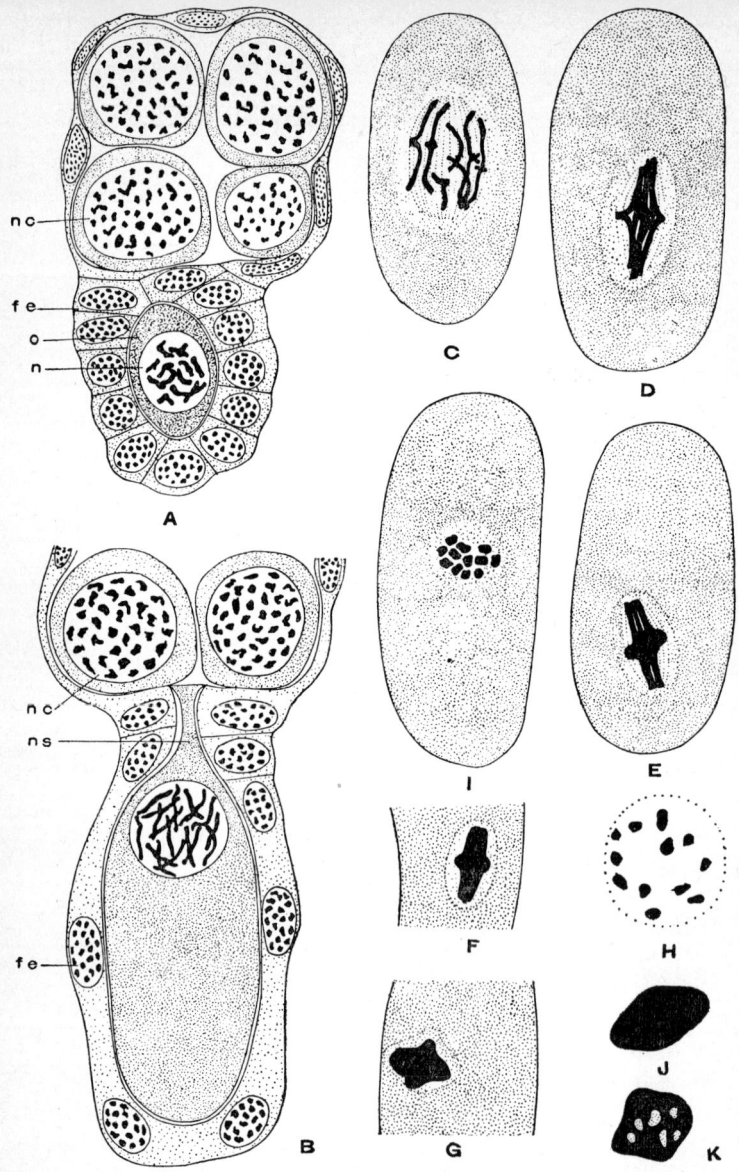

Fig. 46.—*Copidosoma gelechiæ.* *A.* Young oöcyte (*o*) surrounded by an epithelium (*f.e*) and accompanied by nurse cells (*n.c*). *B.* Older oöcyte with nurse string (*n.s*). *C.* Oöcyte containing spindle on which are pairs of chromosomes. *D–G.* Stages in condensation of this spindle. *H.* Cross section of spindle in stage shown in *C*. *I.* Cross section of spindle in stage shown in *D*. *J–K.* Late stages in condensation of spindle.

(150)

by a cellular envelope. Increase in size takes place synchronously in both the nucleus and the cytoplasm of the oöcyte, and a number of stages in this process are illustrated in the accompanying figures. In Fig. 46, *B* a strand of cytoplasm is shown extending forward to the nurse chamber, and it is evidently by means of this pathway that nutritive material is conveyed to the oöcyte. During the growth period the nurse cells decrease in size until they occupy but a very small space and the follicular epithelium becomes very much attenuated (compare Figs. 46, *A* and 47, *D*).

The fully developed oöcytes (Fig. 47, *D*) are more or less vase-shaped with a broad base (posterior), a narrower " waist-line," and a slightly thicker distal (anterior) portion. They are not so long and slender as those illustrated by Silvestri, but perhaps this shape is attained later when the eggs are laid. Within the oöcyte are two conspicuous bodies. At the anterior end is a very large nucleus (*n*) which almost completely fills that portion of the egg; it contains a few scattered rods of chromatin. Near the posterior end is a smaller but even more conspicuous body (Fig. 47, *D*, *k*) which stains very deeply with iron-hæmatoxylin. This may be vacuolated and irregular, showing signs of disintegration, as shown in Fig. 47, or may possess a smooth outline and be entirely homogeneous. It is undoubtedly of a very tough nature, since it not infrequently tears out of the egg substance when struck by the sectioning knife. This obviously represents the "nucleolo" of

152 GERM-CELL CYCLE IN ANIMALS

Silvestri. Silvestri claims that this "nucleolo" is a plasmosome which was cast out of the oöcyte nucleus at an early stage in the growth period, but an examination of my material proves that it really contains all of the chromatin of the oöcyte nucleus. Since it is

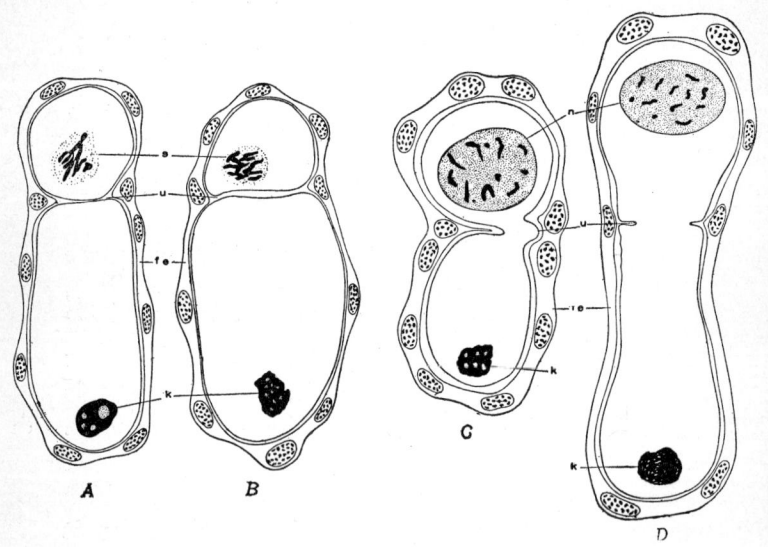

Fig. 47. — *Copidosoma gelechiæ*. Stages in fusion of two contiguous oöcytes end to end. *fe* = epithelium; *k* = keimbahn-chromatin; *n* = nucleus; *s* = spindle breaking down; *u* = point of union of oöcytes.

not a nucleolus, at least in the species I have studied, it can no longer be called a "nucleolo" and therefore the term 'keimbahn-chromatin' will be applied to it.

Figure 46, *A* was drawn from a longitudinal section through an oöcyte (*o*) in an early stage of growth. It is surrounded by follicle cells (*fe*) and accompanied by a group of nurse cells (*n.c*) at the anterior end. A large part of the oöcyte is occupied by the nucleus (*n*) within which are a comparatively few irregular rods of chromatin, forming a group in the center. This nucleus thus differs quite strikingly from those of the follicle and nurse cells. In Fig. 46, *B* is shown an older oöcyte and two of the accompanying nurse cells (*n.c*). The nucleus contains many long slender rods of chromatin which often cross each other near their extremities.

Soon after this stage is reached the nuclear membrane disappears and a sort of spindle is formed as illustrated in Fig. 46, *C*. No asters could be discovered, but the spindle fibers are quite distinct. The chromatin rods are arranged longitudinally on the spindle, and in material fixed in Carnoy's solution and stained in iron-hæmatoxylin followed by eosin, are remarkably distinct. The arrangement of these rods seems to indicate either that entire chromosomes are separating after synapsis or that daughter chromosomes are being pulled apart after a longitudinal split. I am unfortunately unable to state definitely what processes do precede the condition shown here, but it seems probable that the chromatin of the early oöcytes forms a spireme which breaks up into chromosomes, and that these chromosomes become united in pairs at or near their ends, and are there drawn out upon the spindle as represented in Fig. 46, *C*. It seems also certain that a definite number of these chromosome-pairs are present. Only a few cross sections of spindles were found in my preparations, but in these the chromosomes are widely separated and consequently easily counted. Apparently there are twelve double rods in each spindle (Fig. 46, *H*, *I*).

Instead of continuing its activity and forming two daughter nuclei this spindle persists for a long time, undergoing a gradual contraction and condensation. Thus in the stage succeeding that just described the chromatin rods are close together and the entire spindle has decreased in diameter although not in length (Fig. 46, *D*). Spindles in this condition are not always parallel to the long axis of the egg but may be oblique or, more rarely, almost perpendicular to this axis. Hence several transverse sections were obtained, one of which is illustrated in Fig. 46, *I*. Here also is shown a closer proximity of the chromosomes as compared with the cross section of the younger spindle represented in Fig. 46, *H*. The number of chromosomes also appears to be constant, namely, twelve. During succeeding stages the spindle continues to shorten and condense. That shown in Fig. 46, *E* still exhibits spaces between the rods and the presence of only a few spindle fibers. A further contraction is indicated in Fig. 46, *F*, where the chromosomes have become so closely crowded as to form an apparently solid body in the shape of a cross. This chromatin body still continues to contract as shown in Fig. 46, *G*, *J*, and *K*. At about this time vacuoles begin to appear within it (Fig. 46, *K*) and its shape becomes more or less irregular, most often assuming a nearly spherical condition. This may now be recognized as the "nucleolo" of Silvestri or the keimbahn-chromatin as we have decided to call it.

The spindle at first lies nearer the anterior than the posterior part of the oöcyte. As it shortens and condenses it is more often found below the middle of the cell, and finally reaches a position near the posterior end. The conclusion is thus reached that the "nucleolo" of Silvestri is not a plasmosome (metanucleolus) which escapes from the oöcyte nucleus, but consists of all of the chromatin of this nucleus condensed into a more or less spherical body during a peculiar process of spindle formation.

The discovery of the origin and nature of the keimbahn-chromatin brought forth a new problem, namely, that of the origin of the egg nucleus. It was early noted that the oöcytes containing this peculiar spindle were free from any other inclusions in the cytoplasm. How then do they acquire a nucleus? Two hypotheses have been considered, one of which has a considerable body of evidence in its support. In the first place the nucleus might arise from chromatin granules which break away from the chromosomes during the formation or condensation of the spindle. There is, however, no evidence for this view, since the entire chromatin content of the oöcyte nucleus seems to take part in the formation of the spindle and later the keimbahn-chromatin. The second hypothesis was suggested when a number of cases were discovered of two oöcytes lying end to end without any intervening follicular epithelium.

This hypothesis is that pairs of oöcytes unite end to end, the posterior oöcyte containing the keimbahn-chromatin and the anterior furnishing the egg nucleus. Stages in this process are shown in Fig. 47, *A*, *B*, *C*, and *D*.

As the oöcytes increase in size and age the follicular epithelium becomes gradually thinner and in several instances only a delicate strand could be observed between the ends of adjoining oöcytes. In Fig. 47, *A* two oöcytes are shown without any cellular layer between them, although the follicular epithelium extends in a short distance at the point of contact. The posterior cell is much the larger and older, and possesses keimbahn-chromatin, but no nucleus. The other oöcyte is younger and smaller and contains what has been interpreted as a disintegrating spindle (*s*). The condition illustrated in Fig. 47, *B* is similar except that the keimbahn-chromatin in the posterior oöcyte is less regular, having already begun to break up, and the chromatin rods in the anterior cell represent a further stage in the transformation of a spindle into a nucleus. Figure 47, *C* illustrates what is considered a later stage in the fusion process. The anterior part, which contains a definite nucleus, is connected with the posterior position by a thick strand. The nuclear membrane is not very distinct in the preparation indicating that the nucleus is not yet completely formed. The posterior part is not as large as in the other figures, since the section was not exactly in the longitudinal axis, but slightly oblique. The keimbahn-chromatin has been added in the figure from a part of the oöcyte three sections away. A still further stage of fusion is indicated in Fig. 47, *D*.

In all these cases and in fully developed eggs there is a distinct "waist line" which can be accounted for upon the view that two oöcytes fuse end to end as above described, the narrow part corresponding to the region of union. The conclusion seems warranted, therefore, that every egg when laid consists of two oöcytes which have united end to end, the posterior or older oöcyte being provided with keimbahn-chromatin derived from the chromatin of its nucleus, and the anterior supplied with a nucleus which has arisen from the disintegration of a spindle similar to that from which the keimbahn-chromatin originated.

A number of references are present in literature to what have been termed "uterine," "disappearing," or "aborting" spindles. Such a spindle was first noted by Selenka (1881) in the turbellarian, *Thysanozoön diesingii*. Here apparently a completely developed maturation spindle was observed in the fully grown eggs after they had entered the uterus; then, just before the metaphase of mitosis, the spindle broke down and the nucleus returned to a resting condition. This same nucleus later gave rise to polar bodies as in the eggs of other animals. Similar aborting spindles have been described by Lang (1884) in several species of polyclads, by Wheeler (1894) in *Planocera inquilina*, by Gardiner (1895, 1898) in *Polychœrus caudatus*, by Surface (1907) in *Planocera*, by Patterson (1912) in *Graffilla gemellipara*, and by Patterson and Wieman (1912) in *Planocera inquilina*. Patterson and Wieman have given the uterine spindle in *Planocera* careful study, and have established the fact that in this species it is simply a maturation spindle which forms near the center of the egg and later moves to the periphery, undergoing during this migration a distinct contraction. They further suggest that the uterine spindles described in the eggs of other animals are really one phase in a typical maturation process.

It has thus been shown that the first maturation spindle in certain eggs may remain practically inactive for a considerable period. It should be noted, however, that in *Copidosoma* the spindle arises not in the fully grown egg but in very young oöcytes, and that it appears to lack asters at every period of its history. While therefore this structure may be a precocious maturation spindle, it differs markedly from any other such spindle that I have been able to find described in cytological literature.

The second view is that the oöcyte spindle represents a special mechanism leading to an accurate distribution of chromatin in the keimbahn-chromatin mass. The position of the contracted and condensed spindle, however, is not definite, since it has been found to occupy almost any part of the oöcyte and to lie with its long axis parallel to the long axis of the oöcyte, or oblique or even perpendicular to this axis (Fig. 46, *E*, *G*). Furthermore the keimbahn-chromatin does not seem to be of a definite structure, but soon after it reaches a sphere-like shape it begins to vacuolate and becomes irregular (Figs. 46, *K*; 47). It also seems probable that in some oöcytes the oöcyte spindle gives rise to the keimbahn-chromatin, whereas in others it becomes disorganized, forming the nucleus of the egg (Fig. 47, *A*, *B*, *C*). What causes the difference in the history of the oöcyte spindles? No definite answer can be given to this question, but there are two possibilities, (1) external and (2) internal influences. It seems very improbable that any internal mechanism exists which determines what the history of the oöcyte spindle shall be. On the other hand, the arrangement of the oöcytes in the ovary might cause the spindle of those most posteriorly situated to become keimbahn-chromatin and of those next in order to transform into nuclei. According to this view the oöcytes depend upon chance for their final position in the ovary, and the fate of the spindle is decided by the environment of the oöcyte.

There are numerous cases of cell fusion in both PROTOZOA and METAZOA, and germ cells and somatic cells. For example, PROTOZOA engulf other cells; the fully grown ova of *Hydra* consist of several germ cells fused together; and leucocytes may fuse with one another. In all such cases the nucleus of one cell persists, whereas those of the other cells disintegrate and disappear. Among certain leucocytes of *Axolotl*, however, Walker (1907) has described a sort of fusion which results in the transference of the chromatin from one cell to another without the disintegration of the migrating chromatin. In plants also Gates (1911) has shown that chromatin may migrate from one pollen mother-cell of *Œnothera gigas* into a neighboring mother-cell where it remains visible for some time before becoming incorporated with the surrounding cytoplasm. Many more cases of cellular fusion might be mentioned, but in no instance so far as I am aware has the union of two well-developed oöcytes to form one egg been reported. It is true that in *Copidosoma* the chromatin in one (the proximal) oöcyte (the keimbahn-chromatin) finally disintegrates and disappears in the cytoplasm, and thus the condition here may be compared with that in the cases mentioned above, but the stage of fusion in *Copidosoma* is extremely late in the growth period, and the chromatin material remains visible for a remarkably long interval of the germ-cell cycle.

According to Silvestri the first cleavage cell of *Copidosoma* consists of the egg nucleus surrounded by only a small portion of the substance in the posterior end of the egg in which is embedded the keimbahn-chromatin. If the two materials within the oöcytes do not become intimately fused, it is obvious therefore that the cells of the embryo which are descended from the first cleavage cell are derived from the nucleus of the anterior of the two fused oöcytes and cytoplasm from the posterior oöcyte with the addition of the keimbahn-chromatin.

The history of the germ cells after their segregation is not known for any polyembryonic animal.

Polyembryony has been described in an earthworm. *Lumbricus trapezoides* (Kleinenberg, 1879), in certain BRYOZOA (Harmer, 1893; Robertson, 1903), in the armadillo (Patterson, 1913), and in parasitic HYMENOPTERA (Marchal, 1904; Silvestri, 1906, 1908). In every case cleavage is of the indeterminate type, and the cell lineage is unknown. Various theories have been advanced to account for polyembryony, such as (1) blastotomy or the early separation of blastomeres, each giving rise to a single individual as has been brought about by Driesch (1892) and others by separating the blastomeres of the eggs of certain animals; (2) polyovular follicles may occur in mammals and by some (Rosner, 1901) are considered sufficient to account for polyembryony among the members of this class; and (3) precocious budding has been suggested to account for the production of many individuals from a single egg, most recently by Patterson (1913), who has shown that in the armadillo the blastoderm produces two primary buds from each of which two secondary buds arise, and hence four young develop from each egg. According to the theory of germinal continuity each of the buds must be supplied with germ cells or with germ-plasm which has not yet been segregated into germ cells. Silvestri's investigations seem to indicate that the former is true for parasitic HYMENOPTERA, but it is difficult to see how a definite number of germ cells can be supplied to each bud during a process of development which is apparently so indeterminate. If, however, a definite number is not required, and the germ cells become generally distributed throughout the cellular mass before budding begins, the chances are that every bud will contain one or more germ cells. For example, if germ cells occur in all parts of the blastoderm of the armadillo, as is quite possible, each of the four embryos must become provided with a portion of them. On the other hand, the germ-plasm may be rather widely distributed among the cells and only becomes segregated in germ cells after budding takes place. Careful studies of the germ-cell history in polyembryonic species are much needed and would no doubt produce important results.

The data presented in this chapter are sufficient to prove that in many insects a complete germ-cell cycle can be demonstrated. There are many species, however, in which no early segregation of germ cells has been discovered even after very careful examination. It is therefore too early to make any general statements for the entire class, but we must base our conclusions regarding the germ-cell cycle upon our knowledge of those forms in which the keimbahn actually can be traced. Finally one point should be emphasized; in every case the segregation of the primordial germ cells is intimately associated with a substance which can be made visible by proper staining methods. In *Miastor* this is the poleplasm; in *Chironomus* the "Keimwulst" or "Keimbahnplasma"; in *Calliphora* the "Dotterplatte"; in chrysomelid beetles the pole-disc; and in parasitic HYMENOPTERA, the keimbahn-chromatin. The nature and significance of these substances will be discussed later.

2. THE KEIMBAHN IN THE CRUSTACEA

The keimbahn in the CRUSTACEA is best known in certain CLADOCERA and COPEPODA. Of special interest are the investigations of Grobben (1879), Weismann and Ischikawa (1889), Haecker (1897), Amma (1911), Kühn (1911, 1913), and Fuchs (1913).

Grobben (1879) studied the embryology of *Moina rectirostris* and gives a remarkably fine account of early cleavage stages, considering the early date when the work was done. He figures stages showing a foreign body which he considered a polar body, segregated in one of the early blastomeres, the segregation and characteristics of the primordial germ cell and the first entoderm cell, and the division and later history of the germ cells. His results have been, in the main, confirmed by Kühn (1911, 1913).

Weismann and Ischikawa (1889) have contributed an interesting account of the primary cellular differentiation in the fertilized winter eggs of six species of the DAPHNIDÆ, belonging to four genera. The germinal vesicle in the eggs of these species casts part of its chromatin contents into the cytoplasm which there became organized into a "Paranucleus." This paranucleus then acquired a cell body and in this condition was termed the "Copulationszelle" because of its future history. In two of the species examined this Copulationszelle united with one of the first two cleavage cells; in the other four species it united with one of the first eight cells. Furthermore, it apparently always fused with a certain definite cleavage cell. The authors conclude that the Copulationszelle has some important relation to the history of the germ cells.

The keimbahn of *Cyclops* and some closely allied forms has been very carefully investigated by Haecker

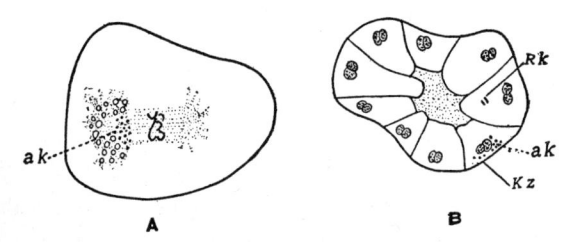

Fig. 48.—*Cyclops*. *A*. Egg showing "Aussenkörnchen" (*ak*) at one end of first cleavage spindle. *B*. Thirty-two-cell stage showing "Aussenkörnchen" (*ak*) in the primordial germ cell (*Kz*). *Rk* = polar bodies. (*From Haecker, 1897*.)

(1897), Amma (1911), and Fuchs (1913) with results which are of particular interest. In *Cyclops*, according to Haecker, "Aussenkörnchen" arise at one pole of the first cleavage spindle (Fig. 48, *A*, *ak*); these are derived from disintegrated nucleolar material and are attracted to one pole of the spindle by a dissimilar influence of the centrosomes. During the first four cleavage divisions the granules are segregated always in one cell (Fig. 48, *B*, *Kz*); at the end of the fourth division these "Aussenkörnchen" disappear, but the cell which contained them can be traced by its delayed mitotic phase and is shown to be the primordial germ cell.

The most recent and complete accounts of the keimbahn in the COPEPODA are those of Amma (1911) and Fuchs (1913). Amma studied the early cleavage stages of eleven species of *Cyclops* (Fig. 49, *A–G*), three species of *Diaptomus* (Fig. 49, *H*), one species of *Canthocamptus*, and one species of *Heterocope*. *Cyclops fucus* var. *distinctus* is made the basis for the most detailed study, but short descriptions and figures are presented of the others. In all of the sixteen species examined the stem-cell which gives rise to the primordial germ cell may be recognized, as Haecker (1897) discovered in *Cyclops*, first by the presence of granules which do not occur in the other cleavage cells, and later by a delayed mitotic division. The process is essentially as described by Haecker.[1]

[1] The following summary of the keimbahn in *Cyclops fuscus* var. *distinctus* is given by Amma:

"1. Während der ersten Furchungsteilungen ist eine bestimmte Folge von Zellen, die Keimbahn, durch das Auftreten von Körnchen, die sich bei der Teilung jewels um einen Spindelpol der Teilungsfigur ansammeln gekennzeichnet (Fig. 49, *A*).

"2. Die Körnchen oder Ectosomen entstehen immer erstmals während des Stadiums der Diakinese, vermehren sich während der nächst folgenden Phasen noch bedeutend und verschmelzen gegen das Ende der Teilung zu grösseren, unförmigen Brocken, welche allmählich während des Ruheperiode der Zelle aufgelöst werden (Fig. 49, *B*).

"3. Die neue Körnchenzelle geht stets vom körnchenführenden Produkte der alten Körnchenzelle hervor, was direkt dadurch bewiesen werden kann, dass sich in der neuen Körnchenzelle immer noch unaufgelöste Überreste der Ectosomen der alten Körnchenzelle vorfinden; alle Körnchenzellen stammen somit in direkter Linie von einander ab (Fig. 49, *C*).

"4. Vom II — Zellenstadium an bleibt die Körnchenzelle immer in der Teilung hinter den andern Furchungszellen zurück; es ergibt sich

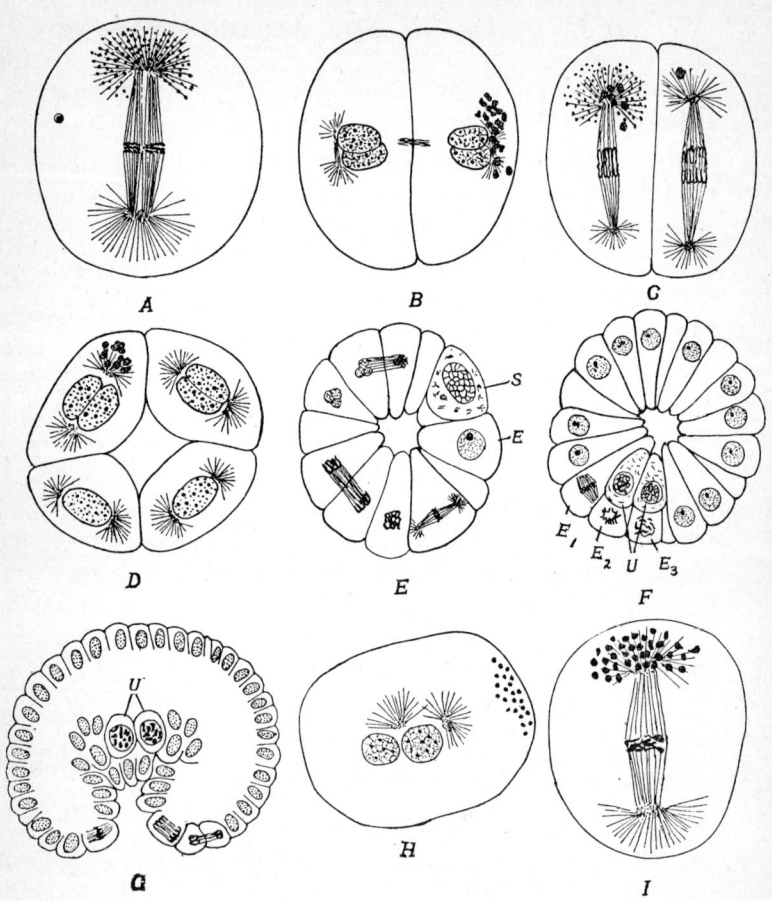

Fig. 49. — Stages in the keimbahn of copepods. *A–G. Cyclops fuscus* var. *distinctus*. *H. Diaptomus cœruleus*. *I. Cyclops viridis*. *A.* Ectosomes at end of first cleavage spindle. *B.* Two-cell stage; ectosomes dissolving. *C.* Old and newly formed ectosomes at end of one of second cleavage spindles. *D.* Eight-cell stage; ectosomes dissolving in stem-cell. *E.* Sixteen- to twenty-eight-cell stage. *S* = cell with, *E* = cell without, granules. *F.* One hundred and twelve-cell stage with two primordial germ cells (*u*) and three entoderm cells (*E*). *G.* Two hundred and forty-cell stage. *u* = primordial germ cells. *H.* Appearance of ectosomes before cleavage spindle forms. *I.* Increased production of ectosomes due to carbonic acid gas. (*From Amma, 1911.*)

(166)

An important departure from the usual method of origin of the "Ectosomen" is recorded for *Diaptomus cœruleus*. Amma says concerning the process in this species that " whereas in other forms the Ectosomen first appear during the stage of diakinesis of the first cleavage spindle, in this species they are already present before the pronuclei unite" (Fig. 49, *H*).

The origin and nature of the Ectosomen are considered by Amma at some length. The hypothesis that these granules arise by the splitting off of particles of chromatin from the chromosomes as occurs in *Ascaris* is rejected (1) because in one species, *Diaptomus cœruleus* (Fig. 49, *H*), the Ectosomen appear before the nuclear membrane breaks down in preparation for the formation of the first cleavage spindle, and (2) because the Ectosomen do not stain as deeply as chromatin but only slightly darker than the cytoplasm. The origin of the Aussenkörnchen (Ectosomen) from the nucleolus, as considered probable by

eine Phasendifferenz, welche in immer stärkeren Masse in den höheren Furchungsteilungen zunimmt (Fig. 49, *C*).

"5. Aus dem körnchenführenden Produkte der Körnchenzelle des vierten Teilungsakts, der Stammzelle *S*, gehen, nachdem diese sich an dem fünften Furchungsschritte nicht beteiligte, gegen Ende des sechsten, im LX — Zellenstadium, die beiden definitiven Urgeschlechtszellen hervor; bei dieser Teilung der *S*-Zelle erscheinen die Ectosomen in ganzen Zellraume (Fig. 49, *E*, *F*).

"6. In Ausnahmefällen beginnt die *S*-Zelle sich etwas früher zu teilen, nämlich schon während des Übergangs des XXX — zum LX — Zellenstadium.

"7. Die Urgeschlechtszellen verlieren den Verband mit dem Blastoderm, sie werden allmählich in die Tiefe gedrängt (Fig. 49, *G*)" (pp. 529–530).

Haecker (1897), could not be confirmed. The condition in *Diaptomus cœruleus* (Fig. 49, *H*) is also a serious objection to this theory. The Ectosomen are different from chromidia, since chromidia arise from the nucleus and no connection could be discovered between the Ectosomen and the nuclei. The hypothesis that they may represent chondriosomes is also rejected.

Amma finally decides [1] that the Ectosomen represent the "Endprodukte des Kern-Zelle-Stoffwechsels," in which case a greater amount of Ectosomen would be present if an egg were allowed to develop in carbonic acid gas. The results of a number of experi-

[1] "Aus dem ganzen Verlaufe der Körnchenentwicklung geht nun soviel mit Sicherheit hervor, dass man es bei den Ectosomen mit vergänglichen Gebilden zu tun hat, denen keine weiteren Funktionen zukommen, die im Leben der Zelle nicht weiter verwendet werden. In den Prophasen der Kernteilung entstehen die Körnchen zunächst als feine Tröpfchen im Zellplasma; im weiteren Verlauf der Teilung erfahren sie dann noch eine Zunahme, bis sie ungefähr im Stadium des Dyasters ihre höchste Entwicklung erreicht haben. Von hier ab beginnt der regressive Prozess der Körnchen: sie fliessen zu grösseren, unförmigen Klumpen zusammen, welche vom Zellplasma allmählich vollständig resorbiert und aufgelöst werden. Bei der nächsten Teilung der Keimbahnzelle erscheinen dann die Ectosomen wieder von neuem. Um ein einfaches Unsichtborwerden während der Zellenruhe, wie es. z. B. vom Centrosoma von vielen Forschern angenommen wird, kann es sich bei den Ectosomen nicht handeln, denn vielfach konnten ja neben den neuen, frisch entstandenen Ectosomen noch die Überreste der Ectosomen der letzen Körnchenzelle nachgewiesen werden. Es erfolgt also bei jedem neuen Teilungsschritte tatsächlich eine *Neubildung und Wiederauflösung* der Körnchen.

"Gestützt auf diese Tatsachen, möchte ich nun die Ansicht vertreten, dass die Ectosomen als *Abscheidungen, Endprodukte des Kern-Zelle Stoffwechsels* aufzufassen sind, welche zu bestimmten Zeiten im Plasma der Zelle zur Abscheidung gelangen und wieder aufgelöst werden" (p. 557).

ments with oxygen and carbonic acid gas indicate that a greater amount of Ectosomen occur when the egg is developed in the latter, as shown by Fig. 49, I, which is from an egg of *Cyclops viridis* placed one hour after deposition into carbonic acid gas for one hour.

When various stains were used it was found that the Ectosomen became colored much like the cytoplasm. For example, when stained in methylene blue followed by eosin the chromosomes were blue and the Ectosomen and cytoplasm red, and when stained by the methyl green-fuchsin-orange G method of Heidenhain the chromosomes were green and the cytoplasm and Ectosomen red.

Amma also attempts to explain the fact that the Ectosomen appear at only one end of the first cleavage spindle and in only one of the cleavage cells until the two primordial germ cells are formed. He rejects the hypothesis Haecker advanced that the centrosomes possess an unequal influence upon the Ectosomen and that one centrosome attracts all of them because it is stronger than the other, and is inclined to favor the idea that the Ectosomen are the visible evidence of an organ-forming substance which is thus distinguished from the rest of the cytoplasm as "Körnchenplasma." [1]

Fuchs (1913) has confirmed for *Cyclops viridis*

---

[1] Amma's statement is, "dass *im Zellplasma des noch ungefurchten Copepodeneies ein vom übrigen Eiplasma qualitativ verschiedenes Körnchenplasma existiert, welches die organbildende Substanz, die Anlagesubstanz für die Geschlechtsorgane darstellt*" (p. 564).

many of Amma's results and has pointed out the similarities between the cell lineage of the COPEPODA and CLADOCERA. Kühn (1913) has studied the keimbahn in the summer egg of a cladoceron, *Polyphemus pediculus*, and has confirmed certain parts and cor-

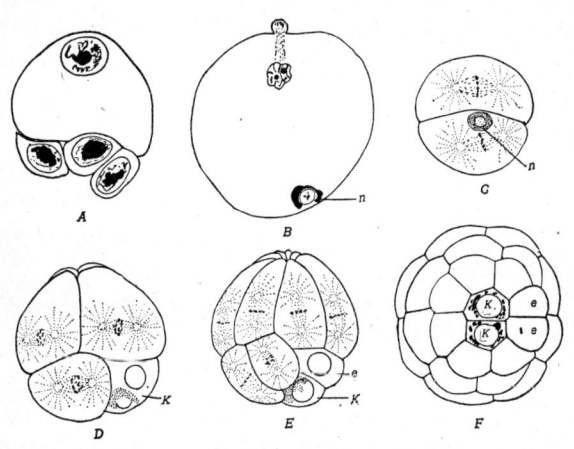

FIG. 50. — *Polyphemus pediculus*. *A*. Egg with three nurse cells. *B*. Egg at close of maturation. n = "Nahrzellenkern." *C*. Two-cell stage; view of vegetative pole. *D*. Eight- to sixteen-cell stage. K = "keimbahnzelle." *E*. Sixteen- to thirty-cell stage. e = entoderm cell. *F*. Thirty-two-cell stage from vegetative pole. K = primordial germ cells; e = entoderm cells. (*From Kühn, 1911, 1913.*)

rected other portions of the work done by earlier investigators — Grobben (1879), Samassa (1893), and Weismann and Ischikawa (1889). In this species usually one (but sometimes two or three) of the nurse cells (Fig. 50) pass into the egg before cleavage. This cell (or cells) becomes embedded near the periphery at the vegetative pole (Fig. 50, *B*, *n*). During each of the early cleavage divisions this nurse cell is confined to one cell (Fig. 50, C–E) which gives rise during the third cleavage (8- to 16-cell stage) to the primordial germ cell, containing the remains of the nurse cell (Fig. 50, E, K), and to the primordial entoderm cell which does not receive any part of the nurse cell (Fig. 50, E, e). The primordial germ cell and primordial entoderm cell do not divide as quickly as the other blastomeres during the succeeding cleavage stages — a fact that aids in their identification. While the egg is undergoing cleavage the nurse cell is gradually changing, so that when the sixteen-cell stage is reached it has become disintegrated into dark staining granules and fragments of various forms and sizes (Fig. 50, E). During the division of the "Keimbahnzelle" (from 16–32-cell stage) these granules and fragments are about equally distributed between the daughter cells (Fig. 50, F). A similar distribution takes place in succeeding divisions of the primordial germ cells, and this is accompanied by a further decrease in the size of the dark staining granules. A blastula of 236 cells is figured by Kühn which shows at the vegetative pole four primordial germ cells lying next to eight entoderm cells and bordered by twelve mesoderm cells. During gastrulation this group of twenty-four cells becomes surrounded by the ectoderm cells, and the primordial germ cells may then be recognized as the anlage of the reproductive organs.

Kühn discusses the origin and significance of the "Nahrzellenkern" and compares this body with similar bodies which have been found in the primordial germ cells of other animals, but is unable to arrive at any final conclusion.

In certain CLADOCERA and COPEPODA, as we have seen, there are visible substances within the cytoplasm of the egg which become segregated in, and render distinguishable, the primordial germ cell. Some species belonging to these and other groups of CRUSTACEA have been studied in which such a visible substance peculiar to the primordial germ cell is absent.

Samassa (1893) not only failed to find the primordial germ cell during the cleavage stages of *Moina rectirostris*, but claims that the germ cells arise from four mesoderm cells. Kühn (1908), from a study of the parthenogenetic generation of *Daphnia pulex* and *Polyphemus pediculus*, also derives the germ cells from the mesoderm. Vollmer (1912) could not distinguish the germ cells of *Daphnia magna* and *D. pulex* in the developing winter eggs until the blastoderm was almost completed and Müller-Calé (1913) could not find these cells in *Cypris incongruens* until the germ layers were fully formed. McClendon (1906a) has shown that in two parasitic copepods, *Pandarus sinuatus* and an unnamed species, the primordial germ cell is established at the end of the fifth cleavage (32-cell stage) instead of at the end of the fourth as Haecker (1897) found in *Cyclops*. It is suggested that this delay may be due to the large amount of yolk present. The stem-cell from which it arises is, however, not made visibly different from the rest of the blastoderm by peculiar granules as is the case in *Cyclops*.

Bigelow (1902) has described in *Lepas anatifera* and *L. fascicularis* certain stages which may bring the forms in which no early segregation of the germ cells has been discovered into line with the apparently more determinate species. In *Lepas* the yolk, which at first is evenly distributed within the egg, passes to the vegetative pole and becomes segregated in one of the first two cleavage cells (cd^2). At the 16-cell stage the yolk lies within the single entoblast cell ($d^{5.1}$), which occupies a position corresponding to that of the primordial germ cell in *Moina*. In this connection may be mentioned the fact that in many animals the germ cells are supposed to come from the entoderm and are characterized by the possession of much yolk.

CHAPTER VI

THE SEGREGATION OF THE GERM CELLS IN NEMATODES, SAGITTA, AND CERTAIN OTHER METAZOA

1. THE KEIMBAHN IN THE NEMATODA

THE classical example of the keimbahn in animals is that of *Ascaris megalocephala* as described by Boveri (1887, 1892). The first cleavage division of the egg of *Ascaris* results in two daughter cells, each containing two long chromosomes (Fig. 51, *A*). In the second division the chromosomes of one cell divide normally and each daughter cell receives one half of each (Fig. 51, *B, S*). The chromosomes of the other cell behave differently; the thin middle portion of each breaks up into granules (Fig. 51, *A*) which split, half going to each daughter cell, but the swollen ends (Fig. 51, *B, C*) are cast off into the cytoplasm. In the four-cell stage there are consequently two cells with the full amount of chromatin and two with a reduced amount. This inequality in the amount of chromatin results in different-sized nuclei (Fig. 51, *C*); those with entire chromosomes (*S*) are larger than those that have lost the swollen ends (*C*). In the third division one of the two cells with the two entire chromosomes loses the swollen ends of each; the other (Fig. 51, *D, S*) retains its chromosomes intact. A similar reduction in the amount of chromatin takes place in the fourth and fifth divisions and then ceases. The single cell in the 32-cell stage which contains the full amount of chromatin

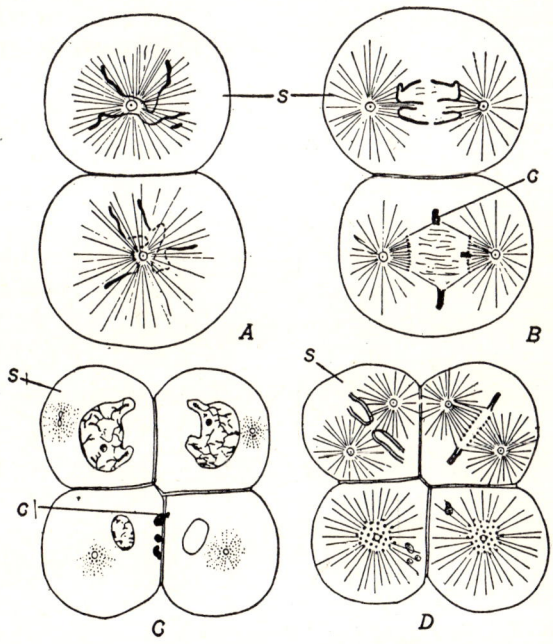

Fig. 51. — *Ascaris*. Stages in early cleavage showing the chromatin-diminution process in all cells except the stem cell (*S*). (*From Boveri, 1892.*)

has a larger nucleus than the other thirty-one cells and gives rise to all of the germ cells, whereas the other cells are for the production of somatic cells only. The cell lineage of *Ascaris* is shown in the accompanying diagram (Fig. 52).

Meyer (1895) extended the study of chromatin-diminution to other species of *Ascaris*. In *A. lumbricoides* no diminution takes place until the four-cell stage; then three of the nuclei become deprived of part of their chromatin. A diminution of this

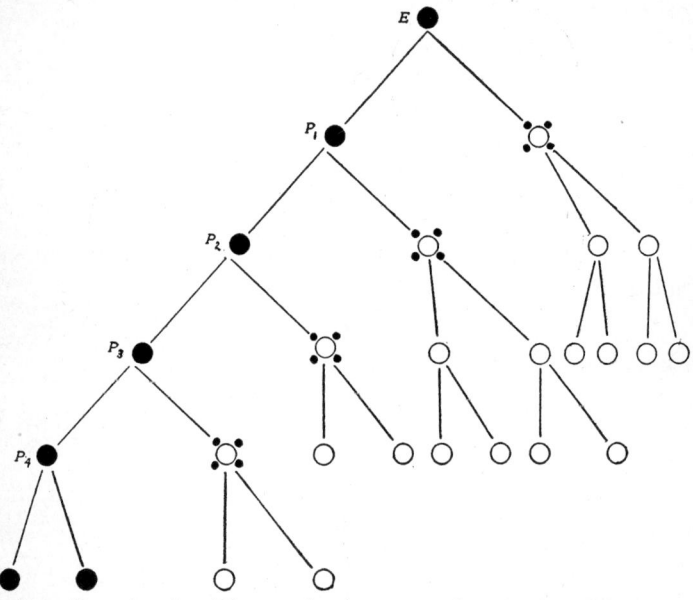

Fig. 52. — *Ascaris.* Diagram showing segregation of primordial germ cell. E = egg; P_1, P_2, P_3 = stem cells; P_4 = primordial germ cell. Circles represent somatic cells. (*From Boveri, 1910.*)

sort had been described by Boveri as a variation in the process observed in *A. megalocephala*. In *A. rubicunda* the differentiation of the cleavage cells seems to resemble *A. megalocephala* more than it does *A. lumbricoides*. Only late cleavage stages of *A. labiata* were obtained by Meyer, but there is no doubt that a similar process occurs here. The general conclusion is reached that the cleavage cells of all ASCARIDÆ undergo a chromatin diminution.

Bonnevie (1901), however, while able to confirm Meyer's results so far as *A. lumbricoides* is concerned, could discover no process of diminution in *Strongylus paradoxus* and *Rhabdonema nigrovenosa*.

The elimination of chromatin from all of the somatic cells of *Ascaris* and not from the germ cells led to the conclusion that the germ-plasm must reside in the chromatin of the nucleus. The more recent experimental investigations of Boveri (1910*a*, 1910*b*), however, indicate that it is not the chromatin alone that determines the initiation of the diminution process, but that the cytoplasm plays a very important rôle. Dispermic eggs were found to segment so as to produce three types as follows:

Type I, with one stem cell (P) and three primordial somatic cells (AB);

Type II, with two stem cells and two primordial somatic cells; and

Type III with three stem cells and one primordial somatic cell.

Fig. 53, B shows a cleavage stage of Type II. Here are represented two stem cells (P) with the complete amount of chromatin, both of which are preparing to divide to form the stem cells (P_2) of the next generation. From the study of these dispermic eggs Boveri (1910) concludes [1] that it is "die *unrich-*

[1] "Durch die simultane Vierteilung eines dispermen Ascaris-Eies entstehen (vielleicht mit ganz seltenen Ansnahmen) Zellen, welche die

tigen plasmatischen Qualitäten des sich entwickelnden Zellenkomplexes" that cause the injurious results of dispermy, and that if, of the three types of dispermic eggs described, the cells could be isolated in pairs, one AB-cell paired with one P_1-cell,

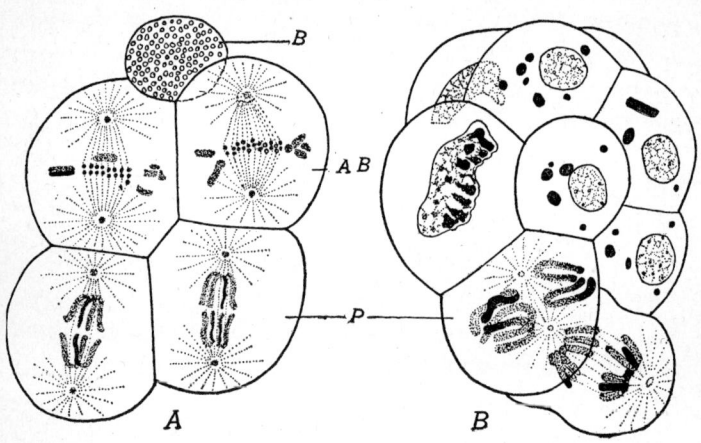

Fig. 53.— *Ascaris.* A. Chromatin-diminution in a centrifuged egg. B. In a dispermic egg. (*From Boveri, 1910.*)

an embryo, normal except in size, would result from each pair.

Eggs that were strongly centrifuged cut off at the beginning of the first cleavage at the heavy pole a

gleiche Wertigkeit besitzen, wie diejenigen, die durch Zweiteilung eines normal-befruchteten Eies gebildet werden, nämlich die Wertigkeit AB oder P_1. Es können drei Zellen die Qualität AB besitzen oder zwei oder eine; dem jeweiligen Rest kommt die Qualität P_1 zu. Schon beim Uebergang vom vierzelligen zum achtzelligen Stadium lässt sich aus der Teilungsrichtung mit sicherheit diagnostizieren, welche der vier primären Blastomeren als AB, welche als P_1 aufzufassen sind; und diese Wertbestimmung wird durch die weiteren Schicksale der vier Zellfamilien in jeder Hinsicht bestätigt " (p. 157).

granular ball (Fig. 53, *A*, *B*). This phenomenon was reported by Hogue (1910) and such eggs were termed "Balleier." In these eggs the two cells of the four-cell stage which are adjacent to the "Ball" undergo the diminution process (Fig. 53, *A*, *AB*); the remaining two are stem cells which give rise to the germ cells (Fig. 53, *A*, *P*). Thus there are two "Keimbahnen" proceeding side by side in a single egg and four primordial germ cells are produced instead of two as in normal eggs (see Fig. 51). Miss Hogue's experiments with centrifugal force led her to conclude that these must be an "unsichtbare Polarität" or "Protoplasmaachse" in the egg of the *Ascaris*. Boveri agrees with this and considers further that the initiation of the diminution process is not determined by the chromatin but by the cytoplasm of the egg.[1]

2. The Keimbahn in Sagitta

Sagitta has proved to be of considerable importance to those interested in the keimbahn of animals. Hertwig (1880) figures the four primitive germ cells in the gastrula and later stages, proving that these cells are early set aside in embryonic development. Recently the work of Elpatiewsky (1909, 1910) has

[1] He states that, "Was aber auch hier durch weitere Untersuchungen noch erreicht werden mag, Eines halte ich für sicher, dass sich alles, was über die Wertigkeit der primären Blastomeren bei abnormer Furchung ermittelt worden ist, durch die Annahme sehr einfacher Plasmadifferenzen erklären lässt, wogegen die Hypothese einer differenzierenden Wirkung des Kerns in jeder Form auf imüberwindliche Schwierigkeiten stösst" (p. 206).

given *Sagitta* a new importance, since this writer has found within the fertilized egg a cytoplasmic inclusion which is intimately associated with the segregation of the germ cells. The presence of this inclusion has been confirmed by Buchner (1910a, 1910b)

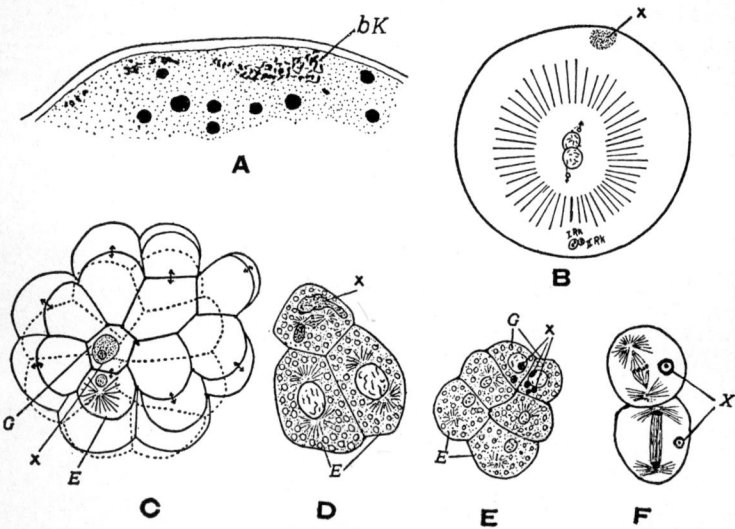

Fig. 54. — *Sagitta*. *A*. First appearance of the "besondere Körper" (*bK*) in the egg. *B*. Egg with germ nuclei fusing. *X* = "besondere Körper." *C*. Thirty-two-cell stage; the primordial germ cell (*G*) contains the "besondere Körper" (*X*). *D*. Two entoderm cells (*E*) and dividing primordial germ cell. *E*. Two primordial germ cells showing unequal distribution of "besondere Körper" (*X*). *F*. Division of first two primordial germ cells; one dividing more rapidly than the other. (*From Elpatiewsky, 1909, 1910.*)

and Stevens (1910b), and several ideas have been expressed regarding its origin, fate, and significance.

Elpatiewsky (1909) found in *Sagitta*, at the time when the male and female nuclei were lying side by side in the middle of the egg, a body situated near the periphery at the vegetative pole (Fig. 54, B, x). This body, which he called the "besondere Körper," consists at first of "grobkörnigen" plasma which stains like chromatin but not so intensely; later it condenses into a round homogeneous body with a sharp contour. During the first five cleavage divisions the "besondere Körper" is always confined to a single cell. At the completion of this fifth cleavage (32-cell stage), the blastomere containing this cytoplasmic inclusion is recognizable as the first "Urgeschlechtszelle" (Fig. 54, C, G) and its larger sister cell as the first "Urentodermzelle" (Fig. 54, C, E). The primordial germ cell is the last to divide during the sixth cleavage and the "besondere Körper" does not, as before, pass entire into one of the daughter cells, but breaks up into a number of pieces, part of which are included in each of the two daughter cells (Fig. 54, D, X). One of these daughter cells apparently acquires more of the "besondere Körper" than the other. This division appears to Elpatiewsky to be differential, separating the primordial oögonium from the primordial spermatogonium, the latter being the cell which receives the larger portion of the "besondere Körper" and which during the next (seventh) division is slightly delayed (Fig. 54, F). Subsequent to the seventh cleavage the remains of the "besondere Körper" become pale and gradually disappear, apparently dissolving, and in the four germ cells resulting from the next division only occasionally can stained granules from this body be distinguished.

Buchner (1910a, 1910b) had no difficulty in finding the "besondere Körper" of Elpatiewsky and in tracing it during the cleavage stages. He claims that it originates from the "accessory fertilization cell" described by Stevens (1904) as degenerating after the egg breaks away from the oviduct wall, and that it is chromidial in nature and should therefore be called "Keimbahnchromidien." Stevens (1910), however, has carefully examined abundant material from *Sagitta elegans* and *S. bipunctata*, and no connection between the "accessory fertilization cell" and the "besondere Körper" could be traced, the latter appearing for the first time at the stage when the egg and sperm nuclei lie side by side in the middle of the egg, thus confirming Elpatiewsky's conclusions. She admits the possibility of the origin of the "besondere Körper" from granules of the accessory fertilization cell, provided this material loses its staining capacity for a period, and suggests also that the granules of chromatin-like material extruded from the nucleus of the egg during maturation may take part in its formation. Miss Stevens also believes with Elpatiewsky that the "besondere Körper" divides unequally between the two daughter cells of the primordial germ cell and that this is a differential division. She was unable, however, to detect any constant difference between either the cytoplasm or the nuclei of oögonia and spermatogonia. It is worthy of mention that Elpatiewsky (1910) believes that the "besondere Körper" may originate "aus dem achromatischen Kernkörper."

3. The Keimbahn in Other Metazoa

Certain phenomena have been reported in the early development of the eggs of many other animals which have either been compared or can be compared with conditions such as we have described in the preceding portions of this book.

The large nucleolus in the germinal vesicle of the medusa, *Æquorea forskalea* (Fig. 55, *A*), according to Haecker (1892), disappears from the germinal vesicle about half an hour after the egg is laid, and a similar body becomes evident near the egg nucleus which has in the meantime become smaller (Fig. 55, *B*). These two bodies are considered by Haecker to be identical, and the term "Metanucleolus" has been applied to them. The metanucleolus is, in each division up to the sixty-four cell stage, segregated intact in one cell. Its further history was not traced, but in the blastula (Fig. 55, *D*) when the cells at the posterior pole begin to differentiate, nucleolar-like bodies appear in some of them which are absent from the undifferentiated blastula elements. These may be the descendants of the metanucleolus.

A body similar to the metanucleolus was also discovered by Haecker near the copulating germ nuclei in the egg of *Aurelia aurita*, but its history could not be determined because of the large amount of yolk present. Haecker identifies the metanucleolus of *Æquorea* with the spherical body described by Metchnikoff (1886) near the egg nucleus of *Mitrocoma annæ*, and considered by him as a sperm nucleus.

A similar interpretation is given by Haecker for the cytoplasmic inclusion ("Spermakern") found by Boveri (1890) in *Tiara*. Similarly the "Kleinkern" which Chun (1891) discovered in the egg cells of *Stephanophyes superba*, and the bodies described by Hertwig (1878) near the maturation spindles of *Mytilus* and *Sagitta*, resemble very closely the metanucleolus of *Æquorea*.

Furthermore, the metanucleolus is considered by Haecker homologous to the "Paracopulationszelle" described by Weismann and Ischikawa in the winter eggs of certain DAPHNIDÆ, and in both cases it is considered probable that these peculiar bodies are restricted to the "Keimbahnzellen" of the embryo.

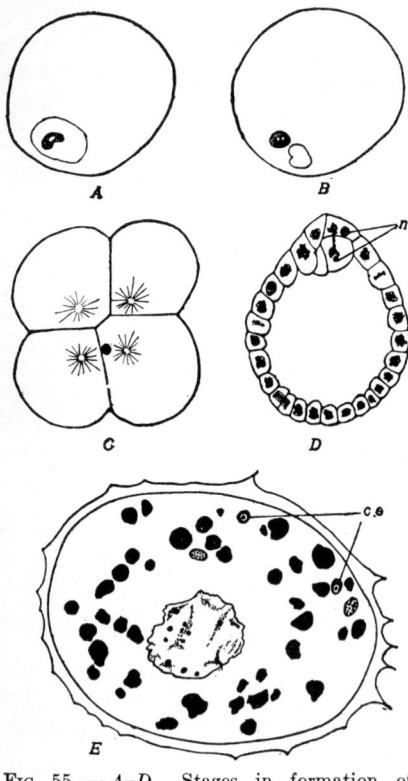

FIG. 55. — *A–D*. Stages in formation of blastula of *Æquorea forskalea* showing segregation of metanucleolus. (*From Haecker, 1892.*) *E*. Oöcyte of the cat containing the "corps enigmatique" (*c.e*). (*From Vander Stricht, 1911.*)

In the eggs of *Myzostoma*, Wheeler (1897) found that the nucleolus of the germinal vesicle does not dissolve soon after it is cast out into the cytoplasm during the formation of the first maturation spindle, but remains visible at least until the eight-cell stage, at which time it lies in the large posterior macromere, a cell which "very probably gives rise to the entoderm of the embryo." Later embryonic stages were not studied. According to Wheeler "the nucleoli are relegated to the entoderm cells as the place where they would be least liable to interfere in the further course of development and where they may perhaps be utilized as food material after their disintegration" (p. 49).

McClendon (1906b) has likewise described a body embedded in the cytoplasm of the egg of *Myzostoma clarki* which he derives from the "accessory cells" which, as Wheeler (1896) has shown, attach themselves to either pole of the oöcytes. These "accessory" cells are really the "Nährzellen" of other authors. The cleavage of the egg was not studied. Buchner (1910b) suggests that this body described by McClendon and the "nucleolus" of Wheeler are identical and that through them the keimbahn may be determined.

Granules of various sorts have been noted in the eggs of various animals which are segregated in particular blastomeres and may have some relation to the keimbahn. For example, among the mollusks, Blockmann (1881) has described the appearance of a group of granules in the early cleavage cells of

Neritina which finally reach the velar cells. It is also probable that Fol (1880) observed similar granules in the 16-cell stage of *Planorbis*. In the same category, no doubt, belong the bodies figured by Fujita (1904) in the 4-cell to the 16-cell stages of *Siphonaria* lying at the vegetative pole, and the "Ectosomen" described and figured by Wierzejski (1906) in *Physa*. These granules appear at the vegetal pole in the blastomeres of *Physa* during the second cleavage; are at first embedded in the entoderm mother cells, but finally become localized in the ectoderm cells. They periodically appear and disappear, and may, as suggested by Wierzejski, represent only "eine besondere Erscheinung des Stoffwechsels" (p. 536).

Similarly in the rotifer, *Asplanchna*, Jennings (1896) has traced a "cloud of granules" from the eight-cell stage until the seventh cleavage, when this mass forms part of the smaller entodermal cell. In *Lepas* there has also been recorded (Bigelow, 1902) a segregation of granules in one blastomere. Many other substances granular in form have been described in the eggs of animals, some of them at least having migrated there from the somatic tissue. Blockmann (1887) discovered a number of bacteria-like rods in the undeveloped eggs of *Blatta germanica;* these rods multiplied by division and were considered symbiotic bacteria. "Bacterienartige Stäbchen" were also noted by Heymons (1895) in the eggs of *Periplanata orientalis* and *Ectobia livida;* these sink into the yolk and disappear. More recently a report of

Buchner (1912) indicates that these bodies are really organisms which seem to be symbiotic and not parasitic, although it remains to be proved what advantage the host receives from their presence. Of a similar sort are the Zoöxanthellæ which Mangan (1909) has shown enter the developing ovum from the parental tissues. All of these organisms become in some way embedded in the germ cells, but so far as we know never serve to distinguish the keimbahn, although a more selective distribution within the developing animal would obviously be greatly to their advantage.

Vander Stricht (1911) has compared the "besondere Körper" found by Elpatiewsky (1909, 1910) in the egg of *Sagitta* with several bodies, the "corps enigmatique," which he discovered in the oöcyte of the cat (Fig. 55, E). One or two of these "corps enigmatique" are present in the young oöcyte originating from a few (one to five) cytoplasmic safranophile granules which are visible at the beginning of the growth period. They at first lie near the nucleus, but as the size of the oöcyte increases they become situated near the periphery. Usually three parts can be recognized in the "corps enigmatique": "granulation centrole, couche intermediaire et couche corticale foncée." As the term applied to them indicates, the functions of these bodies were not determined. The following suggestion is, however, made: "il est possible que cet élément nous montre, des l'origine, la 'Keimbahn' ainsi que les premieres cellules génitales constituées." A body stained deeply by nuclear dyes which was found by O. Van der Stricht (1909) in the bat at the time of the first cleavage mitosis may be similar to the "corps enigmatique" of the cat.

In many animals no keimbahn-determinants nor similar bodies have as yet been discovered. The best we can do in cases of this sort is to determine from what cleavage cell or cells the germinal epithelium probably originates. For example, in *Arenicola*, Lillie (1905) has shown that the part of the peritoneum from which the germ cells arise develops from teloblast cells which are probably derived (Child, 1900) from cell 4d. At present, however, no characteristics have been discovered which enable us to distinguish between the germ cells and the somatic cells in the early embryonic stages of such animals (Downing, 1911).

CHAPTER VII

THE GERM CELLS OF HERMAPHRODITIC ANIMALS

Many of the most interesting biological problems are those connected with the phenomenon of sex. The term "sex" is applied to the soma or body of an organism; it indicates the presence of certain morphological and physiological characteristics, which may be separated into primary and secondary sexual characters. The primary sexual characters are those immediately connected with the reproductive organs; the secondary sexual characters, such as the beard of man, the brilliant feathers and beautiful songs of many male birds, and the antlers of the moose, represent differences between male and female individuals not directly concerned with the production of germ cells. It is customary to speak of male germ cells and female germ cells; this is not strictly proper, since in only a few special cases can we predict the sex of the individual which will develop from an egg. Moreover, every germ cell must contain the potentiality of both sexes since sooner or later its descendants will give rise, some to male, some to female or perhaps to hermaphroditic offspring. Thus the egg is an initial hermaphrodite; it may or may not become an eventual hermaphrodite according to the sexual condition of the individual to which it gives rise.

190   GERM–CELL CYCLE IN ANIMALS

All the species of METAZOA may be separated into two groups. The individuals in one group of species

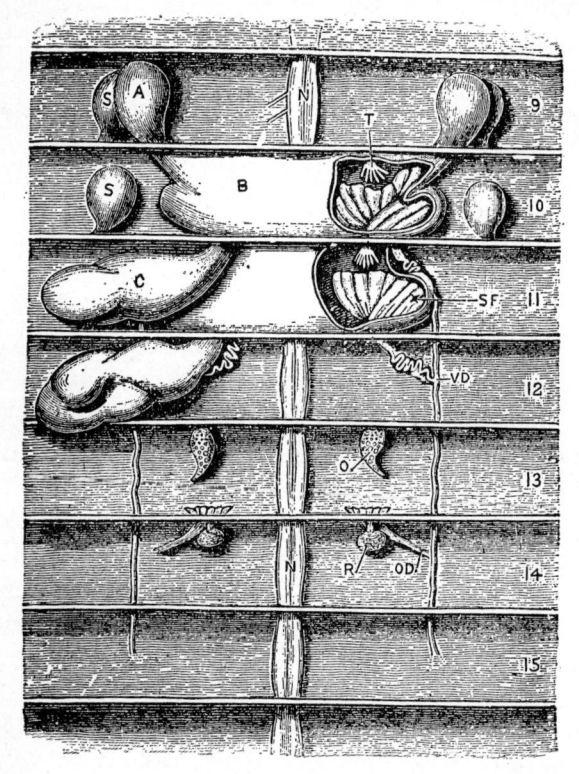

Fig. 56. — Diagram of the reproductive organs of the earthworm, dorsal view. *A, B, C*, seminal vesicles; *N*, nerve-cord; *O*, ovary; *OD*, oviduct; *R*, egg sac; *S*, spermatheca; *SF*, seminal funnel; *T*, testes; *VD*, vas deferens. (*From Marshall and Hurst.*)

possess only one sort of reproductive organs (male or female) and produce only one sort of germ cells (eggs or spermatozoa); these species are said to be diœ-

GERM CELLS OF HERMAPHRODITES

cious or gonochoristic. In the other group both male and female reproductive organs occur in each individual; and such species are called monœcious or hermaphroditic. The majority of animals are gonochoristic, but a number of classes and orders consist almost entirely of hermaphroditic species, and probably no large group of animals is free from species which are monœcious. A study of hermaphroditism is necessary for the elucidation of many biological problems; and some of those dealing more directly with the germ-cell cycle will be considered in this chapter.

There are many variations in the morphology of the reproductive organs in hermaphrodites. In some, such as the earthworm (Fig. 56), the male and female organs, consisting of all the parts typically present in gonochoristic animals, are present and entirely separate from each other. All gradations between such a state and an intimate association of male and female germ cells are known. Perhaps the most interesting series occurs among the mollusks. Here the germ gland may consist of two regions, as in *Pecten maximus*, one of which gives rise to ova, the other to spermatozoa; or certain cysts may contain only female germ cells and other cysts only male germ cells, or both sorts of germ cells may occur in a single cyst.

Hermaphroditism has been shown to be prevalent among animals that are parasitic or sedentary, or for some other reason may become isolated from their fellows. Thus, it is of advantage for a parasite, such as the tapeworm, to be able to form both male and female germ cells, since it may at any time become the only one of its species to occupy the alimentary canal of a host. Hermaphroditism in such a case, however, is of no benefit if self-fertilization is not possible. Although there are thousands of hermaphroditic species of animals there are comparatively few whose eggs are known to be fertilized by spermatozoa from the same individual. We must therefore distinguish between morphological and physiological hermaphroditism and recognize the fact that the former condition is much more prevalent than the latter. Among the species in which self-fertilization normally occurs are certain rhabdocœls, digenetic trematodes, cestodes, ascidians, and mollusks. Van Baer, in 1835, claims to have observed self-copulation in the snail, *Lymnæa auricularia;* that is, an individual with its penis inserted in its own female opening. That species of this genus fertilize their own eggs has frequently been stated by investigators. Frequently the spermatozoa of an hermaphrodite are capable of fertilizing the eggs of the same individual, but penetrate more readily the eggs of other individuals. Such is the case in the ascidian, *Ciona intestinalis* (Castle, 1896; Morgan, 1905).

Both sorts of germ cells are seldom produced at the same time by hermaphrodites. Those species in which spermatozoa mature first are called protandric; this is the usual condition. In a few cases eggs are formed first and later spermatozoa; individuals in which this occurs are called protogynic.

Proterogyny has been described in certain ascidians (*Salpa*), pulmonate gasteropods, and corals. That hermaphrodites are not sexless but really animals with double sex is well shown by the life history of a worm, *Myzostoma pulminar*, which passes through a short male stage during which spermatozoa are produced, then a stage when no functional germ cells are formed, and finally a female stage, characterized by the development of eggs (Wheeler, 1896). Thus, in this species, although hermaphroditic, there is no functional hermaphroditic stage. All variations between this entire separation of the periods of germ-cell development and the simultaneous production of male and female germ cells have been recorded. Some degree of protandry has been observed among the sponges, cœlenterates, flatworms, segmented round-worms, mollusks, echinoderms, crustacea, and chordates.

Hermaphroditism may occur in only a few families, genera, or species in a class. This is true, for example, among the anthropods and vertebrates. Normally the insects are called diœcious, but among bees, ants, and butterflies, and more rarely other groups, individuals appear which exhibit male characters on one side of the body and female characters on the other, or the anterior part may be male, the posterior female, etc. (von Siebolt, 1864; Schultze, 1903; Morgan, 1907, 1913). Such a phenomenon is known as gynandromorphism. Several hypotheses have been proposed to account for this condition. Boveri has suggested that if the egg nucleus should chance to divide before the sperm nucleus fuses with it, the latter may unite with one of the daughter nuclei of the egg nucleus; this cell with this double nucleus might then produce female structures, whereas the other cell with only a single nucleus representing one-half of the egg nucleus might give rise to male characters. Morgan has proposed another theory which is based on the fact that more than one spermatozoön is known to penetrate the eggs of insects. If one of these supernumerary spermatozoa should chance to divide, it might result in the formation of male structures, whereas the cells containing descendants of the egg nucleus fused with another sperm nucleus would exhibit female characteristics.

There is some evidence that true hermaphroditism may exist among insects, at least during their embryonic and larval stages. Thus Heymons (1890) has described in a young larva of the cockroach, *Phyllodromia germanica*, what appear to be rudimentary egg-tubes, and in another larva eggs were found in the testes which resembled those present in the egg-tubes of female larvæ of the same size (1 mm. in length). More recently, Schönemund (1912) has reported the presence of egg-tubes attached to the anterior end of the testes of stone-fly nymphs (*Perla marginata*).

True hermaphroditism is rare in man and other mammals, but several cases have been described in the pig by Sauerbeck (1909) and Pick (1914), and in man by Simon (1903), Uffreduzzi (1910), Gudernatsch (1911), and Pick (1914).

One of the problems connected with hermaphroditism that has caused a great amount of discussion is whether the diœcious or the monœcious condition is the more primitive. The majority of zoölogists are inclined to consider the hermaphroditic condition more primitive, but a number of careful investigators have decided in favor of gonochorism. Among these are Delage (1884), F. Müller (1885), Pelseener (1894), Montgomery (1895, 1906), and Caullery (1913).

Very little is known regarding the segregation and early history of the germ cells of hermaphrodites. The principal results have been obtained from studies on *Sagitta* by Elpatiewsky (1909), Stevens (1910*b*), and Buchner (1910*a*, 1910*b*), and on *Helix* by Ancel (1903), Buresch (1911), and Demoll (1912). Boveri (1911), Schleip (1911), and Kruger (1912) have made some interesting discoveries on the chromosome cycle in nematodes, and likewise Zarnik (1911) on pteropod mollusks. To this list we may add such investigations as those of King (1910), Kuschakewitsch (1910), and Champy (1913), on amphibians.

The segregation of the germ cells in *Sagitta* was described and figured in Chapter VI (Fig. 54). Here the first division of the primordial germ cell is probably differential; one daughter cell becomes the ancestor of all the ova, the other of all the spermatozoa in the hermaphroditic adult. None of the three investigators who have studied this subject in *Sagitta* have been able to discover with certainty any visible differences between the first two germ cells, but Elpatiewsky thinks the peculiar cytoplasmic inclusion, called by him the "besondere Körper," may be unequally distributed between these cells, and that the one which procures the larger portion is the progenitor of the spermatozoa, the other of the ova. The evidence for this view is, however, insufficient.

In *Helix* both eggs and spermatozoa originate in every acinus of the ovo-testis; it is therefore an excellent species for the study of the differentiation of the sex cells. According to Ancel (1903) the anlage of the hermaphroditic gland of *Helix pomatia* appears a few hours before the larva hatches; it consists of a group of cells situated in the midst of the mesoderm, from which germ layer it seems to originate. It soon loses its rounded form and becomes elongate; then a lumen appears within it, thus changing it into a vesicle whose wall consists of a single layer of cells — a true germinal epithelium. Secondary, tertiary, etc., vesicles bud off from the single original vesicle, forming the acini of the fully developed gland. Cellular differentiation takes place by the transformation of the germinal epithelial cells into male, nurse, and female elements. An indifferent epithelial cell is shown in Fig. 57, *A*; the chromatin granules are condensed to form irregular clumps. Some of these indifferent epithelial cells increase in size and give rise to indifferent progerminative cells; the chromatin clumps fuse, forming more or less spherical masses (Fig. 57, *E*). From cells of this sort originate both the oögonia and spermatogonia. The progerminative male cell passes through the stages shown in Fig. 57, *B–D*; part of the chromatin of the progermi-

GERM CELLS OF HERMAPHRODITES

native cell loses its affinity for nuclear dyes; the chromatin masses become less numerous and more nearly spherical; and the entire cell increases in size, the nucleus growing much more than the cytoplasm. These progerminative male cells divide mitotically

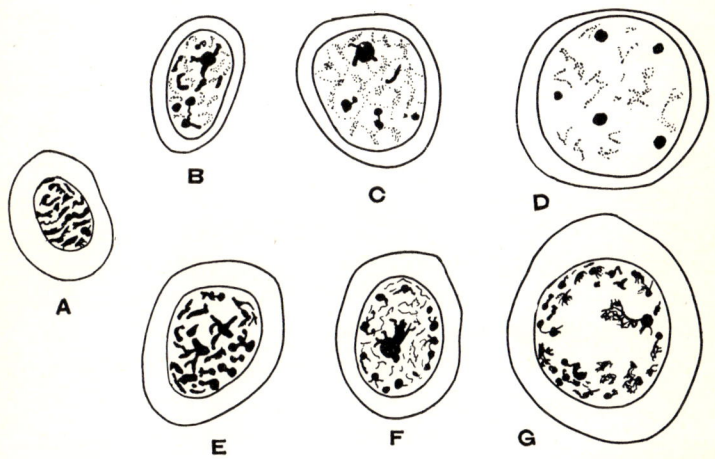

FIG. 57.—*Helix pomatia.* Stages in differentiation of male and female sex cells from indifferent cells. *A.* Epithelial indifferent cell. *E.* Progerminative indifferent cell. *B–D.* Stages in transformation of progerminative cell into a spermatogonium. *F–G.* Stages in transformation of progerminative cell into an oöcyte. (*From Ancel, 1903.*)

and then pass into the lumen of the acinus, where they may be recognized as spermatogonia of the first order.

After the spermatogonia have passed into the lumen of the acinus the wall is seen to consist of two groups of cells; those of one group are central and in contact with the spermatogonia, the others are peripheral. The centrally situated cells now increase in size; but their nuclei retain the original condition; that is, the chromatin is present in irregular clumps. These are nurse cells. After the nurse cells have formed, certain of the peripheral cells increase in volume and pass through an indifferent progerminative stage (Fig. 57, *E*). Then they transform into female progerminative cells, as shown in Fig. 57, *F*, *G*. The chromatin clumps break up and become oriented near the nuclear membrane, where they form a layer of more or less rounded bodies bearing chromatic filaments. In the meantime, both nucleus and cytoplasm increase in amount, especially the cytoplasm. This (Fig. 57, *G*) represents an oöcyte, which does not divide before maturation.

Ancel concludes from these observations that there are three successive periods of cellular differentiation in the hermaphroditic gland of *Helix*: (1) the appearance of spermatogonia, (2) nurse cells, and (3) oöcytes. Both spermatogonia and oöcytes pass through the indifferent progerminative-cell stage, but the nurse cells do not; there are therefore two sorts of differentiation of the indifferent epithelial cells. Regarding the cyto-sexual determination, the following hypothesis is advanced: A progerminative indifferent cell becomes a male or female element according to its environment at the time of its transformation; if it appears before the nurse cells are formed it becomes a spermatogonium; if nurse cells are already present it grows into an oöcyte. The discovery of certain individuals containing only male elements is explained by Ancel by supposing the transformation of the cells into sex cells to cease

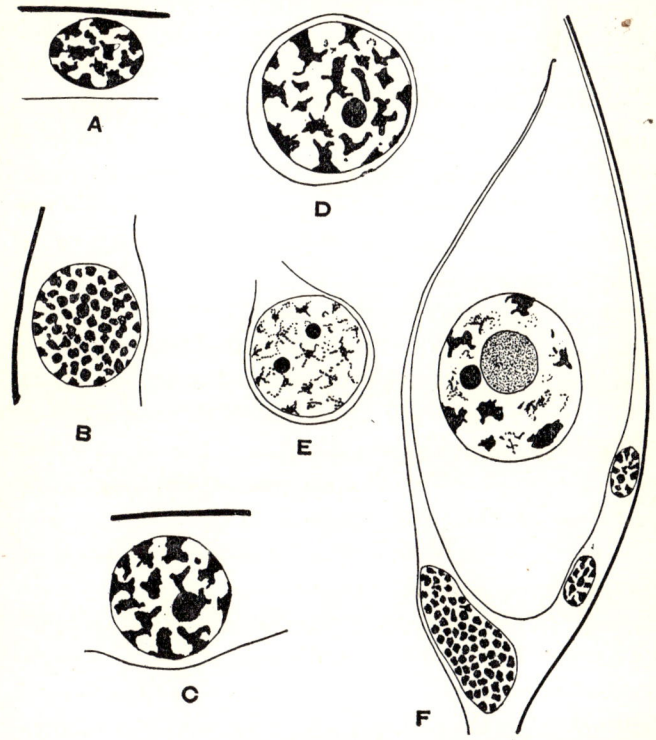

Fig. 58. — *Helix arbustorum.* Stages in the differentiation of male and female sex cells. *A.* Nucleus of germinal epithelium. *B.* Nucleus of nurse cell. *C.* Nucleus of indifferent sex cell. *D.* Spermatogonium of first order. *E.* Spermatogonium of second order. *F.* Growing oöcyte. (*From Buresch, 1911.*)

before nurse cells are formed; thus all the sex cells would become spermatogonia.

More recently Buresch (1911) has repeated the

200 GERM–CELL CYCLE IN ANIMALS

work of Ancel, using *Helix arbustorum* for his material. He confirms many of Ancel's results, objects to others, and adds certain new observations. The germinal epithelium is considered by Buresch to be a syncytium containing both in young and old specimens three sorts of cells, indifferent cells, egg cells, and nurse cells. Likewise spermatogonia are present not only in young but also in fully developed hermaphroditic glands. This is contrary to Ancel's idea of successive transformation. Buresch's view is indicated in Fig. 59. Here the vertical row of circles represents the nuclei of the syncytial germinal epithelium, some of which, as at *m*, change to indifferent germ cells. These may pass into the lumen of the acinus as spermatogonia of the first order (*Sg. I*) and divide to form spermatogonia of the second order (*Sg. II*) which grow into spermatocytes (*Sc*); spermatozoa are derived from these in the usual manner. Other indifferent germ cells remain in the wall, as at *w*, and grow into oöcytes, and a third class of cells become nurse cells (*n*). In Fig. 58, *A* is shown a nucleus of the germinal epithelium about 4 microns by 6 microns in size. During differentiation into an indifferent germ cell (Fig. 58, *C*) the chromatin forms a nucleolus, and both nucleus and nucleolus increase in size until the former reaches a diameter of about 7 microns. Those indifferent germ cells that are to produce spermatozoa separate from the epithelium with a small amount of cytoplasm and fall into the lumen of the acinus as spermatogonia of the first order (Fig. 58, *D*). These divide to form spermato-

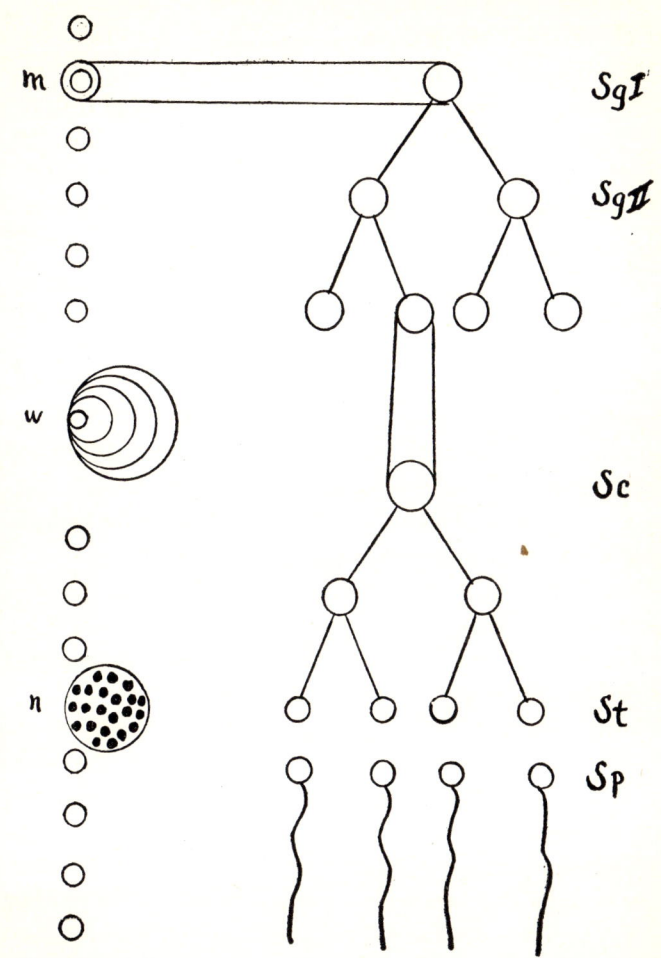

Fig. 59. — *Helix arbustorum.* Diagram showing row of germinal epithelial cells some of which, as at *m*, become spermatogonia and drop into lumen of germ gland; others become nurse cells (*n*); and still others oöcytes (*w*). *SgI* = spermatogonium of first order; *SgII* = spermatogonium of second order; *Sc* = spermatocyte; *St* = spermatid; *Sp* = spermatozoa. (*From Buresch, 1911.*)

gonia of the second order (Fig. 58, *E*). Those indifferent germ cells that are to form oöcytes grow large, remain in the germinal epithelium, and do not divide. They possess a double nucleolus (Fig. 58, *F*). When a diameter of 36 microns is attained, the oöcyte passes out of the hermaphroditic gland into the uterus.

The nurse cells, like the oöcytes, remain in the wall and do not divide; their nuclei grow to be about 15 microns in diameter and the chromatin forms irregular clumps more or less evenly distributed (Fig. 48, *B*). No differences could be discovered in the indifferent germ cells by means of which the future history of these cells could be determined. It was noted, however, that egg cells were never present without a neighboring nurse cell, and the conclusion was reached that a favorable position with regard to a nurse cell determines whether an indifferent germ cell shall develop into a spermatogonium or an egg. If Buresch's observations are correct, *Helix* is not protandric, but both sorts of germ cells mature at the same time, and the fate of an indifferent germ cell depends upon nutrition, that is, its proximity to a nurse cell.

Demoll (1912*b*) has proposed a new hypothesis regarding sex determination and has selected certain events in the oögenesis and spermatogenesis of *Helix pomatia* as arguments in its favor. The hypothesis is that the accessory chromosome (see Chapter IX) contains the anlagen of the male sexual characters, whereas the female sexual characters are localized

GERM CELLS OF HERMAPHRODITES 203

in the autosomes. In *Helix* the oögonia and spermatogonia arise from cells that are similar in size and constitution (Fig. 60, *A*). When the germ-cell nuclei reach the bouquet stage, a Nebenkern appears near the side against which the chromatin threads

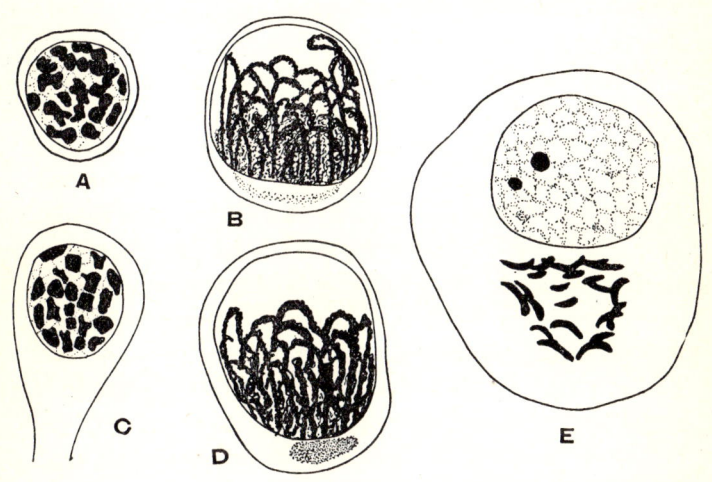

Fig. 60.—*Helix pomatia*. Stages in the differentiation of male and female sex cells. *A*. Young oöcyte. *B*. Later stage of oöcyte showing faint Nebenkern. *C*. Young spermatocyte. *D*. Later stage of spermatocyte showing well-marked Nebenkern. *E*. Still later stage of spermatocyte containing Nebenkern consisting of banana-shaped rods. (*From Demoll, 1912.*)

become packed. This Nebenkern is probably a product of the nucleus; it appears in the female cell only as a slightly darker area of cytoplasm (Fig. 60, *B*) but in the male cell is more dense (*D*), later consisting of a number of darkly staining banana-shaped pieces (*E*). With the appearance of the Nebenkern the specific growth of the female cells is initiated. The Nebenkern disappears in the oöcyte soon after the yolk begins to form. The chromatin threads in the spermatocytes break down and lose their affinity for dyes, but later reappear. In the oöcyte, on the contrary, the chromatin threads persist. Demoll concludes from these observations that the Nebenkern always determines the character of the germ cells, which, up to its formation, may be called indifferent germ cells. He further concludes, that, since in diœcious animals sex is determined by the accessory chromosomes, in *Helix* the sexual specificity of the Nebenkern must be determined by the accessory chromosomes. Such chromosomes were described by Demoll (1912a) in a previous contribution.

A similar idea has been expressed by von Voss (1914) regarding the differentiation of indifferent germ cells in a flat-worm, *Mesostoma ehrenbergi*. In the embryo of this hermaphrodite the germ gland is a syncytium containing both the nuclei of future oögonia and future spermatogonia. The cytoplasm is apparently homogeneous throughout. The formation of the oögonia from indifferent germ cells begins with the appearance of a "germinal-vesicle stage"; this is followed by an increase in the amount of cytoplasm surrounding them. Since the cytoplasm appears to be similar in all parts of the syncytium, differentiation must be initiated by the nucleus, and the suggestion is made that perhaps the accessory chromosome may be responsible for the separation of the germ cells into oögonia and spermatogonia.

The investigators whose results have been described above have thus furnished three theories regarding the differentiation of male and female germ cells in hermaphrodites: (1) In *Sagitta*, according to Elpatiewsky, it is an unequal distribution of the "besondere Körper," (2) in *Helix*, according to Ancel and Buresch, it is due to the presence or absence of a nurse cell in the immediate neighborhood, and (3) in *Helix*, Demoll considers it a result of the influence of the accessory chromosome. It is perfectly obvious that hermaphrodites offer exceptionally fine material for the study of the differentiation of germ cells, but that thus far the results have not furnished an adequate explanation of the phenomenon. The investigations of Boveri (1911), Schleip (1911), and Krueger (1912) on the chromosomes in hermaphroditic nematodes may be discussed more profitably during the consideration of the chromosome cycle in the next chapter.

Certain morphological and experimental studies on the germ glands of amphibians are of interest because both oögonia and spermatogonia are sometimes more or less closely associated in a single individual during the developmental stages, and may persist even in the adult germ glands of a number of species which are commonly considered diœcious. Pflüger, for example, was able to separate the young of the frog, *Rana temporaria*, into three groups, males, females, and hermaphrodites; the hermaphrodites developed into either males or females. Similar results were obtained by Schmidt-Marcel (1908) and Kuschakewitsch (1910), who refer to the hermaphroditic individuals as intermediates.

There is no consensus of opinion regarding the origin of the germ cells in amphibians; one group of investigators, including Allen (1907) and King (1908), recognize a definite keimbahn, whereas many others (Semon, 1891; Bouin, 1900; Dustin, 1907; Kuschakewitsch, 1910; Champy, 1913) believe they arise from the germinal epithelium or near-by cells. Very few students have attempted to determine the stages in or causes of the differentiation of male and female cells from the primordial germ cells. Kuschakewitsch (1910) concludes from his extensive studies on the history of the germ cells in frogs that at first all of the germ cells are indifferent but subsequently become differentiated in two directions. Champy (1913) has studied this differentiation in a number of amphibians and has concluded that if the characteristically lobed or polymorphic nuclei of the primordial germ cells in *Bufo*, *Hyla*, and *Rana temporaria* lose their original shape and become spherical and clear, the germ gland will form an ovary; but if the nuclei retain their primitive condition, a testis will result. Champy believes with Kuschakewitsch that both sorts of germ cells arise from sexually indifferent cells, that is, sex is not irrevocably fixed in the fertilized egg. Furthermore Champy's observations have led to the conclusion that the germ cells in the sexually indifferent germ glands are morphologically identical with primitive spermatogonia. These indifferent germ cells become differentiated into ova or spermatozoa as a result of various causes, some general and others local in nature, which probably are most influential at certain definite stages in the cellular activity. A new equilibrium is thereby established between the different cell organs which initiates new processes resulting in differentiation. The undifferentiated cells in the testis of the adult appear also to be identical with the primitive spermatogonia, and have still the power of producing either ova or spermatozoa. Thus the male amphibians are also females "en puissance," but the reverse is not true. This accounts for the numerous discoveries of ova in the testes of these animals.

Reports of so-called hermaphroditism in amphibians are abundant in the literature. Cases have been reported in frogs by Cole (1895), Friedmann (1898), Gerhartz (1905), Ognew (1906), Yung (1907), Schmidt-Marcel (1908), Youngman (1910), Hooker (1912), and many others. Hooker has reviewed the literature of the subject. Hermaphroditism in other amphibians is more rare, but it has been noted in salamanders by La Vallett St. George (1895) and Feistmantel (1902). Usually the condition spoken of as hermaphroditism consists in the presence of ova in the testis, and it is probable that true hermaphroditism is rare in these animals as it is in other vertebrates. In the toad, however, a condition exists which is of particular interest. The genital ridge of every toad tadpole 15 to 18 days old becomes visibly differentiated into two regions, an anterior portion which develops into Bidder's Organ, and a posterior region which becomes an ovary or testis. Bidder's Organ persists in the adult of males, where it lies just anterior to the testis, but in the females of *Bufo variabilis*, *B. cinereus*, *B. clamita*, and *B. lentiginosus* it disappears at the end of the second year. *Bufo vulgaris* seems to differ from the other species since here Bidder's Organ persists, becoming small and shrunken during the winter (Ognew, 1906) and regenerating during the summer months (Knappe, 1886). At first the cells in both the anterior and posterior portions of the genital ridge are similar, all possessing a polymorphic nucleus, and dividing mitotically, but later those of Bidder's Organ begin to divide amitotically and assume the characteristics of young oöcytes with rounded nuclei. Knappe (1886) claims that these cells never become functional ova because they are unable to form yolk. King (1908), however, does not consider this probable, but traces their differentiation to irregularities in the synizesis stage.

By most investigators Bidder's Organ is regarded as a rudimentary ovary. Others believe that the AMPHIBIA were derived from hermaphroditic ancestors and that in the male it is a rudimentary ovary and in the female a rudimentary testis. This seems more probable than Marshall's suggestion that this organ is the result of degenerative processes proceeding backward from the anterior end of the genital ridge, or than that it represents the remains of a sex gland possessed by the larvæ of ancestral toads when they were pædogenetic, as Axolotl is at the present time. Champy (1913) has found that the cells of Bidder's Organ in *Bufo pantherina* pass through stages in their transformation similar to those of the primitive germ cells of *Rana esculenta* which become ova, and is inclined to the view that the principal difference between the toad and the intermediate type of young frogs lies in the fact that in the former the oviform cells are localized in Bidder's Organ, whereas in the frog they are scattered throughout the germ gland.

The development of the germ glands in the hagfish, *Myxine glutinosa*, resembles that in the toad in many respects. Cunningham (1886) and Nansen (1886) considered Myxine to be a protandric hermaphrodite. Schreiner (1904), however, was able to show that every adult is functionally male or female with a rudimentary ovary anteriorly situated and a posterior, mature testis, or a functional ovary anterior to a rudimentary testis. These results were confirmed by Cole (1905).

Similar conditions have been found by Okkelberg (1914) in the young of the brook lamprey, *Entosphenus wilderi*. Of fifty larvæ ranging from $7\frac{1}{2}$ cm. to 20 cm. in length, 46 per cent were true females, 10 per cent were true males, and 44 per cent were hermaphrodites. Since male and female adults are approximately equal in numbers, it was concluded that the juvenile hermaphrodites become adult males. In favor of this conclusion is also the fact that the adult males frequently possess ova in their gonads which resemble those present in the hermaphroditic larvæ.

Regarding the differentiation of the germ cells in hermaphrodites then we may recognize two principal views: (1) that there is some material within the cell which initiates specialization, or (2) that differentiation is due to general or local causes outside of the germ cells. The former is favored by Elpatiewsky (1909, 1910) from studies on *Sagitta* and by Demoll (1912) from studies on *Helix*. The second view is more widely advocated. The conclusions derived by Kuschakewitsch (1910) and Champy (1913) on amphibians, and of Ancel (1903) and Buresch (1911) on *Helix* agree in their essential features. All of these investigators maintain that the sex cells pass through an indifferent stage and are differentiated into oöcytes or spermatocytes because of influences external to themselves. Buresch and Champy also believe that even in the fully developed germ glands of the adult these primitive cells are present. The causes of their differentiation, however, have not been definitely determined.

CHAPTER VIII

KEIMBAHN-DETERMINANTS AND THEIR SIGNIFICANCE

It is customary to be suspicious of any peculiar bodies revealed to us in fixed and stained material under high magnification. There can be no doubt, however, that most, if not all, of the cytoplasmic inclusions mentioned in the preceding chapters are realities and not artifacts. Some of them have been seen in the living eggs; most of them have been described by several investigators; they occur after being fixed and stained in many different solutions; and their presence is perfectly constant. The genesis, localization, and fate of these bodies are difficult to determine, and their significance is problematical; but the writer has attempted in the following pages to draw at least tentative conclusions from the evidence available and to indicate what still needs to be done.

A. The Genesis of the Keimbahn-determinants

The writers who have discussed the origin of the keimbahn-determinants have derived them from many different sources. In a few cases they are known to be nuclear in origin, consisting of nucleolar or chromatic materials; they are considered differentiated parts of the cytoplasm by some investigators; in some species they are extra-cellular bodies, such as nurse cells.

The accompanying table indicates the number and diversity of the animals in which keimbahn-determinants have been described, and shows the increasing interest that has been given to this subject within recent years, over half of the papers listed having been published since 1908. Several cases have been referred to in the text, but omitted from the table because of insufficient evidence regarding their connection with the primordial germ cells. The list as given includes representatives of the CŒLENTERATA, CHÆTOGNATHA, NEMATODA, ARTHROPODA, and VERTEBRATA. The terms applied to the various substances have been chosen evidently because of their genesis, position in the egg, or supposed function.

TABLE OF PRINCIPAL CASES OF VISIBLE SUBSTANCES CONCERNED IN DIFFERENTIATION OF GERM CELLS (IN CHRONOLOGICAL ORDER)

Name of Species, Genus, or Group	Name Applied to Substance	Authority	Date
Chironomus nigroviridis	Dotterkörnchen	Weismann	1863
Miastor	Dottermasse	Metchnikoff	1866
Moina rectirostris	Richtungskörper	Grobben	1879
Chironomus	Keimwulst	Ritter	1890
Daphnidæ	Paracopulationszelle	Weismann and Ischikawa	1889
Æquorea	Metanucleolus	Haecker	1892
Ascaris megalocephala	Chromatin	Boveri	1892

A. lumbricoides A. rubicunda A. labiata	Chromatin	O. Meyer	1895
Cyclops	Aussenkörnchen	Haecker	1897
	Ektosomen	Haecker	1903
Calliphora	Dotterplatte	Noack	1901
Dytiscus	Anello cromatico	Giardina	1901
Apis mellifica	Richtungskörper	Petrunkewitsch	1902
Parasitic Hymenoptera	Nucleolo	Silvestri	1906 1908
Chrysomelidæ	Pole-disc	Hegner	1908
Miastor metraloas	polares Plasma	Kahle	1908
Sagitta	besondere Körper	Elpatiewsky	1909
Guinea-pig	Chondriosomes	Rubaschkin	1910
Chick	Chondriosomes	Tschaschkin	1910
Lophius	extruded plasmosome	Dodds	1910
Ascaris	Plasmadifferenzen	Boveri	1910
Chironomus	Keimbahnplasma	Hasper	1911
Copepoda	Ectosomen	Amma	1911
Polyphemus	Nahrzellenkern	Kühn	1911 1913
Sagitta	Keimbahnchromidien	Buchner	1910
Man	Sertoli cell determinant	Montgomery	1911
Chick	Attractionsphere	Swift	1914
Parasitic Hymenoptera	Keimbahnchromatin	Hegner	1914

a. NUCLEAR. NUCLEOLI. It seems certain that bodies of a nucleolar nature behave as keimbahn-determinants. There are three or more kinds of bodies that are spoken of as nucleoli. Of these may be mentioned (1) the *true nucleoli* or *plasmosomes*, (2) *karyosomes* or *chromatin-nucleoli*, and (3) *double-nu-*

cleoli, consisting of usually a single *principal nucleolus* (Hauptnucleolus of Flemming), and one or more *accessory nucleoli* (Nebennucleoli of Flemming). Many nucleoli have been described that may perhaps represent intermediate stages in the evolution of one of the types mentioned above into another.

The young ovarian egg of most animals contains a single spherical nucleolus ("Keimfleck," or "germinal spot"), but the number may increase greatly during the growth period. Usually during the formation of the first maturation spindle the nucleolus escapes from the nucleus into the cytoplasm, where it disappears, often after breaking up into fragments. Many theories have been advanced regarding the origin, function, and fate of the nucleoli of the germinal vesicle. They are considered by some of chromatic origin, arising as an accumulation of the chromatin, or from the chromatin by chemical transformation. Others consider them extra-nuclear in origin (Montgomery, 1899).

Many functions have been attributed to the nucleoli; of these the following may be mentioned: (1) They function as excretory organs (Balbiani, 1864; Hodge, 1894); (2) nucleoli play an active rôle in the cell, since they serve as storehouses of material which is contributed to the formation of the chromosomes (Flemming, 1882; Lubosch, 1902; Jordan, 1910; Foot and Strobell, 1912) and may give rise to kinoplasm (Strasburger, 1895) or "Kinetochromidien" (Schaxel, 1910); (3) nucleoli are passive by-products of chromatic activity; they become absorbed by active substances (Haecker, 1895, 1899); (4) nucleoli represent nutritive material used by the nucleus into which it is taken from the cytoplasm (Montgomery, 1899).

Undoubtedly the various bodies known as nucleoli originate in different ways, have different histories, and perform different functions.

In the particular cases to be discussed here the nucleoli are not temporary structures, as is usually true, but persist for a comparatively long interval after the germinal vesicle breaks down. What seemed to be the most important and convincing evidence of the functioning of a nucleolus as a keimbahn-determinant is that furnished by Silvestri (1906, 1908) in parasitic Hymenoptera. As shown in Chapter V, however, the "nucleolo" of Silvestri is really not a nucleolus but consists of chromatin.

As we have already noted, in a few instances the nucleolus does not disappear during the maturation divisions but persists for a time as a "metanucleolus" (see p. 183). These metanucleoli are evidently of a different nature from the usual type and are hence saved from immediate disintegration in the cytoplasm. The localization of the metanucleolus in the egg is the result of either its own activity, or that of the surrounding cytoplasm, or a combination of these. Gravity can have no decided effect upon it (Herrick, 1895), since its position is constant, whereas the position of the egg with respect to gravity is not. It also seems hardly possible that oxygenotactic stimuli are the cause of its localization, as has been suggested by Herbst (1894, 1895) for the migration of the blastoderm-forming cells from the center to the surface of the eggs of certain arthropods.

Haecker (1897) has suggested that the "Aussenkörnchen" which appear in the egg of *Cyclops* during the formation of the first cleavage spindle may be nucleolar in nature. Later (1903) this idea was withdrawn, and more recently Amma (1911) has likewise been unable to sustain this hypothesis. The most convincing data furnished by Amma are that in an allied form, *Diaptomus cœruleus* (Fig. 49, *H*), these granules appear before the cleavage spindle is formed and before the nucleoli of the pronuclei have disappeared.

The remaining forms in which nucleoli have been considered as keimbahn-determinants are merely suggestive. In *Æquorea*, Haecker (1892) traced the metanucleolus, which arises from the germinal vesicle, into certain cells of the blastula. Similar bodies appear in *Mitrocoma* (Metchnikoff, 1886), *Tiara* (Boveri, 1890), *Stephanophyes* (Chun, 1891), *Myzostoma* (Wheeler, 1897), and *Asterias* (Hartmann, 1902), but their ultimate fate has not been determined. Meves (1914), however, has traced the middle piece of the sperm of the sea urchin, *Parechinus miliaris*, into one of the cells of the animal half of the egg at the thirty-two-cell stage. This middle piece is of a plastochondrial nature.

It seems probable that in all these cases the same influences may be at work regulating the time, the place, and the method of localization of the nucleoli.

The writer can only conclude (1) that the metanucleoli differ in nature from ordinary plasmosomes, chromatin-nucleoli, and double-nucleoli; (2) that these bodies are definitely segregated in a certain part of the egg or in a certain blastomere, probably by protoplasmic movements; (3) and that their disintegration and the distribution of the resulting fragments or granules are controlled by reactions between them and the substances in which they are embedded.

CHROMATIN. In two genera of animals the differentiation of the primordial germ cells is accompanied by a diminution of the chromatin in the nuclei of the somatic cells, so that eventually the nucleus of every germ cell is provided with the full complement of chromatin, whereas the nucleus of every somatic cell lacks a considerable portion of this substance, which remains behind in the cytoplasm when the daughter nuclei are reconstituted. These two genera are *Ascaris* and *Miastor*. This diminution process was described by Boveri (1892) in the former and confirmed by O. Meyer (1895) and Bonnevie (1902), and by Kahle (1908) in *Miastor* and confirmed by Hegner (1912, 1914a). For details of these processes reference should be made to Figs. 15–16, 51–52, and pp. 57 and 174. It may be pointed out here that although the final results are similar the process differs in the two genera. In *Ascaris* both ends of each chromosome are split off, whereas in *Miastor* approximately one-half of each daughter chromosome is left behind to form the "Chromosomenmittelplatte" (Fig. 16) and later the "Chromatinreste" (Fig. 18).

The elimination of chromatin during the maturation and early cleavage divisions of the egg, as well as during the mitotic divisions of other kinds of cells, has often been recorded. For example, Wilson (1895, p. 458) estimates that only about one-tenth of the chromatin in the germinal vesicle of the starfish is retained to form the chromosomes during the first maturation division, and Conklin (1902) finds that "in Crepidula the outflow of nuclear material occurs at each and every mitosis" (p. 51). Furthermore, Rhode (1911) argues that chromatin-diminution is a normal histological process, and describes such phenomena in blood cells, nerve cells, and cleavage cells of several AMPHIBIA, comparing conditions with the chromatin-diminution in *Ascaris* and *Dysticus*.[1]

Diminution processes similar to those in *Ascaris* and *Miastor* have not been discovered in other animals, although investigators have been on the watch for such phenomena and have studied allied species, *e.g.*, the work of Hasper (1911) on *Chironomus* and my own work on the chrysomelid beetles (see pp. 108

---

[1] His conclusion is as follows: "In der Histogenese der allerverschiedensten Gewebe tritt uns also die Erscheinung entgegen, dass die sich entwickelnden Zellen, bzw. Kerne einen Teil ihres Chromatins abstossen, d. h. also eine Chromatindiminution erfolgt, wenn auch die Befunde selbst im speziellen von den bisher beobachteten in der Einleitung beschriebenen Fällen der Chromatindiminution etwas abweichen.

"Eine Chromatindiminution tritt also nicht nur am Anfang und Ende der Keimbahn, wie es bisher angegeben worden ist, sondern in den verschiedensten Entwicklungsstadien und bei den verschiedensten Geweben und Tieren ein, sie hat also offenbar eine allgemeine Bedeutung." (p. 25.)

to 118). If, therefore, there is a similar difference in all animals in chromatin content between the germ cells and somatic cells, the elimination of chromatin from the latter must take place by the transformation of the basichromatin of the chromosomes into oxychromatin which passes into the cytoplasm during mitosis, or else by the more direct method advocated by the believers in the chromidia hypothesis.

The causes of the diminution of chromatin in *Ascaris* and *Miastor* are unknown. Recently Boveri (1910) has concluded from certain experiments on the eggs of *Ascaris* (see p. 177) that in this form it is the cytoplasm in which the nuclei are embedded that determines whether or not the latter shall undergo this process. Kahle (1908) does not explain the cause of the diminution in *Miastor*. To the writer it seems more important to discover why the nuclei of the keimbahn cells *do not* lose part of their chromatin, since the elimination of chromatin during mitosis is apparently such a universal phenomenon. I would attribute this failure of certain cells to undergo the diminution process not to the contents of the nucleus alone but to the reaction between the nucleus and the surrounding cytoplasm. As stated in a former paper (Hegner, 1909a), "In *Calligrapha* all the nuclei of the egg are apparently alike, potentially, until in their migration toward the surface they reach the 'Keimhautblastem'; then those which chance to encounter the granules of the pole-disc are differentiated by their environment, *i.e.*, the granules, into germ cells. In other words, whether or not a cell will become a germ cell depends on its position in the egg just previous to the formation of the blastoderm."

Similarly in *Ascaris* the cleavage nuclei are conceived as similar so far as their "prospective potency" is concerned, their future depending upon the character of their environment, *i.e.*, the cytoplasm. In the egg of *Miastor* cleavage nucleus IV (Fig. 15) does not lose part of its chromatin because of the character of the reaction between it and the substance of the "polares Plasma." In chrysomelid beetles (Hegner, 1908, 1909, 1914a) and *Chironomus* (Hasper, 1911), however, although no diminution process has been discovered in the nuclei that encounter the pole-disc or "Keimbahnplasma," the other nuclei in the egg, so far as known, are similar in this respect. The nuclei of the primordial germ cells, however, may be distinguished easily from those of the blastoderm cells in chrysomelid beetles, proving conclusively that a differentiation has taken place either in one or the other. This differentiation probably occurs in the nuclei that take part in the formation of the blastoderm, since the nuclei of the germ cells retain more nearly the characteristic features of the pre-blastodermic nuclei, whereas those of the blastoderm cells change considerably.

In some cases the eliminated chromatin may have some influence upon the histological differentiation of the cell, since it is differentially distributed to the daughter cells, but in *Ascaris* and *Miastor* no mechanism exists for regulating the distribution of the cast-out chromatin, and there is consequently no grounds for the hypothesis that "in *Ascaris* those cells which become body cells are the ones that include the cast-off chromosome ends in their cytoplasm, and it will probably be found that these ejected chromosome parts engender such cytoplasmic differentiations as characterize the body cells" (Montgomery, 1911, p. 192).

CHROMIDIA. To several of the bodies listed in the table on page 88 as keimbahn-determinants has been ascribed an origin from the chromatin of the germinal vesicle. Many cases of the elimination of chromatin from the nuclei of growing oöcytes are to be found in the literature. Blochmann (1886) discovered a process of "budding" in the oöcytes of *Camponotus ligniperda* resulting in the formation of "Nebenkerne." These appear first as small vacuoles lying near the nucleus; later they contain small staining granules and acquire a membrane. The "Nebenkerne" grow in size and increase in number, while the nucleus of the oöcyte becomes smaller. Stuhlmann (1886) described a similar phenomenon in about a dozen different species of HYMENOPTERA. The oöcyte nucleus in all species examined becomes localized near the anterior end; then the small nuclear-like bodies form around it at its expense. The time of their production varies in the different species; in some they appear in the very young eggs; in others not until a much later stage has been reached. Sometimes they fuse to form a large "Dotterkern" lying at the posterior pole of the egg;

or they may remain separate and later become scattered. Paulcke (1900) also noted nuclear-like bodies near the oöcyte nucleus of the queen bee, and Marshall (1907) has likewise found them in *Polistes pallipes*. In this species the nuclear-like bodies form a single layer around the nucleus; later they come to lie near the periphery of the oöcyte and finally disappear. Loewenthal (1888) has described what appears to be chromatin in the cytoplasm of the egg of the cat, and an elimination of chromatin was noted by van Bambeke (1893) in the ovarian egg of *Scorpæna scrofa*. In none of these species, however, have keimbahn-determinants been discovered.

According to Buchner (1910) the "besondere Körper" in the egg of *Sagitta*, and in fact keimbahn-determinants in most other animals are of a chromidial nature, representing the tropho-chromatin demanded by the binuclearity hypothesis. The term chromidia was introduced by R. Hertwig in 1902 and applied to certain chromatin strands and granules of nuclear origin in the cytoplasm of *Actinosphærium*. Goldschmidt (1904) transferred the chromidia hypothesis to the tissue cells of *Ascaris*. Since then chromidia have been described in the cells of many animals, including both somatic and germ cells. Thus far the group of zoölogists that favor the chromidia idea have not received very extensive backing, but the fact remains that chromatin particles are in some cases cast out of the nuclei in the oöcytes of certain animals and continue to exist as such in the cytoplasm for a considerable period. It is also possible that, as Buchner (1910) maintains, the keimbahn-determinants may be in reality "Keimbahnchromidien."

This view was suggested by the writer in 1909 (p. 274) to account for the origin of the pole-disc granules in the eggs of chrysomelid beetles. It was thought that here as in the HYMENOPTERA (Blochmann, 1886; *et al.*) chromatin granules might be cast out of the nuclei of the oöcytes, and that these granules might gather at the posterior end to form the pole-disc. It was also suggested that chromatin granules from the nurse-cell nuclei might make their way into the oöcyte and later become the granules of the pole-disc. It should not be forgotten, moreover, that these granules stain like chromatin. Finally, mention should be made of the "anello cromatico" of Giardina (1901) which is associated with the differentiation of the oöcytes in *Dytiscus* (see p. 120, Fig. 38), and the keimbahn-chromatin which I have recently described (Hegner, 1914*b*) in the eggs of the parasitic hymenopteron, *Copidosoma* (p. 151, Figs. 46–47).

CONCLUSION. Certain keimbahn-determinants may consist of nucleolar material which is derived from the germinal vesicle and persists until the primordial germ cells are established. In some cases the keimbahn cells are characterized by the possession of the complete amount of chromatin in contrast to the somatic cells which lose a part of this substance. Since, however, the chromatin-diminution process does not occur in many species, it is probably not a universal phenomenon, and consequently cannot be of fundamental importance. Most of the evidence, on the other hand, points toward the conclusion that all of the cleavage nuclei are qualitatively alike, and that the cytoplasm is the controlling factor.

b. CYTOPLASMIC OR EXTRACELLULAR NUTRITIVE SUBSTANCES. It was pointed out on a preceding page (p. 101) that one of the characteristics used to distinguish primordial germ cells from other embryonic cells is the presence within them of yolk material. In many vertebrates the yolk globules persist in the primordial germ cells until a comparatively late stage, and indeed are often so numerous as to practically conceal the nuclei of these cells. A large number of the keimbahn-determinants that have been described are supposed to consist of nutritive substances. Some of the earliest investigators were aware of the yolk content of the primordial germ cells. For example, in *Chironomus* Weismann (1863) found four oval nuclei lying in the "Keimhautblastem" at the posterior end of the egg, each of which is associated with one or two yolk granules; these are the "Polzellen." In another Dipteron, *Simula* sp., Metchnikoff (1866) records four or five polecells which possess fine yolk granules in their cell substance. The same author (1866) also states that when the pseudovum in the pædogenetic larva of *Miastor* contains twelve to fifteen nuclei, one of these, together with the dark yolk-mass in which it lies, is cut off as a cell which gives rise to the pole-cells.

In certain DAPHNIDÆ, Weismann and Ischikawa (1889) describe a "Paracopulationszelle" which is derived from the contents of the germinal vesicle (see p. 163); but the recent work of Kühn (1911, 1913) renders it probable that this body is nothing but the remains of a nurse cell. The "Dotterplatte" discovered by Noack (1901) at the posterior end of the egg of *Calliphora* (Fig. 34) is considered by this investigator to consist of yolk elements. In previous communications (Hegner, 1908, 1909, 1911) the writer has discussed the probability that the pole-disc in chrysomelid eggs consists of nutritive material, and Weiman (1910*a*) also has offered arguments for this view.

The granules segregated in certain cleavage cells of *Neritina* (Blochmann, 1881), *Asplanchna* (Jennings, 1896), *Lepas* (Bigelow, 1902), *Siphonaria* (Fujita, 1904), and *Physa* (Wierzejski, 1906) may be of a nutritive nature, and these cells may be the stem cells from which the germ cells of these animals eventually arise. The hypothesis that the nucleoli consist of food substance also argues in favor of the idea that the keimbahn-determinants are nutritive.

The importance of these nutritive substances to the primordial germ cells can be stated with some degree of certainty. According to some authorities the primordial germ cells remain in the primitive condition and do not undergo differentiation at the same time, or at least at the same rate, as do the other embryonic cells. On this account their yolk contents are not at first utilized, since their metabolic activities are so slight. This is more especially true of the vertebrates in which, it has been suggested (Hegner, 1909a, p. 276), the yolk contents of the germ cells are transformed into the energy of motion during the characteristic migration of these cells into the germinal epithelium. Why these nutritive substances are segregated in the primordial germ cells is more difficult to answer. Finally, it is interesting to note that the differentiation of the indifferent germ cells of *Helix arbustorum* into spermatogonia or oögonia has been found to depend upon nutrition (Buresch, 1911).[1]

YOLK NUCLEUS. There are many bodies in the cytoplasm of growing oöcytes that have been called yolk nuclei and that may be responsible for the origin of the keimbahn-determinants. Some of these bodies have already been considered, but the term 'yolk nucleus' has been applied to so many different cytoplasmic inclusions (Munson, 1912) that no attempt will be made here to describe them nor to trace their history.

MITOCHONDRIA. The condition of the chondriosomes in the primordial germ cells of certain vertebrates (Rubaschkin, 1910, 1912; Tschaschkin, 1910; Swift, 1914) and the theories that have been pro-

---

[1] "Ob aber eine indifferente Geschlechtszelle sich in männlicher oder weiblicher Richtung weiter entwickeln wird, das können wir schon sehr früh sagen, nämlich nach der Lage dieser Zelle näher oder weiter von einer Nährzelle " (p. 327).

posed regarding the rôle of these bodies in heredity make it necessary to refer to them briefly here. At the present time it is difficult to make any definite statement regarding the origin, nature, and significance of the various cytoplasmic inclusions that have been grouped under the general title of mitochondria. It seems probable that we are concerned with a number of different sorts of inclusions, and with various stages in their evolution. In the guinea pig (Rubaschkin, 1910, 1912) and chick (Tschaschkin, 1910) the chondriosomes of the cleavage cells are spherical and all similar, but, as development proceeds, those of the cells which become differentiated to produce the germ layers unite to form chains and threads, whereas those of the primordial germ cells remain in a spherical and therefore primitive condition (Fig. 31, *B*). Swift (1914) has found, however, that in the chick the mitochondria in the primordial germ cells are not at all characteristic, resembling those of the somatic cells. The germ cells nevertheless can be distinguished from the latter by the presence of an especially large attraction-sphere (Fig. 31, *D*). This distinction between the primordial germ cells and the surrounding somatic cells may enable us to trace the keimbahn in vertebrates back into cleavage stages — something that has not been accomplished as yet.

An examination of the various keimbahn-determinants listed in the table (p. 212) has led the writer to conclude that none of them is of a mitochondrial nature, but the results obtained by the special methods employed by students who are studying mitochondria give us good reason to hope that other substances may be made visible which will help to clear up the problem of primary cellular differentiation.

METABOLIC PRODUCTS. Among the most difficult cases to explain are those of *Sagitta* and certain copepods, since here the keimbahn-determinants apparently arise *de novo* in the cytoplasm. Buchner's (1910) contention that the "besondere Körper" of *Sagitta* is the remains of the "accessory fertilization cell" of Stevens (1904) is not sustained by either Stevens (1910) or Elpatiewsky (1910). The idea of the nucleolar nature of the "Aussenkörnchen" in *Cyclops* has been discarded by Haecker (1903) and the conclusion reached that these granules are similar to nucleoli in one respect, namely, they are by-products of activities within the cell. Amma (1911) has considered this subject at some length, and after rejecting the possibilities of these being of (1) chromatic, (2) nucleolar, (3) chromidial, and (4) mitochondrial origin likewise concludes that they are transitory by-products. In this way the keimbahn-determinants in copepods are satisfactorily explained, and a similar explanation may be applied to *Sagitta*, although with less certainty.

c. DISCUSSION. A review of the literature on the keimbahn-determinants and the investigation of these substances in the eggs of insects force me to conclude that the fundamental organization of the egg is responsible for the segregation of the primordial germ cells, whereas the visible substances simply furnish evidence of this underlying organization. As I have stated elsewhere (Hegner, 1908, p. 21) regarding the keimbahn-determinants in beetles' eggs, "the granules of the pole-disc are therefore either the germ-cell determinants or the visible sign of the germ-cell determinants." The writer's experiments have thus far failed to determine the exact function of these granules. When the posterior end of a freshly laid beetle's egg is pricked with a needle, not only the pole-disc granules flow out, but also the cytoplasm in which they are embedded (Hegner, 1908). If a small region at the posterior end is killed with a hot needle, the pole-disc is prevented from taking part in the development of the egg, but so also is the surrounding cytoplasm (Fig. 37, c). Eggs thus treated continue to develop and produce embryos without germ cells, but as a rule a part of the posterior end of the abdomen is also absent (Hegner, 1911a). The pole-disc granules and the cytoplasm containing them is moved by centrifugal force toward the heavy end of the egg and is proved to be quite rigid, but eggs thus treated do not develop sufficiently normally to enable one to decide whether the pole-disc produces germ cells in its new environment or not.

That the germ cells of *Chironomus* arise from a prelocalized substance was stated by Balbiani (1885) in these words, "the genital glands of the two sexes have an absolutely identical origin, arising from the same substance and at the same region of the egg." Ritter (1890) expressed the opinion that the "Keimwulst" of *Chironomus* consists of fine granulated protoplasm, an opinion concurred in by Hasper (1911), who terms it "Keimbahnplasma." The similar material in *Miastor metraloas*, the "polares Plasma," is considered a special sort of protoplasm by Kahle (1908), and I can confirm this for *Miastor americana*. Further evidence of the protoplasmic nature of the substances which become segregated in the primordial germ cells is furnished by Boveri's experiments on *Ascaris*. In 1904 this investigator concluded from a study of dispermic eggs that the diminution process is controlled by the cytoplasm and not by an intrinsic property of the chromosomes, and that the chromosomes of nuclei lying in the vegetative cytoplasm remain intact, whereas those of nuclei embedded in the animal cytoplasm undergo diminution. This conclusion has been strengthened by more recent experimental evidence (Boveri, 1910) both from observation on the development of dispermic eggs and from a study of centrifuged eggs (see p. 178, Fig. 53). Boveri's results furnish a remarkable confirmation of the conclusions reached by the writer from a morphological study of the germ cells of chrysomelid beetles and expressed in the following words: "All the cleavage nuclei in the eggs of the above-named beetles (*Calligrapha multipunctata*, etc.) are potentially alike until in their migration toward the periphery they reach the 'keimhautblastem.' Then those which chance to encounter the granules of the pole-disc are differentiated by their environment, *i.e.*, the granules, into germ cells; all the other cleavage products become somatic cells." Here, however, the pole-disc granules were considered the essential substance.

The appearance of the keimbahn-determinants at a certain time and in a certain place, and their determinate segregation, point unmistakably to an underlying regulating mechanism. These phenomena have some definite relation to the fundamental organization of the egg and require an investigation of our present knowledge of this subject.

The isotropism of the egg as postulated by Pflüger and the "cell interaction" idea especially developed by O. Hertwig and Driesch have given way before the beautiful researches tending to uphold the hypothesis of "germinal localization" proposed by His and championed by so many investigators within the past two decades. The starting point for embryological studies has shifted from the germ layers to the cleavage cells and from these to the undivided egg. Organization, which Whitman (1893) maintains precedes cell-formation and regulates it, is now traced back to very early stages in the germ-cell cycle and held responsible for the cytoplasmic localization in the egg.

One of the fundamental characteristics of the egg is its polarity. It has been known for about thirty years that the eggs of insects are definitely oriented within the ovaries of the adults. Moreover, gravity and the action of centrifugal force have no effect upon the polarity of insect eggs (Hegner, 1909*b*). Giardina (1901) has found that during the divisions of the oögonia in *Dytiscus* a rosette of sixteen cells is produced of which one is the oöcyte and the other fifteen nurse cells. The rosette thus formed possesses a definite polarity coincident with the axis of the oöcyte which is identical with that which was present in the last generation of oögonia. Similarly in *Miastor* (Fig. 12) the polarity of the oöcyte is recognizable as soon as the mesodermal cells, which serve in this species as nurse cells, become associated with it.

The germ cells of other animals also possess a precocious polarity, as evidenced by their implantation in the germinal epithelium (*e.g.*, Wilson, 1903; Zeleny, 1904, in *Cerebratulus*), the position of the nucleus, the formation of the micropyle (Jenkinson, 1911), etc. This is true not only for the invertebrates, but, as Bartelmez (1912) claims, "the polar axis persists unmodified from generation to generation in the vertebrates and is one of the fundamental features of the organization of the protoplasm" (p. 310). Furthermore, experiments with centrifugal force seem to prove that the chief axis of the egg is not altered when substances are shifted about, but is fixed at all stages (Lillie, 1909; Morgan, 1909; Conklin, 1910). Bilaterality also is demonstrable in the early stages of the germ cells of many animals, and, like polarity, seems to be a fundamental characteristic of the protoplasm.

It is somewhat difficult to harmonize the various results that have been obtained, especially by experimental methods, from the study of egg organization. As the oöcytes grow, the apparently homogeneous contents become visibly different in some animals, and when the mature eggs develop normally these "organ-forming substances" are segregated in definite cleavage cells and finally become associated with definite organs of the larva.

Conklin (1905) has shown "that at least five of the substances which are present in the egg (of *Cynthia*) at the close of the first cleavage, viz., ectoplasm, endoplasm, myoplasm, chymoplasm, and chordaneuroplasm, are organ-forming substances." Under experimental conditions "they develop, if they develop at all, into the organs which they would normally produce; and, conversely, embryos which lack these substances, lack also the organs which would form from them." "Three of these substances are clearly distinguishable in the ovarian egg and I do not doubt that even at this stage they are differentiated for particular ends" (p. 220). "The development of ascidians is a mosaic work because there are definitely localized organ-forming substances in the egg; in fact, the mosaic is one of organ-forming substances rather than of cleavage cells. The study of ctenophores, nemertines, annelids, mollusks, ascidians, and amphibians (the frog) shows that the same is probably true of all these forms and it suggests that the mosaic principle may apply to all animals" (p. 221). The same writer has also proved from his study on *Phallusia* (1911) that these various substances exist even when they are not visible in the living egg. It is interesting also to note that Duesberg (1913) finds the "myoplasm" of *Cynthia* to be crowded with plasmosomes, differing in this respect from other egg regions.

Experiments, especially those of Lillie (1906, 1909), Morgan and Spooner (1909), Morgan (1909*a*), and Conklin (1910), have shown that in many eggs the shifting of the supposed organ-forming substances has no influence upon development, and leads to the conclusion that these visible substances play no fundamental rôle in differentiation, but that the invisible ground substance is responsible for determinate development. The eggs of different animals, however, differ both in time and degree of organization, and the conflicting results may be accounted for by the fact that specification is more precocious in some than in others.

The most plausible conclusions from a consideration of these observations and experiments are that every one of the eggs in which keimbahn-determinants have been described consists essentially of a fundamental ground substance which determines the orientation; that the time of appearance of keimbahn-determinants depends upon the precociousness of the egg; that the keimbahn-determinants are the visible evidences of differentiation in the cytoplasm; and that these differentiated portions of the cytoplasm are definitely localized by cytoplasmic movements, especially at about the time of maturation.

B. The Localization of the Keimbahn-Determinants

One of the characteristics of the keimbahn-determinants is their regular appearance at a certain stage in the germ-cell cycle according to the species in which they occur, and their constant localization in a definite part of the egg, or in one or more definite cleavage cells. Keimbahn-determinants are recognizable in many insects' eggs before fertilization is accomplished, and even before the oöcyte has reached its maximum size. We know that in *Chironomus* the "Keimwulst" (Ritter, 1890) or "Keimbahnplasma" (Hasper, 1911) is present when the egg is laid, at which time the pronuclei as a rule have not yet fused. This is true also of the "Dotterplatte" in *Calliphora* (Noack, 1901). There can be little doubt, however, that these substances are present as such in the eggs before fertilization, judging from our knowledge of the history of similar materials in the eggs of other insects. The "pole-disc" in the eggs of chrysomelid beetles (Hegner, 1908; Wieman, 1910a) and the "polares Plasma" in *Miastor* (Kahle, 1908; Hegner, 1912, 1914a) are recognizable some time before fertilization and cannot therefore arise because of any influence exerted by the spermatozoön. Moreover, in *Miastor* the eggs thus far examined have all been parthenogenetic. In parasitic Hymenoptera the Keimbahn-chromatin appears in both fertilized and parthenogenetic eggs at an early growth period. In only one animal not an insect has a similar occurrence been noted, namely, in *Polyphemus*, where, according to Kühn (1911, 1913), the keimbahn-determinants consist of the remains of one or more nurse cells (Fig. 50). In the DAPHNIDÆ (Weismann and Ischikawa, 1889) the "Paracopulationszelle" arises from material cast out by the germinal vesicle; in *Æquora* (Haecker, 1892) the "Metanucleolus" is likewise derived from the germinal vesicle; in *Ascaris* (Boveri, 1892) chromatin-diminution occurs during the two- to four-cell stage; in *Cyclops* (Haecker, 1897, 1903) and other copepods (Amma, 1911) the "Aussenkörnchen" or "Ectosomen" become visible soon after fertilization (*Diaptomus*), but usually not until the pronuclei fuse (other species); in *Sagitta* the "besondere Körper" (Elpatiewsky, 1909, 1910) or "Keimbahnchromidien" (Buchner, 1910) appear to arise *de novo* after fertilization, although if Buchner's contention that they are the remains of the accessory fertilization cells is correct, they should be classed with the "Nahrzellenkern" described by Kühn (1911, 1913) in *Polyphemus*.

It is thus evident that the keimbahn-determinants become visible, wherever they have been described, either just before or just after the eggs are fertilized, or, in parthenogenetic forms, shortly before maturation and cleavage are inaugurated.

The localization of the keimbahn-determinants at the time of their appearance seems to be predetermined. In insects the posterior end of the egg is invariably the place where these bodies occur. In species whose eggs undergo total cleavage they are, under normal conditions, segregated in one definite blastomere from the two-cell stage up to the thirty-two-cell stage, as a rule, and are then distributed among the descendants of the single primordial germ cell. In *Ascaris* it is normally the cell at the posterior (vegetative) pole that fails to undergo the diminution process. It seems therefore that there must be some mechanism in the egg which definitely localizes the keimbahn-determinants.

The segregation of these substances in one blastomere at the first cleavage division is a result of their previous localization, but in later cleavage stages events are more difficult to interpret. Both Haecker (1897) and Amma (1911) have attempted to explain the distribution of the "Ectosomen" in copepods by postulating a dissimilar influence of the centrosomes resulting in the segregation of these granules at one end of the mitotic spindle in the dividing stem cell. According to Zeigler's hypothesis the centrosomes during unequal cell divison are heterodynamic, and Schönfeld (1901) believes that the synizesis stage is due to the attraction of the chromosomes by the centrosomes. It is well known that in many cases where unequal cell division occurs one aster is larger than the other, and this may be the true interpretation of the phenomena, but to the writer it seems more probable that the entire cell contents undergo rearrangement after each cell division, possibly under the influence of the material elaborated within the nucleus and set free during mitosis. Elpatiewsky (1909) also believes in the unequal attractive force of the centrosomes in *Sagitta*.[1]

In *Ascaris*, certain copepods, *Sagitta*, *Polyphemus*, and certain DAPHNIDÆ the keimbahn-determinants are segregated in one cleavage cell until about the thirty-two-cell stage, but their substance is distributed at the next division between the daughter cells. The insects such as *Chironomus*, *Miastor*, and chrysomelid beetles, where, on account of the superficial cleavage the keimbahn-determinants are not segregated in blastomeres, the primordial germ cells from the beginning consist almost entirely of the keimbahn material or this material plus the matrix in which it is embedded. Hence in these cases the keimbahn-determinants are localized at a determined point during each cleavage stage instead of being carried about by the movements of the egg contents or of the blastomeres, but, as in the eggs that undergo total cleavage, the determinants are distributed between the daughter cells as

[1] "Nach der vierten Teilung kommt der besondere Körper in den Wirkungskreis eines Zentrosomos, nämlich desjenigen, welcher näher der Polarfurche liegt. Fast die ganze 'Energie' dieses Zentrosomas wird für die Ueberwindung der vis inertiae des besonderen Körpers verbraucht; dieser wird dem Zentrosoma genähert und umschliesst es wie mit einer Kappe, so dass er im optischen Durchschnitt stets Hufeisen oder Sichelform aufweist. Infolge davon wird die wirkung dieses Zentrosomas auf das Zellplasma nur sehr schwach, dieses Zentrosoma kann nur einen kleinen Plasmateil beherrschen, und die resultierende Zelle wird viel kleiner, als die Schwesterzelle. Diese kleine Zelle, die den besonderen Körper bekommen hat, liegt näher zum vegetativen Poles, als die grössere Schwesterzelle, und stellt die erste Urgeschlechtszelle G(d^{111}), die grössere Schwesterzelle die erste Urentodermzelle E(d^{112}) vor" (p. 231).

soon as the primordial germ cells are established. The reason for this appears to be that localizations occur in holoblastic eggs at each cleavage and that not until the thirty-two-cell stage or thereabouts does the keimbahn material become entirely separated from other organ-forming substances and segregated in a single cell. When this point is finally reached, this keimbahn material must necessarily become divided between the daughter cells.

In practically all known cases the daughter cells of the primordial germ cells are equal in size and each receives an equal portion of the keimbahn-determinants (Fig. 37, *B*). This is certainly to be expected from their constitution and future history. *Sagitta*, however, differs in this respect, for the remains of the "besondere Körper" appear to be unequally distributed between the two daughter cells of the primordial germ cells (Fig. 54) and both Elpatiewsky (1909, 1910) and Stevens (1910), therefore, consider this as probably a differential division whereby in this hermaphroditic animal the substance of the male primordial germ cell is separated from the female. More work is necessary to make certain of this point.

CONCLUSION. Keimbahn-determinants are definitely localized in the egg and in definite cleavage cells. This localization is first observable just before or just after the eggs are fertilized, or, in parthenogenetic forms, shortly before maturation and cleavage are inaugurated. Some mechanism in the egg must be responsible for this localization. Heterodynamic centrosomes may have some influence so far as the segregation of the keimbahn-determinants in cleavage cells is concerned, but the movement of the egg contents seems to be a more probable cause of localization.

C. The Fate of the Keimbahn-determinants

It is unfortunately impossible to trace the keimbahn-determinants throughout the entire germ-cell cycle. The question of their fate, however, is an important one. As we have seen, they become visibly apparent shortly before or just after the inauguration of the maturation divisions, and remain intact for a brief period during the early cleavage stages. They persist in insects as definitely recognizable granules (Fig. 37, *F*) for some time after the primordial germ cells are segregated; then they gradually break up into finer particles, leaving no trace of their existence behind except in so far as they give the cytoplasm of the germ cells a greater affinity for certain dyes. In *Chironomus* they may still form distinct masses after the definitive germ glands have been formed (Fig. 33, *D*). The ectosomes in the copepods are temporary bodies which appear to rise *de novo* during the formation of each mitotic figure in the early cleavage stages, then break down and disappear. Practically all of the other keimbahn-determinants persist during early cleavage and then disappear as distinct visible bodies as soon as the primordial germ cells are definitely segregated. What becomes of them during the comparatively long period between their disappearance in the primordial

KEIMBAHN-DETERMINANTS

germ cells and their reappearance in the oöcytes or mature eggs can only be conjectured. They seem to disintegrate into very fine particles which become thoroughly scattered within the cell body and mixed with the cytoplasm. It has been suggested (p. 68) that they may retain their physiological characteristics and become concentrated again in the growing oöcytes into morphologically similar bodies, increasing in the meantime, by multiplication or in some other way, until they equal in mass those of the preceding generation of germ cells. On the other hand, they may all, like the ectosomes of copepods, be temporary structures produced at a certain time and place under similar metabolic conditions, and, becoming associated with particular parts of the cell contents, thus be constant in their distribution.

Several ideas have been advanced regarding the fate of the eliminated chromatin in *Ascaris*. The ends of the chromosomes which are cast out into the cytoplasm are not equally distributed among the daughter cells nor does there appear to be any mechanism for their definite unequal division. These facts argue against the theory that these cast-out chromatin bodies serve as determinants and also make improbable the hypothesis that they enable the somatic cells to differentiate, whereas the germ cells which do not undergo the diminution process remain in an indifferent condition, since their cytoplasm lacks this material (Montgomery, 1911, p. 792). However, the fact that during the early cleavage divisions in some animals (see p. 218) large amounts of chromatin escape from the nucleus and are differentially distributed to the daughter cells is evidence that nuclear material may play some important rôle in the progressive changes of cleavage cells.

It has been shown that in many animals the germ cells do not multiply for a considerable period during the early developmental stages. This period coincides also with that during which the keimbahn-determinants, as a rule, disappear. For example, the germ cells of chrysomelid beetles multiply until there are about sixty-four present, at which time they constitute a group at the posterior end of the egg and the embryo has just started to form; no further increase in number occurs until the larval stage is reached and the definitive germ glands are established. As soon, however, as the embryo has reached a certain developmental stage, the germ cells migrate into it, and it looks very much as though they remain quiescent until the somatic cells are "able to protect, nourish, and transport" them.

The number of primordial germ cells during the "period of rest" is perhaps most definitely known in *Miastor*, where, as one group of eight and later as two groups of four each, they are present throughout a large part of embryonic development.

In vertebrates also a long period exists during which division of the primordial germ cells does not take place (Fig. 6) and at least in several species certain cell contents (the mitochondria) remain in an indifferent condition (Rubaschkin, 1910; Tschaschkin, 1910; Fig. 31, *B*). These facts all indicate that these cells remain in a primitive condition and do not undergo the histological differentiations characteristic of somatic cells, a view which, however, has been objected to (Eigenmann, 1896). The disappearance of the keimbahn-determinants and the yolk globules of vertebrates during this period have suggested that these substances are nutritive in function, furnishing energy to the migrating germ cells.

The fact of this long rest period, followed by rapid multiplication of the oögonia and spermatogonia during which no important specializations occur, and later succeeded by the remarkable changes that occur in both the oöcytes and spermatocytes, has led to the suggestion (Montgomery, 1911, pp. 790-792) that in the germ-cell cycle there is a series of changes parallel with that of the somatic cycle. In the development of both cycles preformation and epigenesis proceed at the same time. The chromosomes seem to be the preformed elements of the germ cells, since they are apparently the most stable constituents. The cytoplasm, on the other hand, undergoes a series of epigenetic changes such as the formation of an idiozome, the development of mitochondria, the appearance of a sphere, and the metamorphosis of the spermatozoön.

Finally we must inquire into the fate of the keimbahn-determinants in the male germ cells. Does the keimbahn material in these cells increase in amount as has been suggested for the oöcytes and is it localized in the spermatogonia, spermatocytes, or spermatozoa as a definite, visible substance? We know from the investigations of Meves (1911) that the plastosomes in the spermatozoön are carried into the egg, in the case of *Ascaris*, and there fuse with the plastosomes of the ovum. Whether keimbahn-determinants act in a similar manner is unknown. There are, however, certain cytoplasmic inclusions in the male germ cells that have been compared with similar structures in the oöcytes, for example, the chromatic body described by Buchner (1909) in the spermatogenesis of Gryllus (see p. 88), and the plasmosome which is cast out of the nucleus of the second spermatogonia in *Periplaneta* and disintegrates in the cytoplasm (Morse, 1909). That keimbahn-determinants from the spermatozoön are not necessary for the normal production of germ cells is of course evident, since some of the species with which we are best acquainted, for example, *Miastor*, are parthenogenetic.

CHAPTER IX

THE CHROMOSOMES AND MITOCHONDRIA OF GERM CELLS

No account of the germ-cell cycle in animals can be considered complete without at least a brief reference to the history of the chromosomes and mitochondria of germ cells. The chromosomes have for many years been recognized as the most important visible bodies in the cell, and their behavior during the germ-cell cycle has convinced most zoölogists that they may also be regarded as the bearers of hereditary factors. The mitochondria, on the other hand, are cellular constituents which have only comparatively recently come into prominence in cytological literature, and ideas concerning their nature and functions are still in a very chaotic condition.

The Chromosome Cycle in Animals

A few general statements regarding the behavior of the chromosomes during cell division, maturation, and fertilization are contained in Chapters I and II. We may recognize a rather definite chromosome cycle as a part of the germ-cell cycle, and it is to certain events in this chromosome cycle that our attention will be directed in the following paragraphs. It is best to begin our discussion, as in the general review of the germ-cell cycle (Chapter II), with the parthenogenetic or fertilized egg after the maturation processes have been completed, and to exclude all references to the accessory chromosome until later.

It may be pointed out first that the number of chromosomes in the cells of any individual of a species is, with few exceptions, constant. Thus the thread worm of the horse, *Ascaris megalocephala* var. *univalens*, has two; *A. megalocephala* var. *bivalens*, four; the nematod, *Coronilla*, eight; the mole cricket, *Gryllotalpa vulgaris*, twelve; the bug, *Pentatoma*, fourteen; the rat, sixteen; the sea urchin, *Echinus*, eighteen; the salamander, *Salamandra maculosa*, twenty-four; the slug, *Limax agrestis*, thirty-two; and the brine shrimp, *Artemia*, one hundred and sixty-eight. This number, however, is reduced one-half during the maturation of the eggs and spermatozoa so that the mature eggs and spermatozoa possess only half as many chromosomes as the other cells in the body; for example, the body cells, oögonia, and spermatogonia of the rat are provided each with sixteen chromosomes, but the mature eggs and spermatozoa contain only eight. Parthenogenetic eggs differ from those that require fertilization, since in these the complete or diploid number of chromosomes is retained. When cleavage is inaugurated in such eggs, a spindle is formed, the chromosomes are halved, and each daughter cell acquires one-half of each chromosome as in ordinary mitosis. In fertilized eggs, however, the nucleus brought in by the spermatozoön fuses more or less completely with the egg nucleus and the two together become incorporated in the first cleavage

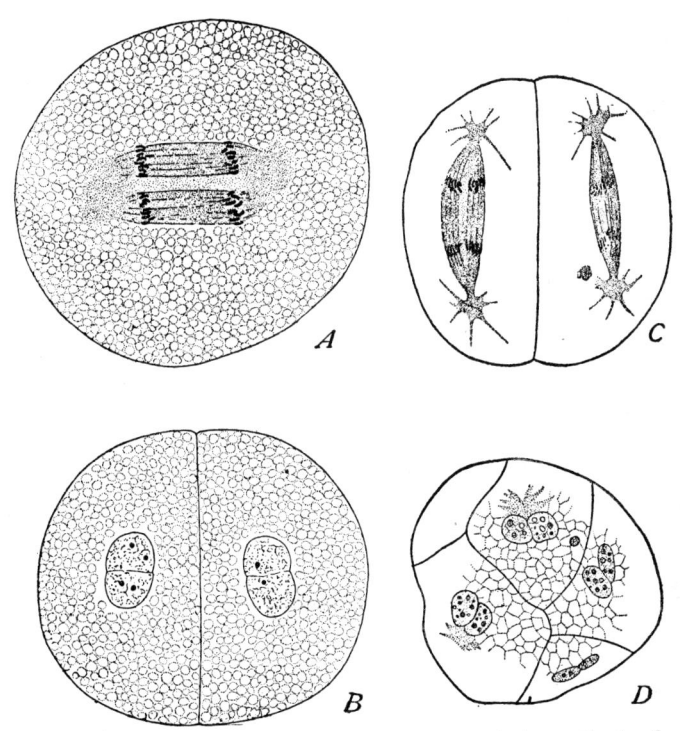

Fig. 61.—Independence of paternal and maternal chromatin in the segmenting eggs of *Cyclops*. *A*. First cleavage-figure in *C. strenuus*; complete independence of paternal and maternal chromosomes. *B*. Resulting two-cell stage with double nuclei. *C*. Second cleavage; chromosomes still in double groups. *D*. Blastomeres with double nuclei from the eight-cell stage of *C. brevicornis*. (*From Wilson, after Haecker.*)

spindle. Each of the two nuclei furnishes an equal (haploid) number of chromosomes to the first cleavage spindle, and thus the diploid (somatic) number is regained. These chromosomes may therefore be considered as forming two groups, one group of paternal origin derived from the sperm nucleus, and one group of maternal origin derived from the egg nucleus; in fact the groups supplied by the two nuclei may remain perfectly distinct (Fig. 61), not only during the first cleavage division, but also during subsequent mitoses.

The chromosomes of the fertilized egg and of the cells to which it gives rise are not always of the same size and shape, but in many cases are known to differ morphologically from one another. It is possible to recognize the different chromosomes during each mitosis, and the evidence is quite convincing that morphologically similar pairs are present in every cell and that one member of each pair is derived from the egg nucleus, the other from the sperm nucleus. Two principal views are held regarding the character of the chromosome divisions during the early cleavage divisions, (1) that the chromatin granules, which represent definite determiners, are divided equally between the daughter chromosomes, and (2) that an unequal distribution of the granules occurs, thus forming daughter cells containing qualitatively different chromosomes. There are no observations which show an unequal distribution.

One of the changes that takes place in the chromosomes at the time of mitosis is the diminution of their chromatin content brought about by the passage of part of their substance into the cytoplasm. This phenomenon has been used as an argument in favor of the theory of nuclear control of cellular activities. Two special cases of chromatin-diminution are known which differ from the usual process; these occur in *Ascaris* and *Miastor* as described and figured in Chapters III and VI. In these animals a large portion of the chromosomes of certain nuclei is cast out into the cytoplasm, whereas all of the chromatin is retained by others; the latter with a complete amount become the nuclei of the germ cells, the rest with a reduced amount are present in all of the somatic cells.

During the cellular divisions which result in the multiplication of the somatic cells and of the primordial germ cells the chromosomes appear at each mitosis in their normal number and are apparently divided equally between the daughter cells. There are, however, certain variations in both the somatic and germinal mitoses. In the somatic cells only one-half the normal number may appear; thus in the snail, *Helix pomatia*, the number may be twenty-four instead of the usual forty-eight. There is reason to believe that each of these twenty-four really consists of two single (univalent) chromosomes, and may therefore be considered bivalent. Even a further reduction in number by the association of univalent chromosomes has been recorded, in which case the combined chromosomes are said to be plurivalent. Other variations in the number of chromosomes, which occur during the maturation of the germ cells, will be referred to later.

Certain cellular phenomena which concern the chromosome cycle have been described in preceding chapters and so need only be mentioned here. First, the occurrence of amitosis in the multiplication of the germ cells has an intimate relation to the specificity of the chromosomes, since if nuclei divide *en masse* it seems improbable that the chromosomes become equally divided between the daughter nuclei (see Chapter V, p. 133); and second, the formation of nurse cells from oögonia may be accompanied, as in *Dytiscus* (Chapter V, p. 120), by a chromatin-diminution process which may be regarded as a differentiation of mother germ cells into somatic cells (nurse cells) and oögonia, a differentiation resembling the segregation of the primordial germ cells in the cleavage stages of the egg.

The most striking and perhaps the most important stages in the chromosome cycle occur during the growth and maturation periods of the germ cells. As briefly described and figured in Chapter II, the mitoses which occur during maturation are meiotic, since the mature germ cells have their chromosome number reduced one-half. The events in this process most worthy of our attention are those which take place during the stages known as synapsis and reduction. Wilson (1912) has summed up the questions that remain to be solved in the following words: "The cytological problem of synapsis and reduction involves four principal questions, as follows: (1) Is synapsis a fact? Do the chromatin-elements actually conjugate or otherwise become associated two by two? (2) Admitting the fact of synapsis, are the conjugating elements chromosomes, and are they individually identical with those of the last diploid or pre-meiotic division? (3) Do they conjugate side by side (parasynapsis, parasyndesis), end to end (telosynapsis, metasyndesis), or in both ways? (4) Does synapsis lead to partial or complete fusion of the conjugating elements to form 'zygosomes' or 'mixochromosomes,' or are they subsequently disjoined by a 'reduction-division'? Upon these questions depends our answer to a fifth and still more important question, namely, (5) Can the Mendelian segregation of unit-factors be explained by the phenomena of synapsis and reduction?"

The behavior of the chromosomes during synapsis in the germ cells of the male is indicated diagrammatically in Fig. 62, the terms used being those proposed by von Winiwarter (1901) in his work on the oögenesis of the rabbit. In the spermatogonia (Fig. 62, *1*) the chromatin is arranged in clumps on an achromatic reticulum; in the spermatocyte (Fig. 62, *2*) it breaks up into granules which become arranged in single rows or filaments (the leptotene threads). These leptotene threads later become paired (synaptene stage, Fig. 62, *3*) and converge toward the side of the nucleus near which the centrosome and centrosphere are situated (Fig. 62, *4*), a condition known as synizesis. The granules of the leptotene filaments approach and finally fuse so as to produce single thick threads (Fig. 62, *5–7*);

this is the pachytene stage. The filaments then begin to unravel (Fig. 62, *6–7*), become distributed

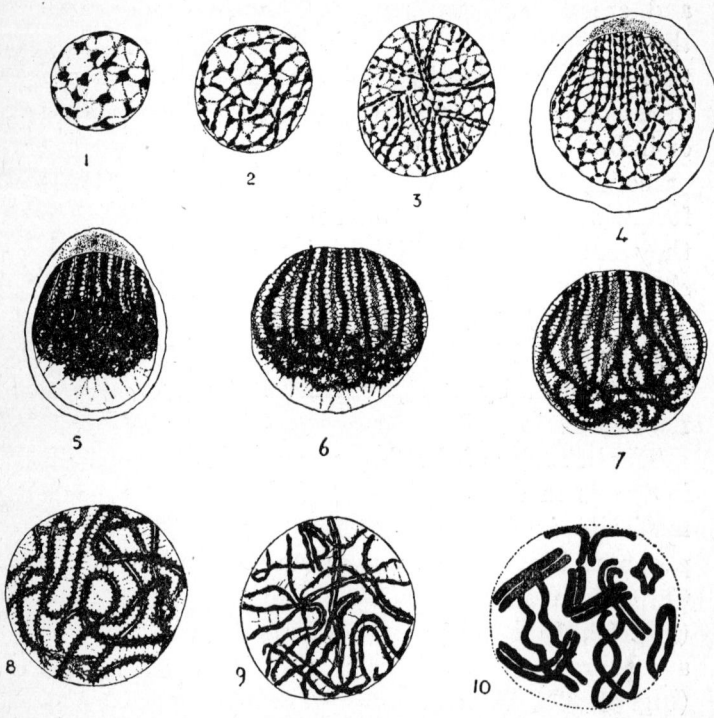

Fig. 62. — Prophases of the heterotype division in the male Axolotl. *1*, nucleus of spermogonium, or young spermocyte; *2*, early leptotene; *3*, transition to synaptene; *4*, synaptene with the double filaments converging towards the centrosome; *5*, contraction figure; *6*, *7*, pachytene; *8*, early; *9*, later diplotene; *10*, the heterotypic double chromosomes; the nuclear membrane is disappearing. (*From Jenkinson, 1913.*)

throughout the nucleus, and finally split into two threads (Fig. 62, *8–9*); this is the diplotene stage. The pairs of filaments finally shorten and thicken, assuming the form of paired chromosomes of various shapes and sizes (Fig. 62, *10*). A spindle then forms; these "heterotypic" chromosomes are drawn upon it; and each daughter cell receives one chromosome of each pair.

This mitosis is called heterotypic because it differs from ordinary indirect nuclear division in two important respects: (1) the chromosomes are present in pairs, and entire chromosomes are separated, and (2) the result is a reduction of chromosomes in the daughter nuclei to one-half the somatic number. According to certain investigators (*e.g.*, Meves, 1907) the union of the leptotene threads in the synaptene stage (Fig. 62, *4*) does not occur, but the two parallel threads are simply the halves of a single longitudinally split filament which fuse in the pachytene stage (Fig. 62, *6–7*), and separate again in the diplotene stage (Fig. 62, *8–9*). The large majority of cytologists, however, believe that the leptotene threads represent chromosomes which actually fuse in pairs in the pachytene stage and separate from each other during the heterotypic mitosis. Furthermore, the chromosomes of each pair are considered to be homologous, that is, the one derived from the spermatozoön is morphologically similar, to its mate, which is derived from the egg nucleus.

Investigators who believe synapsis to be a fact, that the conjugating elements are chromosomes, and these chromosomes are identical with those of the last diploid mitosis are not agreed as to the method of union and subsequent separation of the chromosomes. The chromosomes may unite side by side in parasynapsis or end to end in telosynapsis. Apparently parasynapsis is the rule, although telosynapsis probably occurs in certain species. The results are the same in either case.

The next question to be considered is whether the chromosomes which emerge from the pachytene stage are the same as those that enter it as leptotene filaments, or whether there is a complete fusion into zygosomes or mixochromosomes. It seems probable that at least a partial fusion occurs and that the composition of the chromosomes is changed more or less during synapsis. We know for certain that the peculiar X-chromosomes which have been found in many species of animals become paired in synapsis and later separate in a true reduction division, and we also have evidence which furnishes a mechanical means of effecting a change in the chromosomes during the synaptene stage. This evidence has led to the formulation of the chiasmatype theory (Janssens, 1909). According to this theory the chromosomes which pair in synapsis may twist around each other more or less (Fig. 63), and cross connections are visible. When the paired chromosomes later split apart they represent combinations different from those present before synapsis, because of these cross connections. The results of experimental breeding seem to necessitate some such relation as this during synapsis, and the chiasmatype theory has been used to explain certain results of hybridization that have not been accounted for in any other way (Morgan, 1913, 1914).

The view that the chromosomes are the bearers of factors in heredity is based upon several hypotheses, of which those of their specificity and genetic continuity will be mentioned here. According to the hypothesis of chromosome specificity each chromosome possesses certain functions of a specific kind

Fig. 63. — Twisting of chromosomes according to the chiasmatype theory. *A*. Two twisted chromosomes each divided longitudinally into two. *B*. Twisted chromosomes of *Batracoseps attenuatus*. (*From Janssens, 1909*.)

which determine the character of cellular differentiation and thus the structural and physiological condition of the embryo, larva, and adult. The hypothesis of the genetic continuity was evolved from that of the individuality of the chromosomes. According to the latter theory the chromosomes that appear in mitosis do not become scattered during the resting stage of the nucleus (interkinesis), but retain their identity throughout this period. Lack of evidence has resulted in the substitution of the hypothesis of genetic continuity, according to which there is a definite relation between the chromosomes of successive mitotic divisions.

Much of the cytological literature of the past decade deals with the history of the X- or sex-chromosomes. For many years the number of chromosomes in the cells of the individuals of a species was considered constant and even. Henking, however, in 1891, discovered in the bug, *Pyrrhocoris*, a single chromosome which did not divide in one of the spermatocyte divisions, but passed to one of the daughter cells and hence into only one-half of the spermatozoa. Paulmier (1899) observed similar conditions in the squash bug, and since then one or more odd chromosomes have been discovered in a large number of animals belonging to many different phyla. In 1902, McClung suggested that these peculiar chromosomes might be sex-determinants, and subsequent discoveries have fully demonstrated that they are intimately associated with the phenomena of sex. Most of our knowledge of this subject is due to the investigations of cytologists in this country, especially Montgomery (1898, 1906, 1911), McClung (1899, 1902, 1905), Stevens (1905, 1906, 1910), Wilson (1905, 1906, 1911, 1912), and Morgan (1909, 1911, 1913, 1914). A few of the principal types of sex-chromosome distribution are as follows:

Type I. One X-chromosome. This, the simplest type, has been recently demonstrated in a remarkable fashion by Mulsow (1913) in a nematoid worm, *Ancyracanthus*. Here the chromosomes can be seen not only in stained material but also in the living germ cells. The diploid number of chromosomes in male worms is eleven (Fig. 64, *A*), in female worms, twelve (*E*). Two sorts of spermatozoa are produced, one-half with five and the other half with six chromo-

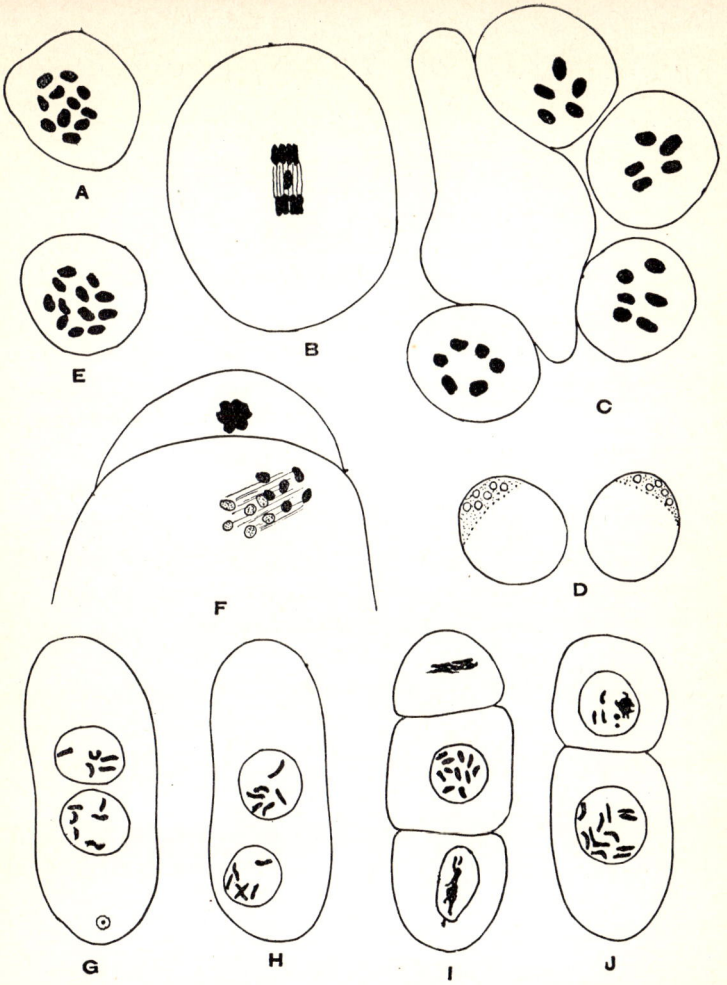

Fig. 64.—Behavior of chromosomes during maturation, fertilization, and cleavage of *Ancyracanthus cystidicola*. (*From Mulsow, 1913.*) *A.* Spermatogonium with eleven chromosomes. *B.* First maturation (spermatocyte) division. The single chromosome finally joins one group. *C.* The four spermatids arising from one spermatocyte; two with six chromosomes, and two with five. *D.* Two spermatozoa drawn while alive; one with six chromosomes, and one with five. *E.* Oögonium with twelve chromosomes. *F.* Second maturation (oöcyte) division. The black mass above is the first polar body; the set of six black chromosomes are those of the second polar body; the six dotted chromosomes are those of the egg. *G.* Fertilized (male producing) egg; sperm nucleus above with five chromosomes; egg nucleus below with six chromosomes. *H.* Fertilized (female producing) egg; both egg and sperm nuclei with six chromosomes. *I.* Cleavage stage of male producing egg; the central cell with nucleus containing eleven chromosomes. *J.* Cleavage stage of female producing egg; the lower cell with nucleus containing twelve chromosomes.

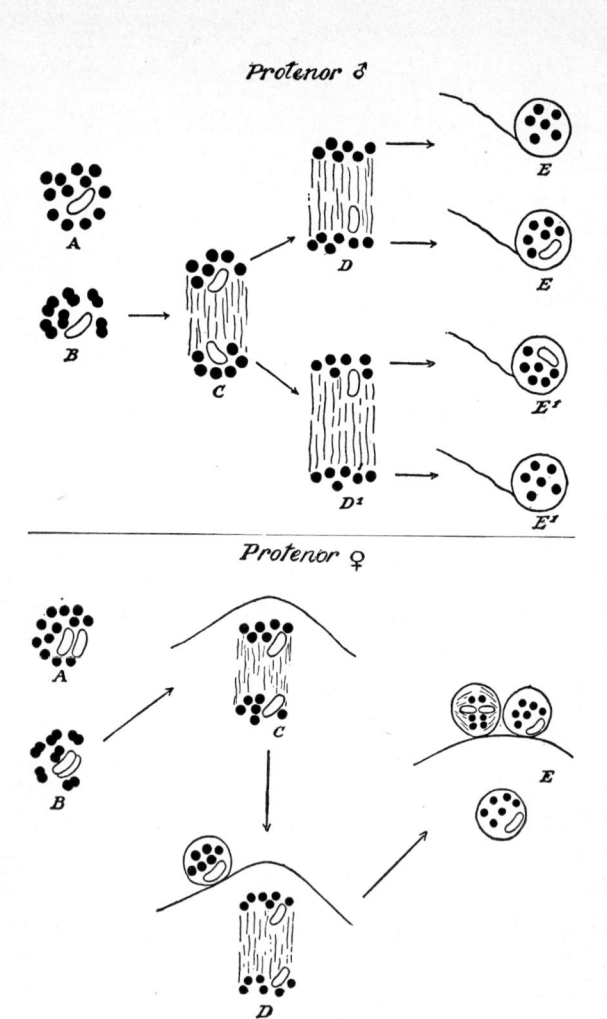

Fig. 65. — Maturation in *Protenor*. *Male above.* A. Spermatogonium. B. Synapsis. C. First maturation division. D, D'. Second maturation division. E, E'. Two sorts of spermatozoa.

Female below. A. Oögonium. B. Synapsis. C. First maturation division. D. Second maturation division. E. Egg nucleus and two polar bodies all alike in chromosome content. First polar body is dividing. (*From Morgan's Heredity and Sex, published by the Columbia University Press.*)

(258)

somes (Fig. 64, *D*). The nuclei of all the mature eggs exhibit six chromosomes. When fertilized the spermatozoön nucleus can be recognized, since it lies near the end away from the polar bodies. On the average one-half of the eggs are fertilized by spermatozoa containing five chromosomes and one-half by spermatozoa containing six. The results are as follows: A zygote resulting from the fusion of an egg with six chromosomes and a spermatozoön with six chromosomes possesses twelve chromosomes and develops into a female (Fig. 64, *H*); and a zygote formed by an egg with six chromosomes and a spermatozoön with five chromosomes contains eleven chromosomes, and hence gives rise to a male (Fig. 64, *G*). The events during the maturation processes in such a case are similar to those in the bug *Protenor*, as illustrated in Fig. 65.

Type II. One X-chromosome and one Y-chromosome. In the bug, *Lygæus bicrucis*, and a number of other species the number of chromosomes in both male and female is the same, but two sex-chromosomes of different sizes are present in the male. As shown in Fig. 66, the eggs are all alike, containing six ordinary and one X-chromosome. The spermatozoa are of two sorts: one-half with the larger, or X-chromosome, the other one-half with the smaller, called by Wilson the Y-chromosome. The zygotes, consequently, produce males if one X-chromosome and one Y-chromosome are present, and females if two X-chromosomes occur.

Type III. Two chromosomes of equal size

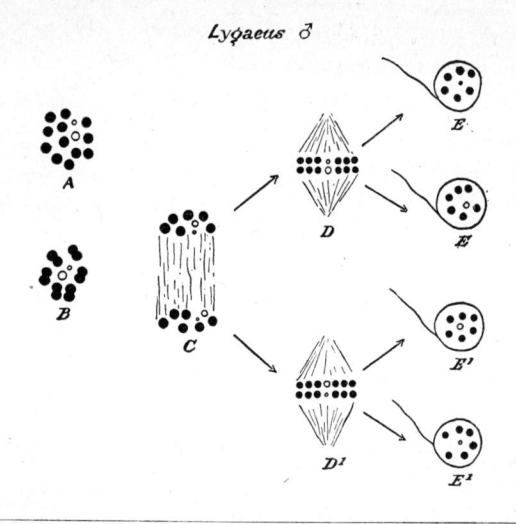

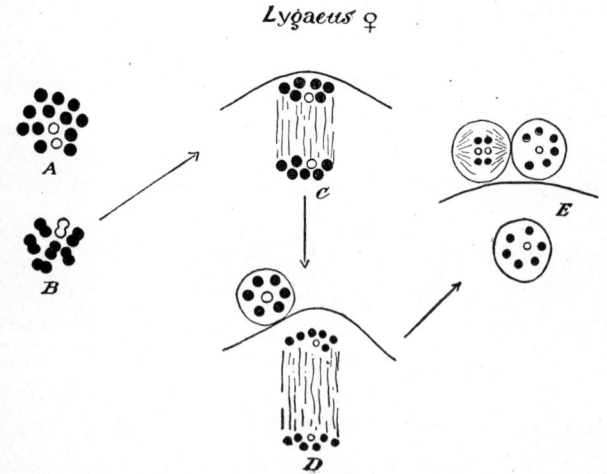

Fig. 66.—Maturation in *Lygæus*. Male above. Female below. Lettering as in Fig. 65. (*From Morgan's Heredity and Sex, published by the Columbia University Press.*)

(Fig. 67). In the bug, *Oncopeltus fasciatus*, the number of chromosomes (16) in both male and female is the same, but they are of equal size in both sexes. It is probable, however, that one of those of the male represents an X-chromosome and the other a Y-chromosome as in Type II, although they are not visibly different.

Type IV. One X-chromosome attached to an ordinary chromosome. There are a number of cases on record in which the X-chromosome is attached to an ordinary chromosome as in *Ascaris megalocephala*. Probably on this account the sex-chromosome was overlooked in these species for many years. The resulting zygotes, as Fig. 68 shows, are comparable to those of Type I (Fig. 65).

Type V. Spermatozoa alike, but eggs of two sorts. In a few animals it has been found that the eggs are dimorphic and the spermatozoa all alike, as represented in Fig. 69.[1]

Numerous variations have been discovered in the number and size of the X- and Y-chromosomes; some of these are illustrated in Fig. 70. When more than one X-chromosome is present they act as a unit, and two sorts of zygotes are produced as in other cases.

Chromosome cycles of more than ordinary interest have been described in the honeybee, in phyloxerans and aphids and in certain hermaphrodites. It has long been known that the female honeybees (queens and workers) develop from fertilized eggs

[1] The recent contributions of Tennent and Baltzer make the occurrence of this type seem very doubtful.

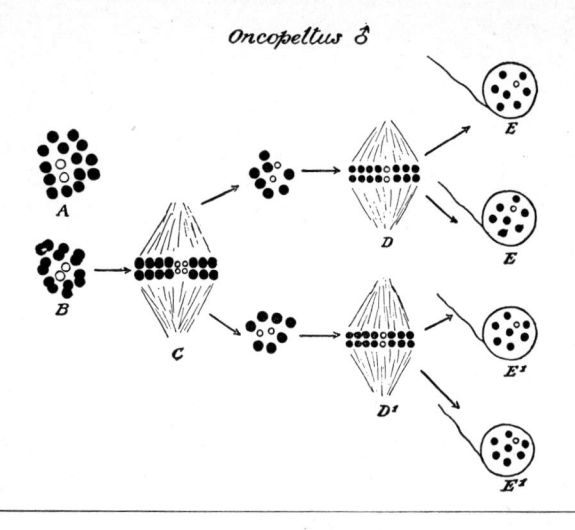

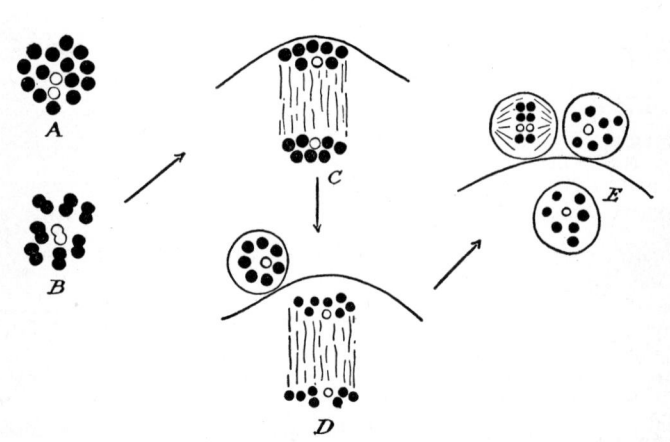

FIG. 67.— Maturation in *Oncopeltus*. Male above. Female below. Lettering as in Fig. 65. (*From Morgan's Heredity and Sex, published by the Columbia University Press.*)

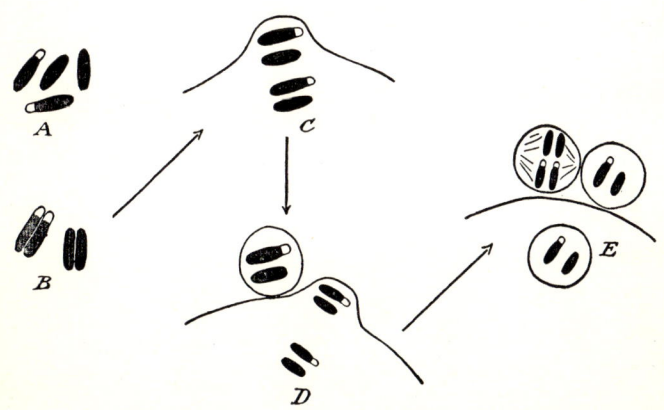

FIG. 68. — Maturation in *Ascaris*. Male above. Female below. Lettering as in Fig. 65. (*From Morgan's Heredity and Sex, published by the Columbia University Press.*)

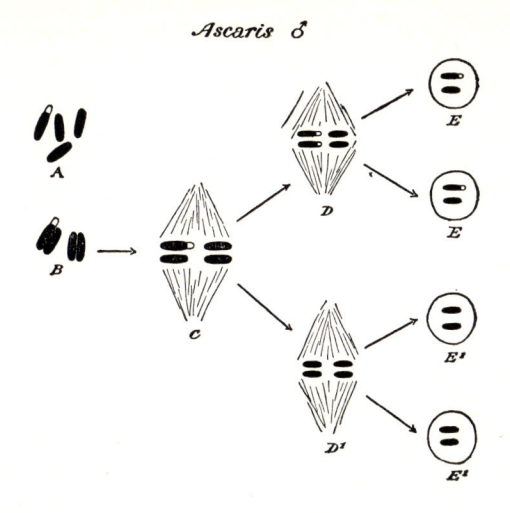

264   GERM–CELL CYCLE IN ANIMALS

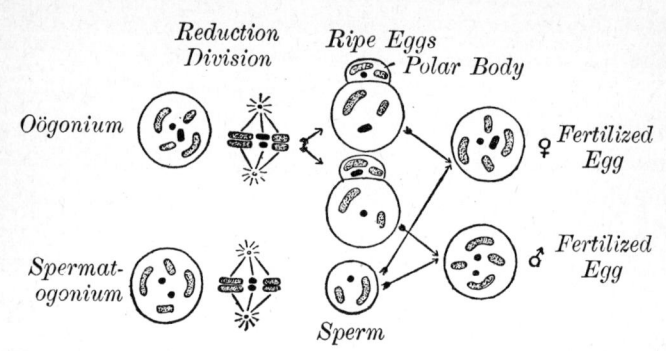

Fig. 69. — Diagrams showing the behavior of the chromosomes during maturation and fertilization in the starfish, *Echinus*. One kind of spermatozoön is formed, but the ripe eggs differ, one containing a large X-element, the other a small Y-element. (*From Schleip, 1913.*)

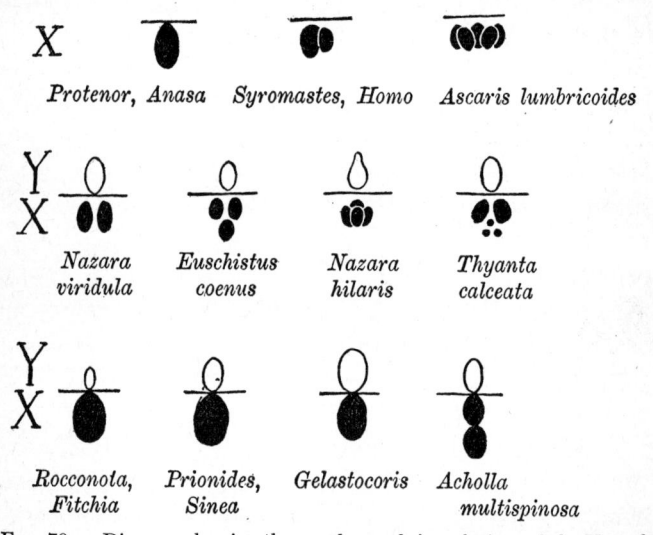

Fig. 70. — Diagram showing the number and size relations of the X- and Y-chromosomes in a number of animals. (*From Wilson, 1911.*)

and the drones parthenogenetically. The history of the chromosomes has here been worked out by Nachtsheim (1913). The primary oöcyte contains sixteen chromosomes in the form of eight tetrads; the mature egg and polar bodies are each provided with eight chromosomes (Fig. 71, E); the inner half of the divided first polar body fuses with the second polar body, forming a "Richtungskopulationskern" (Fig. 71, F) which does not give rise to the male germ cells as Petrunkewitsch (1901) claimed, but degenerates.

The cleavage nucleus in the parthenogenetic egg which produces the male shows sixteen chromosomes which divide to form thirty-two or sixty-four in the somatic cells, but do not increase in number in the spermatogonia. The first maturation division is unequal, and a "polar body" without any chromatin is pinched off (Fig. 71, $A-C$, Rk_1). The spermatids are likewise of two sorts; the smaller (Fig. 71, C, Rk_2) contain as many chromosomes as the larger (16), but degenerate, while the larger transform into spermatozoa. The fertilized (female) eggs possess the same number of chromosomes as the parthenogenetic eggs, plus an equal number which is brought in by the spermatozoön. The cleavage nucleus exhibits thirty-two chromosomes which may become sixty-four in the somatic cells, but unite two by two to form sixteen in the oögonia.

Phylloxera caryæcaulis will serve to illustrate the chromosome cycle in a species with a life cycle composed of parthenogenetic females which alternate with sexual males and females (Morgan, 1909,

266   GERM-CELL CYCLE IN ANIMALS

1910). The eggs laid by the stem-mother (see Chapter I, p. 24) in the spring possess four ordinary and

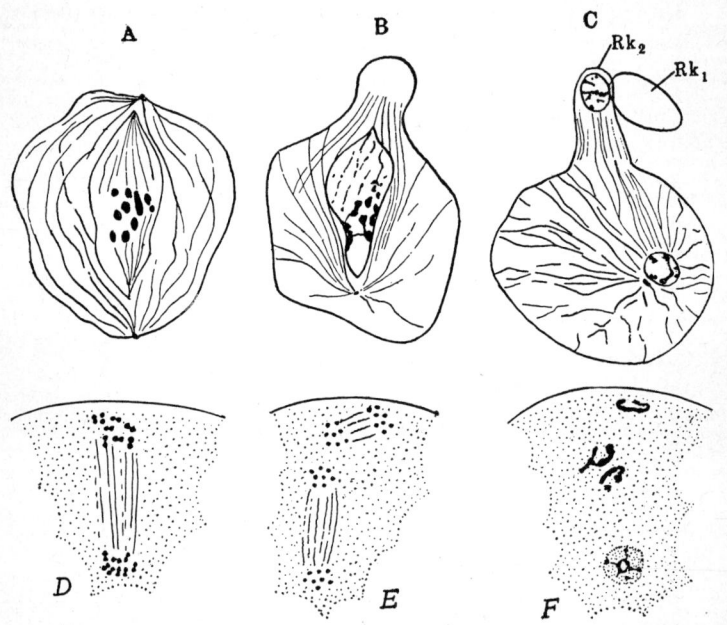

FIG. 71. — Stages in the spermatogenesis and oögenesis of the honeybee. *A, B.* First maturation division in the male. *C.* Second maturation division in the male. Three cells are produced: the first (RK_1) without chromatin; the second (RK_2) with chromatin, but small and functionless; and the third a functional spermatid. (*After Meves, 1907.*)

D. First maturation division in the female showing polar body with eight dyads, and secondary oöcyte with eight dyads. *E.* Second maturation division in the female showing the divided first polar body, the second polar body, and female pronucleus each with eight monads. *F.* Outer end of first polar body disintegrating; inner half of first polar body uniting with second polar body, and female pronucleus. (*After Nachsheim, 1913.*)

two sex chromosomes. These eggs give rise to parthenogenetic females with the same number of chromosomes, and generation after generation of such females appear during the summer; but in the autumn, females, whose eggs must be fertilized before they will develop, and males are produced. The chromosomes of these eggs are distributed during maturation as shown in the diagram (Fig. 72). The eggs that develop into the females possess the usual number of chromosomes, but those that give rise to males cast out in the polar body one chromosome that fails to divide, and hence are provided with one chromosome less than the others. During the maturation of the germ cells of these males two sorts of spermatozoa are formed, one with three chromosomes, the other with only two; the latter degenerate. Therefore, since only one sort of spermatozoa is functional, the fertilized winter eggs are all alike and all give rise to females (stem-mothers) the following spring.

The chromosome distribution in certain nematodes resembles somewhat that of the phylloxcrans. Here, however, we have to deal with organisms that are peculiar in several respects. Maupas (1900) has shown that in the genus *Rhabditis* the number of males per 1000 females ranges from 45.0 to 0.15 according to the species; and that these few males do not copulate with the females and hence are functionless. Furthermore, the females are not true females, but hermaphrodites. Kruger (1912) discovered that in *Rhabditis aberrans* the nuclei of the spermatozoa did not fuse with that of the egg, except in one instance, but disappeared in the cytoplasm;

268   GERM-CELL CYCLE IN ANIMALS

hence the spermatozoa simply initiate development. The chromosome cycle of *Rhabditis nigrovenosa* has been studied by Boveri (1911) and Schleip (1911).

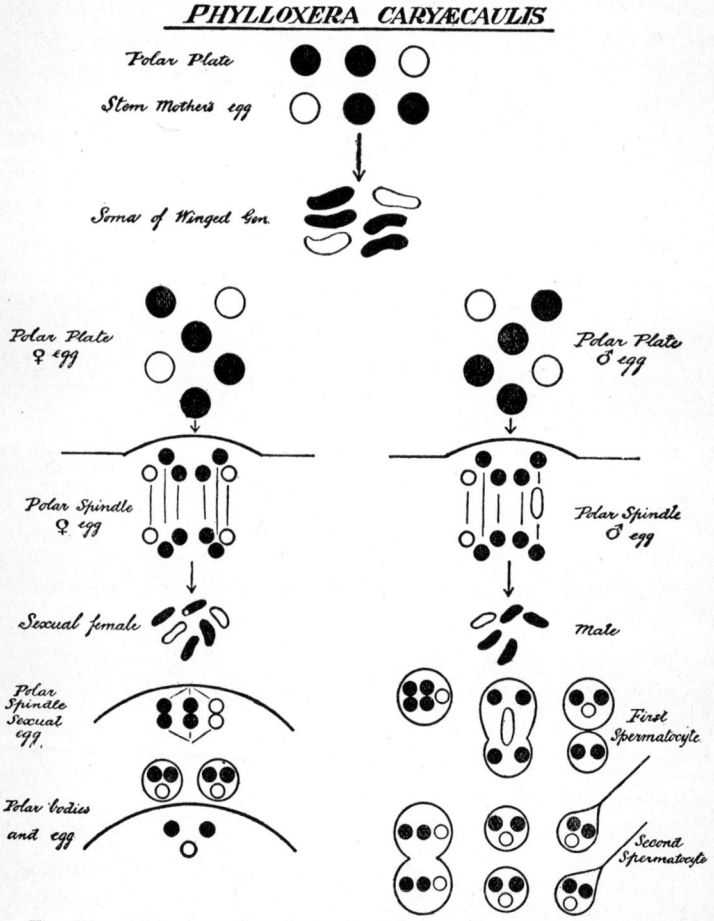

Fig. 72. — Chromosome cycle in *Phylloxera caryæcaulis*. (*From Morgan's Heredity and Sex, published by the Columbia University Press.*)

CHROMOSOMES AND MITOCHONDRIA

This nematode is a parasite in the lung of the frog for part of its life cycle; during this period it resembles the female, but is really hermaphroditic. These hermaphrodites give rise to free-living individuals which are true males and females; the eggs of the latter when fertilized develop into parasitic hermaphrodites. The oögonia and spermatogonia of the hermaphroditic parasites possess twelve chromosomes (Fig. 73, A). The nucleus of the mature egg is provided with six (B). Two sorts of spermatozoa are formed, one-half with six chromosomes, the other half with five; the latter result from the casting out of one chromosome (E) in a manner similar to that described above in *Phylloxera*. The eggs fertilized with the spermatozoa containing six chromosomes (F) produce free-living, true females, whereas those fertilized by the spermatozoa with five (G) develop into free-living, true males. The hermaphroditic condition is regained as follows: The free-living females give rise to eggs all with six chromosomes; the males, whose spermatogonia contain eleven chromosomes, produce spermatozoa with six or five chromosomes; those with the latter number, however, are not functional, hence all fertilized eggs must be provided with twelve chromosomes and develop into the hermaphroditic parasites.

The chromosome cycle in pteropod mollusks as worked out by Zarnik (1911) seems even more remarkable than that described for nematodes. The hermaphroditic species, *Creseis acicula*, possesses twenty chromosomes, sixteen large ordinary chromo-

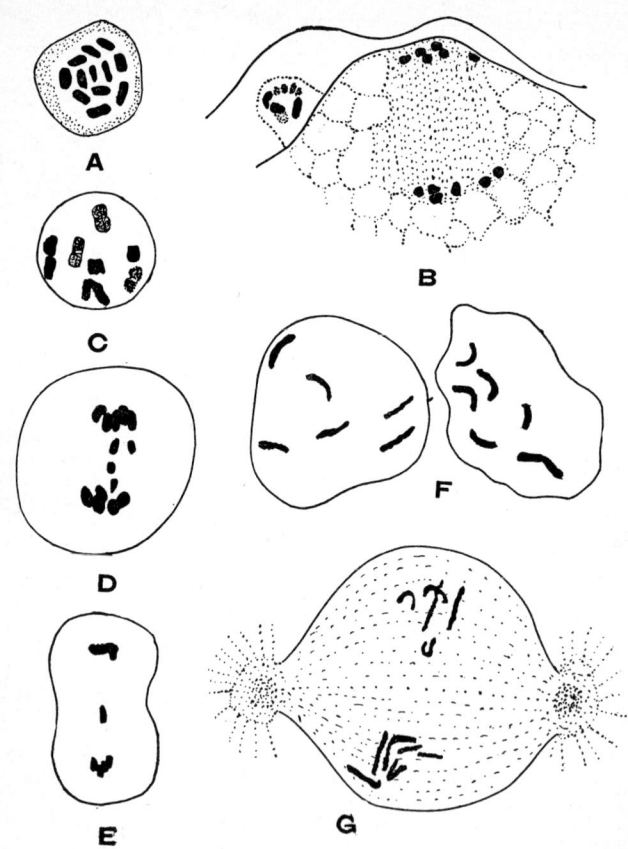

Fig. 73.—*Rhabditis nigrovenosa*. Stages in maturation, fertilization, and cleavage. *A.* Oögonium with twelve chromosomes. *B.* Second maturation division. Pronucleus and second polar body each with six chromosomes. *C.* Primary spermatocyte. *D.* Division of primary spermatocyte. *E.* Second spermatocyte division; one chromosome delayed. *F.* Two spermatozoa each with six chromosomes. *G.* Cleavage spindle of egg showing two groups of chromosomes; one with six contributed by the egg, the other with five contributed by the sperm. (*After Schleip, 1911.*)

somes (shown in black in Fig. 74), two large sex-chromosomes (dotted), and two small sex-chromo-

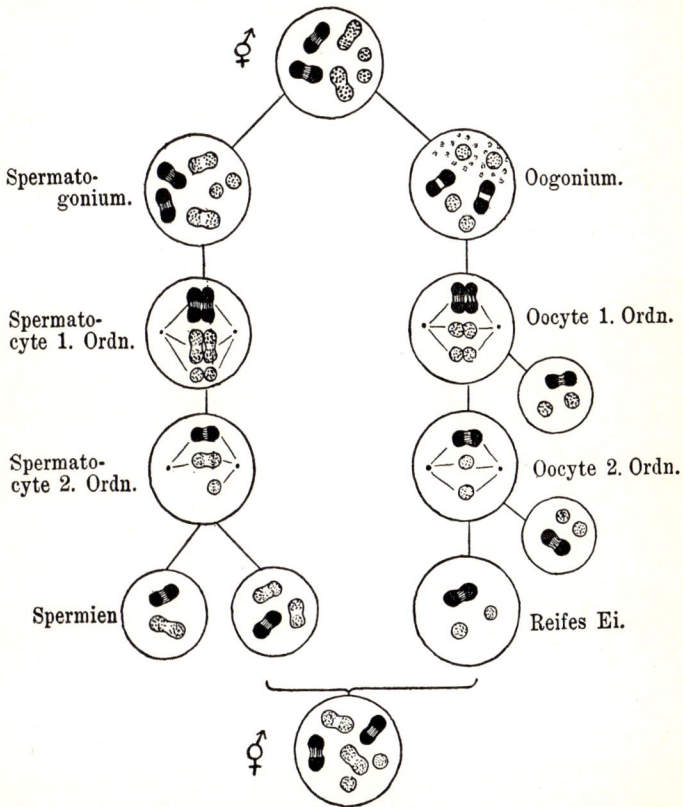

Fig. 74. — Diagrams showing the chromosome cycle in the pteropod mollusk, *Creseis acicula*. In order to simplify the diagrams each black chromosome is made to represent eight ordinary chromosomes. (*After Zarnik, 1911.*)

somes (dotted). The spermatogonia enter the maturation period in this condition. The number of chromosomes is reduced in the first division, resulting in two secondary spermatocytes each with eight large ordinary chromosomes, and one large and one small sex-chromosome. During the second division the small sex-chromosome does not divide, but passes intact into one spermatid; thus two sorts of spermatozoa are formed, one with eight large ordinary and one sex chromosome and the others with eight large ordinary chromosomes and two large sex-chromosomes. The spermatozoa with only one sex chromosome is not functional. The oögonia differ from the spermatogonia and somatic cells in the possession of sixteen large ordinary chromosomes and four small sex-chromosomes; two of the latter arise by the diminution of the chromatin in two of the large sex-chromosomes. The maturation divisions are of the usual sort, and all of the eggs are alike, containing eight large ordinary chromosomes and two small sex-chromosomes. Fertilization, as indicated in Fig. 74, always results in a zygote with sixteen large ordinary chromosomes, two large sex-chromosomes, and two small sex-chromosomes, which develop into a hermaphroditic individual.

Although we know very little about the chromosomes of man, the data available seem to indicate that here also there are chromatin bodies concerned with sex-determination. The following table indicates the state of our knowledge at the present time.

Guyer (1910) was the first to announce the discovery of accessory chromosomes in man. He found twenty-two chromosomes in the spermatogonia,

TABLE SHOWING THE NUMBER OF CHROMOSOMES IN MAN ACCORDING TO VARIOUS INVESTIGATORS

DIPLOID NUMBER	HAPLOID NUMBER	INVESTIGATOR	DATE
		Bardeleben	1892
24		Flemming	1897
	18 (15 or 19) [1]	Wilcox	1900
	12	Duesberg	1906
32		Farmer, Moore, and Walker	1906
	16	Moore and Arnold	1906
	12 or 10	Guyer	1910
	12 or 10	Montgomery	1912
24(?)		Gutherz	1912
47	23 or 24	Winiwarter	1912
34 (33, 38)		Wieman	1913

which became ten bivalent and two accessories in the primary spermatocytes. The latter pass undivided to one pole (Fig. 75, *A*), and hence two classes of spermatozoa result, one with ten ordinary chromosomes, and the other with ten ordinary and two accessory chromosomes. Winiwarter (1912), on the other hand (Fig. 75, *D–E*), reports forty-seven chromosomes in the spermatogonia and two classes of spermatozoa, one with twenty-three and the other with twenty-four. The number in the female, according to Winiwarter, is probably forty-eight, and hence all mature eggs are alike so far as chromosome number is concerned, each being provided with twenty-four. If these data are confirmed, it is evident that sex in man is determined at the time of fertilization and cannot be influenced by changing the environment.

[1] Wilcox doesn't state whether this is the reduced or diploid number.

274   GERM–CELL CYCLE IN ANIMALS

The above illustrations indicate that there is some internal mechanism which controls sex, and that certain chromosomes are, in at least many cases,

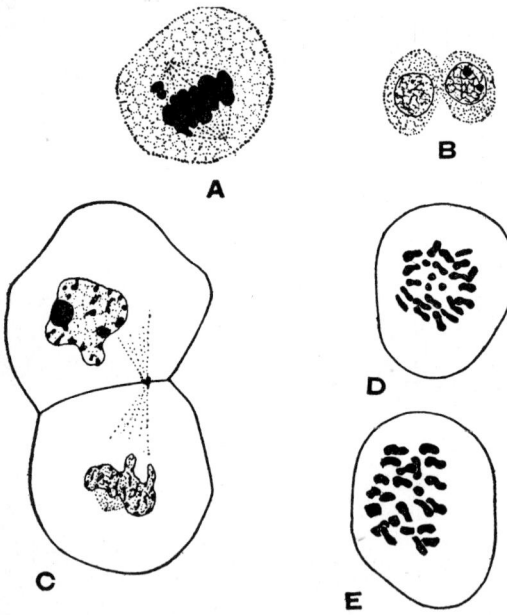

Fig. 75. — Chromosomes in man. *A.* First spermatocyte division showing two accessories passing early to one pole. *B.* Two contiguous spermatids, one without and the other with two accessories. *C.* Two secondary spermatocytes; the one above with an accessory. *D.* Second spermatocyte with twenty-four dyads. *E.* Second spermatocyte with twenty-three dyads. (*A–B, from Guyer, 1910; C–E, from Winiwarter, 1912.*)

factors in sex-determination. Several hypotheses have been suggested as to the relation of these chromosomes to sex, such as that sex is determined by the quantity of chromatin present in the zygote.

No view, however, has won general acceptance, but it seems probable that there are fundamental interrelations between the different parts of the cell which regulate the behavior of the chromosomes. We must, therefore, look further for an explanation of sex-determination. It has been suggested that differences in metabolism may be responsible for the fundamental differences between the sexes. According to this view changes in metabolism may control the behavior of the sex-chromosomes, or the presence of the sex-chromosomes in every cell in the body may influence the metabolism "in such a way that the organism is caused to become of one sex rather than of the other, in consequence of its type of metabolism" (Doncaster, 1914, p. 515).

The Mitochondria of Germ Cells

The study of the relative importance of the nucleus and the cytoplasm in heredity has been given a new impetus within recent years by the more accurate examination and description of certain cytoplasmic inclusions of both germ cells and somatic cells known as mitochondria, chondriosomes, plastosomes, chromidia, etc. Some of the best recent evidence that part of the germ-plasm may be located in the cytoplasm is afforded by the work of Benda, Meves, Regaud, Duesberg, and others on the history of these mitochondrial bodies during maturation, fertilization, early cleavage, and cellular differentiation. As long as forty years ago the cytoplasm of the germ cells was known to contain bodies other than the nucleus; these bodies have been given various names such as sphérules (Kunstler, 1882), cytomicrosomes (La Valette St. George, 1886), bioblasts (Altmann, 1890), and ergastoplasm (Bouin, 1898). In 1897 and 1898 Benda noticed the constant presence of certain granules in the male germ cells of a number of vertebrates and was able to trace their history from the spermatogonia until they formed the spiral filament in the tail of the spermatozoa. These observations were extended the following year (1899) so as to include all stages in the development of the eggs and spermatozoa of many vertebrates and invertebrates and also various tissue cells such as striated muscle-fibers, leucocytes, marrow-cells, etc. This work attracted wide attention chiefly for two reasons: (1) the history of the granules was carefully worked out and the various stages accurately described, and (2) special, rather complicated, staining methods were devised which were supposed to color the mitochondria so that they could be distinguished from all other cell inclusions.

From 1899 until the present time an ever increasing number of investigators have attacked the problems presented by the mitochondria, or referred to these structures incidentally when working upon other histological or cytological problems. The study of mitochondria received its greatest impetus, however, in 1908, when Meves published a paper on these structures in the chick embryo entitled "Die Chondriosomen als Träger erblicher Anlagen." In this paper the chick embryo is described from the fifteen-hour stage up to the three-days-nine-hour stage. The cells of the earliest stage studied contained mitochondria (Fig. 76) which were differently arranged in the germinal layers: the ectoderm and entoderm cells contained, for the most part, rods and threads, the granules being scarce, and the mesoderm cells were characterized by numerous granules and few rods and threads. At the three-day stage the mitochondria of the neuroblasts became difficult to stain by the usual method, but did stain like neurofibrils. These and other observations led Meves to the conclusion that the mitochondria are of considerable importance in cellular differentiation and are in fact the bearers of hereditary Anlagen.

Since this paper of Meves appeared, the zoölogical periodicals have been flooded with the results of investigations of the mitochondria in almost every sort of germ and somatic cell, both normal and abnormal, and in PROTOZOA and METAZOA, INVERTEBRATES and VERTEBRATES. No report on spermatogenesis, oögenesis, or early embryonic development is complete without reference to the mitochondria. In plants, also, cellular bodies have been described of a mitochondrial nature (Meves, 1904; Duesberg and Hoven, 1910; Guilliermond, 1911).

A large number of new terms have been coined for the purpose of describing these cytoplasmic inclusions. Some of them are as follows: (1) mitochondria, applied by Benda (1897, 1898) to certain granules with definite staining reactions; (2) chondriosomes, proposed by Meves (1908) for both single

278   GERM-CELL CYCLE IN ANIMALS

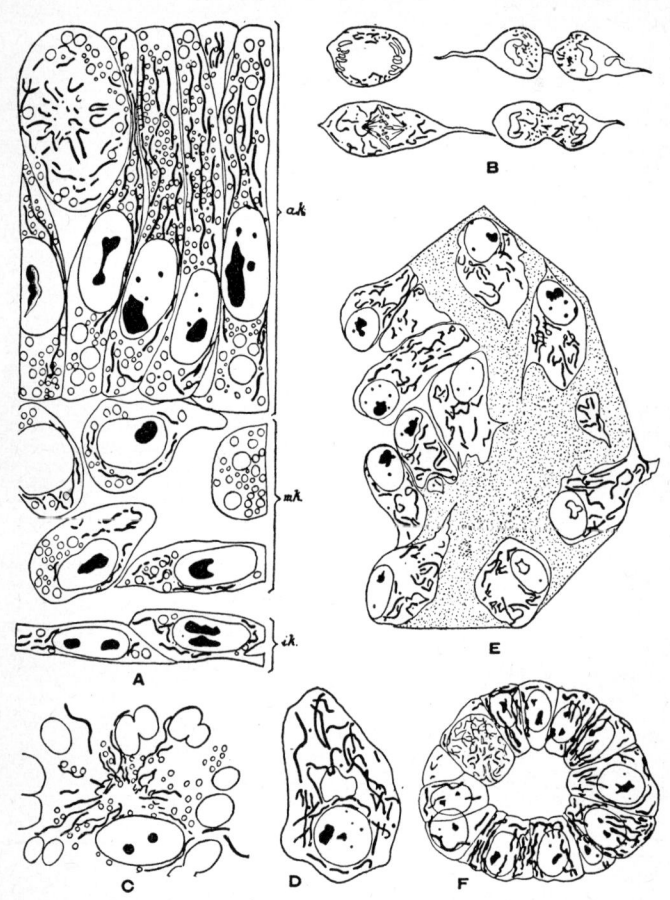

Fig. 76.— Mitochondria in the embryonic cells of the chick. *A.* In cells of the primitive streak. *B.* In dividing connective tissue cells. *C.* In connective tissue cells. *D.* In a cartilage cell. *E.* In osteoblasts and bone cells. *F.* In cells of Wolffian body. (*From Duesberg, 1913; A, B, C, E, after Meves; D, F, after Duesberg.*)

granules and chains of granules; the latter were also called chondriokonts; (3) plastosomes (plastochondria, plastokonta), employed by Meves (1910) because of their supposed rôle in histogenesis; (4) éclectosomes, selected by Regaud (1909) as a general physiological expression for chondriosomes; (5) chondriotaxis, used by Giglios-Tos and Granata (1908) to describe the parallel arrangement of chondriokonts; (6) chondriodiérèse, proposed by the same authors for the division of the chondriokonts during cell division; (7) karyochondria, coined by Wildman (1913) for cytoplasmic inclusions derived from the basichromatin of the nucleus; (8) chromidia, a term considered by Goldschmidt (1904) and others to include the mitochondria.

We are here especially interested in the mitochondria of the germ cells, their origin, fate, and significance, but our ideas regarding the importance of these bodies in heredity depend somewhat upon their behavior in somatic cells. As already stated, Benda (1903) observed mitochondria in both germ cells and somatic cells. Since then they have been recorded in PROTOZOA, in almost every sort of somatic cell in METAZOA, and in many plant cells (Fig. 77). Excellent reviews have been published by Benda (1903), Fauré-Frémiet (1910), Prenant (1910), and Duesberg (1912). These reviews have led to the conclusion already expressed by Regaud (1909, p. 920) that "it is probable that they (mitochondria) exist in all cells, at least at certain stages in their activities." Among the somatic differentiations to which mitochondria are supposed to give rise are neurofibrils and myofibrils. Meves (1907, 1908) considered it probable that neurofibrids were transformed chondriosomes, and Hoven (1910) seemed to have proved it, but Marcora (1911) and Cowdry (1914) find that the neurofibrils arise independently,

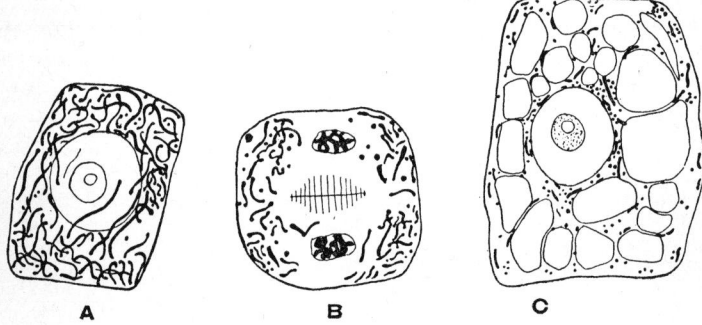

FIG. 77.— Mitochondria in the cells of a plant, *Pisum sativum*. *A*. Young germ cell. *B*. Young germ cell dividing. *C*. Old cell containing vacuoles. (*From Duesberg and Hoven, 1910.*)

although mitochondria are present in the nerve cells. Duesberg (1910) is quite positive that the myofibrils of striated muscle fibers are produced by the metamorphosis of chondriosomes from embryonic muscle cells, and has recently (Duesberg, 1913) strengthened his position by the discovery that the myoplasm described by Conklin (1905) in the egg of the Ascidian, *Cynthia*, is well supplied with chondriosomes.

Mitochondrial structures have been studied in both living and preserved cells. Fauré-Frémiet (1910) describes them in living cells (Fig. 78, *D*) as small, transparent, slightly refringent granules of a pale gray tint, either homogeneous or else vesicular with fluid contents and a thin, denser, refringent periphery. Rod-like mitochondria were likewise observed by Montgomery (1911) in the living male germ cells of *Euschistus* (Fig. 78, *A–B*) which had been teased out in Ringer's solution; and this in-

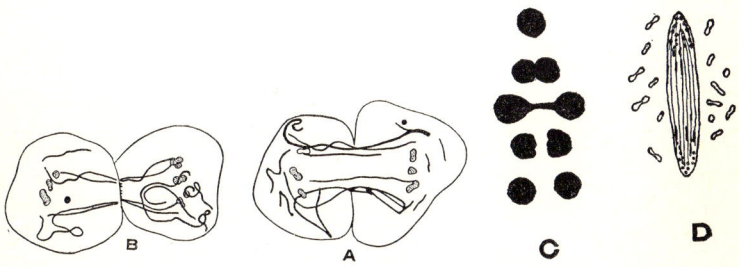

Fig. 78. — Division of mitochondria. *A–B*. Mitochondrial rods dividing during first maturation division in *Euschistus*. *C*. Stages in division of mitochondrial body in *Hydrometra*. *D*. Simultaneous division of micronucleus and mitochondria in *Carchesium* (*in vivo*). (*A–B, from Montgomery, 1911; C, from Wilke, 1913; D, from Fauré-Frémiet, 1910*.)

vestigator concluded that in preserved material "we have been working with images that are very close to the living. . . ." More recently Lewis and Lewis (1914) have made careful studies of mitochondria in living cells from chick embryos. Granules were here seen "to fuse together into rods or chains, and these to elongate into threads, which in turn anastomose with each other and may unite into a complicated network, which in turn may again break down into threads, rods, loops, and rings." Even more remarkable are the movements within the cell described by the same investigators. "The mitochondria are almost never at rest, but are continually changing their position and also their shape. The changes in shape are truly remarkable, not only in the great variety of forms, but also in the rapidity with which they change from one form to another. A single mitochondrium may bend back and forth with a somewhat undulatory movement, or thicken at one end and thin out at the other with an appearance almost like that of pulsation, repeating this process many times. Again, a single mitochondrium sometimes twists and turns rapidly as though attached at one end, like the lashing of a flagellum, then suddenly moves off to another position in the cytoplasm as though some tension had been released." Mitochondria may also be stained *intra vitam*, especially with dahlia violet and Janus green. Most of the fixing solutions ordinarily used for cytological purposes destroy the mitochondria. The methods which seem to give the best results have osmic acid or formalin as a basis, such as those devised by Altmann (see Lee, 1905, p. 43), Benda (Lee, 1905, p. 223), Meves (1908), and Regaud (1908, p. 661). Benda (1903) claimed that all cellular structures which stained violet by his method were of a mitochondrial nature; but this has not been found to hold true. Undoubtedly the many bodies which have been discovered in cells are of several sorts, and only by a thorough study of their staining qualities, morphological aspects, and biological rôles can they be identified. Benda's crystal violet stain seems to be more selective than any other for mitochondria and is of great value for this reason.

Mitochondria most often appear as spherical or elongated granules about 0.001 mm. diameter. These granules may become arranged in a series, thus forming a chain, and the granules in a chain may fuse into a homogeneous rod. Different forms are present in different kinds of cells or even in the same cell at various stages in its evolution or functional activity. Some investigators (Prenant, 1910) maintain that the homogeneous rod is the primitive condition and that the granules are formed by the disintegration of such rods; to others just the reverse seems to be true (Rubaschkin, 1910; Duesberg, 1912).

The chemical constitution of the mitochondria has been studied by a number of investigators. Regaud (1908) has shown that the mitochondria of the seminal epithelium are not histochemically identical. He distinguishes three sorts of granules: (1) those which resist the action of acetic acid and are stainable without being previously immersed in a solution of potassium bichromate, (2) granules which resist acetic acid but require intense chromisation, and (3) granules which do not resist acetic acid and demand chromisation. Fauré-Frémiet, Mayer, and Schäffer (1909) have studied the mitochondria by microchemical and comparative methods and reached the conclusion that they are lecithalbumins.

Mitochondria have been noted in all stages of

284   GERM-CELL CYCLE IN ANIMALS

the male germ-cell cycle, especially in mammals, mollusks, and insects, and appear to be continuous from one generation of cells to the next. During

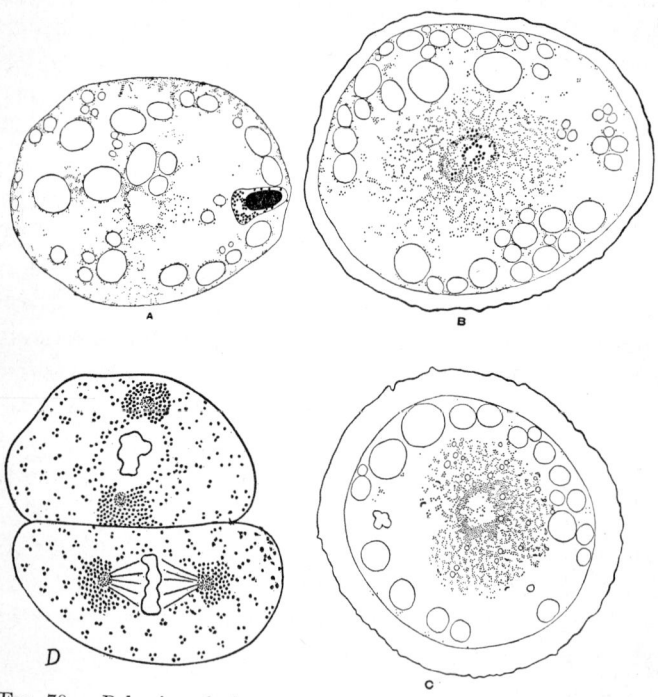

FIG. 79.—Behavior of the mitochondria during the fertilization and early cleavage of the egg of *Ascaris*. *A*. Egg into which a spermatozoön has penetrated. *B, C*. The mixing of the mitochondria of the egg and spermatozoön. *D*. Division stage of the first two blastomeres. (*After Meves, 1911 and 1914.*)

mitosis the plastosomes lie outside of the spindle (Fig. 79, *D*); they may divide autonomously as claimed by Fauré-Frémiet (1910) in PROTOZOA (Fig.

78, *D*) and Wilke (1912) in the spermatocytes of *Hydrometra* or *en masse*, as in the spermatogenesis of *Euschistus* (Fig. 78, *A–B*), thus undergoing a sort of paramitosis (Montgomery, 1911) and *Notonecta* (Browne, 1913). In the former cases each daughter cell is supposed to receive one-half of each granule; in the latter the distribution is largely by chance, but apparently equal (Cowdry, 1914). According to certain observers the centrosomes exert an influence upon the mitochondria as indicated by the aggregation of these bodies around the asters (Fauré-Frémiet, 1910; Meves, 1914); but others have been unable to find any confirmatory evidence in their material (Montgomery, 1911). Duesberg (1908) has pointed out that since there is no rest period between the two maturation divisions there must be a quantitative reduction of plastosomes in the spermatids; a quartering of the mitochondria could not, however, be observed by Montgomery (1912) in *Peripatus*. Montgomery (1911) has suggested that the relative amount of the mitochondrial substance received "might determine the sex-preponderance character of the sperm, a matter unfortunately very difficult to test."

Fauré-Frémiet recognizes four types of mitochondrial distribution in the germ cells: (1) filaments or masses that do not undergo profound morphological changes (Fig. 80); (2) one or more masses which transform into a definite morphological element, the Nebenkern; (3) masses which only partially change into a Nebenkern or yolk nucleus; (4) bodies which transform entirely or in part into deutoplasmic granules of a fatty nature.

The origin of the mitochondria in male cells cannot be stated definitely, since certain investigators (Goldschmidt, Buchner, Wassilieff, etc.) claim that they arise from the nucleus; others (*e.g.*, Meves, Wilke, Duesberg) consider them to be integral parts of the cytoplasm; and a third group (Montgomery, Browne, Wildman) looks upon some of them as the results of chemical interaction between the nucleus and the cytoplasm.

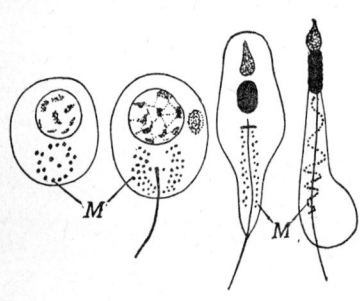

Fig. 80. — Four stages in the formation of the spermatozoön of *Enteroxenos* showing the distribution of the mitochondria (*M*). (*After Bonnevie.*)

Less is known concerning the mitochondria during oögenesis than during spermatogenesis, but certain bodies have been described in the ova of a number of animals which exhibit all of the characteristics of the mitochondria of male cells. As in the latter, they have been considered chromidial by some and of cytoplasmic origin by others.

The importance of the mitochondria depends largely upon their functions. Those of the egg have been observed by Russo (1907), Loyez (1909), Fauré-Frémiet (1910), Van Durme (1914), Hegner (1914a), and others to transform directly into yolk globules. According to Van der Stricht (1904), Lams (1907), etc., they produce yolk elements indirectly; and it is the opinion of Meves, Duesberg, and their followers that they play an important rôle in fertilization. Likewise in the spermatozoa ideas differ regarding their functions. Benda (1899) believed them to be motor organs; Koltzoff (1906), from a study of the spermatozoa of Decapods, maintains that they represent elements which form a sort of cellular skeleton; Regaud (1909) claims that they are the particular cellular organs which exercise a "fonction éclectique," extracting and fixing substances in the cell, and should therefore be called "éclectosomes"; and Meves (1907, 1908) holds that they are cytoplasmic constituents corresponding to the chromosomes of the nucleus. Meves (1907, 1908) came to the conclusion that there must be hereditary substances in the cytoplasm, and by the method of elimination decided in favor of the mitochondria. In his studies on fertilization and cleavage in *Ascaris* (Meves, 1911, 1914) he has shown that granules from the spermatozoön (Fig. 79) fuse with similar granules in the egg, as described previously by L. and R. Zoja (1891), and that these granules are plastosomes. The distribution of the fused granules is followed until the amphiaster is formed in the two-cell stage; here the plastosomes are mainly grouped about the centrosomes, although a few are scattered about in the cytoplasm (Fig. 79, *D*).

Although there are many who believe Meves and his followers to be correct in their contention that the plastosomes are the bearers of hereditary characteristics in the cytoplasm, just as the chromosomes are the bearers of hereditary characteristics in the nucleus, still there are many objections to this view, such as the fact that part or all of the plastosomes may be cast out of the spermatid (*e.g.*, in the opossum, Jordan, 1911; and in *Peripatus*, Montgomery, 1912). It is obvious from the foregoing account that there are a number of opposing views regarding the origin, nature, and rôle of the various cytoplasmic inclusions which have been considered mitochondria. Are they constant, necessary constituents of the living protoplasm, or are they inactive lifeless bodies which may be included under the term metaplasm? If they constitute a part of the living protoplasm, do they form the skeleton of the cell, do they take part in the metabolic activities of the cytoplasm or nucleus, or do they play a rôle in the process of differentiation, and should they be considered as the hereditary substance of the cytoplasm? If they are simply metabolic products, are they excretory in nature, or reserve materials set aside for the later use of the cell? And finally, do they arise from the nucleus, are they strictly cytoplasmic, or do they originate through the interaction of nucleus and cytoplasm? It is impossible in a short space to give an adequate account of the arguments pro and con, and so we must refer the reader to the comprehensive reviews mentioned above. The conclusion, however, is perfectly safe that we shall have to await the results of further investigations before we can come to a definite decision. In the meantime we should thank the mitochondria for focusing the attention of cytologists upon the cytoplasmic elements, since the belief is becoming more and more general that hereditary phenomena are the result of interactions between nucleus and cytoplasm and that the latter may play a more important rôle than is usually supposed.

CHAPTER X

THE GERM-PLASM THEORY

In discussing the germ-plasm theory it is necessary to distinguish between this hypothesis and that of the morphological continuity of the germ cells. The facts and theories involved have grown up together. Owen (1849) was perhaps the first to point out the differences between germ cells and body cells. "Not all of the progeny of the primary impregnated germ cell," he writes, "are required for the formation of the body in all animals; certain of the derivative germ cells may remain unchanged and become included in that body which has been composed of their metamorphosed and diversely combined and confluent brethren; so included, any derivative germ cell or the nucleus of such may commence and repeat the same processes of growth by imbibition, and of propagation by spontaneous fission, as those to which itself owed its origin. . . ." Galton (1872) was among the earliest to recognize the necessity for two sorts of materials in the individual metazoön, "one of which is latent and only known to us by its effects on his posterity, while the other is potent, and constitutes the person manifest to our senses." He at that time believed in the inheritance of acquired characters and conceived the egg as a struc-

THE GERM-PLASM THEORY

tureless body from which both the body and the ova of the individual evolve; and considered these ova to consist of contributions partly from the egg and partly from the body which developed from the egg. Later Jäger (1877) stated the idea of germinal continuity more definitely. He maintained that part of the germ-plasm (Keim Protoplasma) of the animal forms the individual, and the rest is reserved until sexual maturity, when it forms the reproductive material. The reservation of this phylogenetic substance he termed the "continuity of the germ-plasm" ("Continuität des Keimprotoplasmas"). To Weismann (1885) is usually given the credit for originating the germ-plasm theory, but while we are undoubtedly indebted to him for the great influence the hypothesis of germinal continuity has had upon the trend of biological investigations within the past thirty years, we must consider Jäger as the first to clearly enunciate the idea.

Jäger (1878) also expressed a belief in the morphological continuity of the germ cells of succeeding generations, but this idea was first definitely stated by Nussbaum (1880), whose investigations of the germ cells in the trout and frog led him to conclude that the cleavage cells form two groups independent of each other. One group contains the cells which multiply and differentiate and thus build up the body of the individual, but do not produce germ cells; the other group takes no part in the formation of the body and undergoes no differentiations, but multiplies by simple division. The germ cells are thus not derived from the individual in which they lie, but have a common origin with it. The segregated germ cells or species substance is therefore distinct and independent of the individual; this accounts for the constancy of the species. We may distinguish between the two ideas by defining them as follows:

(1) Germinal continuity, or the germ-plasm theory. "In each ontogeny a part of the specific germ-plasm contained in the parent egg-cell is not used up in the construction of the body of the offspring, but is reserved unchanged for the formation of the germ cells of the following generation" (Weismann, 1891, p. 170).

(2) Morphological continuity of the germ cells. The developing egg produces by division two sorts of cells, germ cells which contain the germ-plasm and somatic cells which protect, nourish, and transport the germ cells until they leave the body to give rise to the succeeding generation.

No case of a complete morphological continuity of germ cells has ever been described. Such an occurrence would necessitate the division of the egg into two cells, one of which would give rise to all of the body cells and nothing else, the other only to germ cells. The behavior of the germ-plasm in such a case would be as follows (Weismann, 1904, p. 410): "The germ-plasm of the ovum first doubles itself by growth, as the nuclear substance does at every nuclear division, and then divides into two similar halves, one of which, lying in the primordial somatic cell, becomes at once active and breaks up into smaller and smaller groups of determinants corresponding to the building up of the body, while the germ-plasm in the other remains in a more or less 'bound' or 'set' condition, and is only active to the extent of gradually stamping as germ cells the cells which arise from the primordial germ cell."

According to Weismann this actually occurs in Dipterous insects, but there is no evidence in the literature to warrant this statement. It is consequently necessary to imagine the germ-plasm as present but not definitely localized in a germ cell until some time after the two-cell stage has been reached. Thus in hydroids Weismann explains the situation as follows: "Here the primordial germ cell is separated from the ovum by a long series of cell-generations, and the sole possibility of explaining the presence of germ-plasm in this primordial germ cell is to be found in the assumption that in the divisions of the ovum the whole of the germ-plasm originally contained in it was not broken up into determinant groups, but that a part, perhaps the greater part, was handed on in a latent state from cell to cell, till sooner or later it reached a cell which it stamped as the primordial germ cell."

Evidence that the germ-plasm does become sooner or later localized in the primordial germ cell has accumulated rapidly within recent years. In the pædogenetic fly, *Miastor* (see Chapter III), the first cell to be cut off from the egg is the primordial germ cell (Fig. 17, *p.g.c.*), although at this time there are eight nuclei in the egg. As determined by Kahle (1908) and confirmed by the writer (Hegner, 1912, 1914a), this primordial germ cell gives rise to sixty-four oögonia and to no other cells. This is the nearest approach to a complete morphological continuity of the germ cells that has yet been described, and since this primordial germ cell must contain the germ-plasm of the succeeding generation, the condition in this fly is really comparable to that of the hypothetical case cited above, only in *Miastor* the cell set aside for reproductive purposes is much less than one-half of the egg, the somatic part of the egg being not a single cell, but a syncytium containing seven nuclei.

We may therefore look for the germ-plasm of *Miastor* in the primordial germ cell. So far as we know there are only two sorts of materials in this cell, that contained in the nucleus, and the darkly staining part of the egg which becomes recognizable just before maturation occurs, is situated at the posterior pole, and has been termed the pole-plasm (Fig. 13). If the primordial germ-cell multiplies by simple division and if there is an equal distribution of the contents at every mitosis, then the sixty-four oögonia must each possess one sixty-fourth of both the nucleus and the pole-plasm of the primordial germ cell plus any materials that have been added during the period of multiplication. An enormous enlargement occurs during the growth period both of the nucleus and of the cell. The pole-plasm cannot be recognized at this time, but again becomes

THE GERM-PLASM THEORY

evident just before maturation; it has increased in amount to approximately sixty-four times its former mass. How this increase has been brought about is not known, but it has been suggested (p. 68) that preëxisting particles of pole-plasm may grow and divide, or the dilution of the pole-plasm caused by the growth of the egg might start into action some catalyst which would cause the production of more substance like the pole-plasm and cease its activity when the amount of pole-plasm characteristic of the mature egg had accumulated and brought it to a state of equilibrium. In the midge, *Chironomus*, the primordial germ cell is segregated even earlier than in *Miastor*, namely, at the four-cell stage. The later history of the germ cells is not so well known in this species, however, as in *Miastor*.

The data presented in Chapters V and VI prove that a definite and early segregation of germ cells is known in a sufficient number of groups to indicate that the process is quite general among animals. The morphological continuity of the germ cells, however, cannot be established with such a degree of certainty in the vertebrates, and although most investigators believe that the germ cells are continuous, still the entire keimbahn has never been traced as accurately as it has in many invertebrates. Fortunately almost every new investigation contains additional data and more refined methods which lead us to hope that some time in the near future the primordial germ cells even here may be traced back to early cleavage stages.

One of the distinguishing features of many primordial germ cells is the presence within their cytoplasm of certain stainable bodies to which I have applied the term "keimbahn-determinants." Although, as pointed out in Chapter VIII, these inclusions do not appear to consist of the same sort of material in the eggs of different species and hence their significance is problematical, still they seem to be associated with that particular part of the egg substance which becomes the cytoplasm of the primordial germ cells. For this reason, if for no other, the keimbahn-determinants are of the greatest value, since they enable us to determine the position of this germ-cell substance during the stages before the primordial germ cells are established. It is therefore possible to trace the germ-cell substance in such cases as *Sagitta* (Fig. 54), where there is no morphological continuity of the germ cells. What relation the keimbahn-determinants have to the germ-plasm is not yet definitely known.

There have, of course, been many objections to the germ-plasm theory. The history of the germ cells in the Cœlenterata, upon which Weismann (1882) based a large part of his argument, is considered by Hargitt (see p. 95) to be directly opposed to the hypothesis. According to some zoölogists there is no essential difference between the reproductive cells and the various sorts of somatic cells; they have all arisen as the result of division of labor, and the germ cells have been differentiated for purposes of heredity just as the muscle cells have been differentiated for causing motion and the nerve cells for receiving and conducting stimuli. That the germ cells remain in a primitive condition during a large part of the embryonic period is accounted for by the fact that they become functional at a comparatively late stage in ontogeny (Eigenmann, 1896). Asexual reproduction by means of fission or budding has seemed to some to invalidate the theory of germinal continuity, but as Montgomery (1906, p. 82) has pointed out, "Perhaps in all cases products of asexual generation contain germ cells. If this were so, it might then be the case that the incapacity of any part of the body of an animal to reproduce asexually, or even to regenerate, would be due to the absence of germ cells in it — but this is merely a suggestion." The probability that the regenerating pieces of cœlenterates and the artificial plasmodia formed by dissociated sponge cells contain germ cells has already been noted (p. 79), but there are cases of the regeneration of sex organs that are not so easily explained. For example, Janda (1912) has found that if the anterior part of the hermaphroditic annelid, *Criodrilus lacuum*, is removed, a new anterior end will regenerate containing both ovaries and testes, although not always in their normal positions.

The study of the germ cells in the cestode *Moniezia expansa* convinced Child (1906) that germ cells may develop from tissue cells. In this species the germ cells are derived from the parenchymal syncytium, which has undergone a considerable degree of cytoplasmic differentiation and therefore consists of real tissue cells. Those parenchymal cells that encounter certain conditions become germ cells. Later (1906) the same author gave an account of the development of spermatogonia in the same animal from the differentiated muscle cells. These studies, together with the results from experiments on regeneration, have led Child (1912) to the belief "that this germ-plasm hypothesis and the subsidiary hypotheses which have grown up about it are not only unnecessary and constitute an impediment to biological thought, which has retarded its progress in recent years to a very appreciable extent, but furthermore, that they are not in full accord with observed facts and can be maintained only so long as we ignore the facts." He further maintains that if protoplasm is a physico-chemical substance it is capable of changing its constitution in any direction according to the conditions imposed upon it, and that therefore the continuous existence of a germ-plasm with a given specific constitution is unnecessary.

The evidence in favor of the germ-plasm theory is so strong that the arguments thus far advanced against it have had but little influence. If, then, we accept germinal continuity as a fact and consider the germ-plasm to be a substance that is not contaminated by the body in which it lies, but remains inviolate generation after generation, we should next inquire as to the nature of this substance. The generally accepted idea is that the chromatin of the nucleus represents the physical basis of heredity. In favor of this view are the facts that during mitosis the number and shape of the chromosomes are constant in every species (variations sometimes occur) and the complex series of processes in indirect nuclear division seems to be for the sole purpose of dividing the chromosomes equally between the daughter cells; even during the intervals (interkinesis) between successive mitoses the chromosomes may be recognized in certain species as prochromosomes (see Digby, 1914, for review of literature). During the maturation of the germ cells chromosomes seem to play the most important rôle, uniting in synapsis, and separating in the reducing division. The chromosomes of the minute, motile spermatozoa equal in number those of the comparatively enormous, passive egg; the spermatozoön consists almost entirely of chromatin, and this is the only substance present in the zygote that is equally contributed by both egg and spermatozoön. The processes following the penetration of the spermatozoön into the egg bring about a combination of the chromosomes of the two gametes into a single nucleus; in certain animals at least some characters depend upon the presence of a certain chromosome, the X-chromosome; in certain cases of polyspermy the addition of extra male chromosomes seems to be the cause of the abnormal development of the egg. These and many other facts of chromosome behavior that have been discovered by observations and experiments have convinced most biologists that the chromatin is the germ-plasm.

It is becoming more and more evident, however, that the cytoplasm cannot be entirely excluded. As noted in Chapter IX, the mitochondria appear to be constant cell elements and may actually constitute a part of the essential hereditary substance. Even if these particular cytoplasmic bodies do not represent germ-plasm, still, as pointed out by Guyer (1911) and others, cytoplasm as well as nuclear material is necessary to explain the phenomena which we call heredity. It was shown in Chapter I that the most important primary constituents of protoplasm are the proteins, and the idea is rapidly becoming general that the mechanism of heredity consists of (1) fundamental species substances, probably mainly protein in nature, together with (2) equally specific enzymic substances which regulate the sequences of the various chemical and physical processes incident to development (Guyer, 1911, p. 299). The chromosomes have been suggested as enzymatic in nature (Montgomery, 1910), but enzymes are supposed merely to accelerate reaction already initiated, and hence the substrate must be of as great importance as the enzymes which work upon it. But the substrates must be extremely numerous to supply each species with its specific proteins. That there are enough configurational differences in corresponding protein molecules to supply the number for the thousands of animal species is certain, since some comparatively simple proteins may possess thousands of millions of stereoisomers. Thus the study of heredity substance involves primarily a knowledge of the nature and reactions of the chemical constituents of protoplasm, for, as Wilson (1912, p. 66) says, "The essential conclusion that is indicated by cytological study of the nuclear substance is, that it is an aggregate of many different chemical components which do not constitute a mere mechanical mixture, but a complex organic system, and which undergo perfectly ordered processes of segregation and distribution in the cycle of cell life."

Some of the strongest evidence that the germ-plasm must include cytoplasmic constituents is afforded by the observations and experiments dealing with the differentiation of the germ cells, especially during early embryonic development. The writer's morphological and experimental studies of chrysomelid beetles seem to prove that the nuclei during the cleavage stages are all potentially alike and that it is the cytoplasm which decides their fate. Boveri's experiments on the eggs of *Ascaris* likewise show that the cytoplasm determines the initiation of the chromatin-diminution process and controls the differentiation of the germ cells. Furthermore, much of the data in the preceding chapters indicates that the non-nuclear substance which will become segregated within the primordial germ cell is present in a more or less definite region in the undivided egg, being gradually localized and separated from the other egg substances as cleavage progresses. The position of this germ-cell substance can in many cases be determined because of the presence of inclusions of various sorts, but whether these keimbahn-determinants constitute an important part of the germ-plasm or play a minor rôle in heredity is still uncertain.

Modern cytological studies and the results of experimental breeding both help to solve the problems of the combination and subsequent distribution of the determiners or factors within the germ-plasm. In fact, it has been maintained by certain geneticists that "The modern study of heredity has proven itself to be an instrument even more subtle in the analysis of the materials of the germ cells than actual observations on the germ cells themselves" (Morgan, 1913, p. v). Those who do not wish to commit themselves as to the physical or chemical nature of the germ-plasm are content to speak of determiners, factors, or genes without connecting them with any particular substances. The behavior of the chromosomes, however, enables us to explain so many of the facts of heredity that, as stated above, these bodies are generally considered to constitute the essential hereditary substance.

The study of heredity was wonderfully stimulated by the recognition in 1900 by Correns, Von Tschermak, and de Vries of the results of Mendel's (1866) investigations on plants. One of the simplest of Mendel's experiments is that which he performed with differently colored peas (Fig. 81). A pea bearing green seeds was crossed with a pea bearing yellow seeds. The first (F_1) generation of peas resulting from this cross all bore yellow seeds. When the individual plants of this generation were inbred, three-fourths of the resulting (F_2) generation were yellow

THE GERM-PLASM THEORY

and one-fourth green. This proved that the seeds of the first generation (F_1), although yellow, still possessed within them the factor for greenness in a latent condition. Green was therefore called a re-

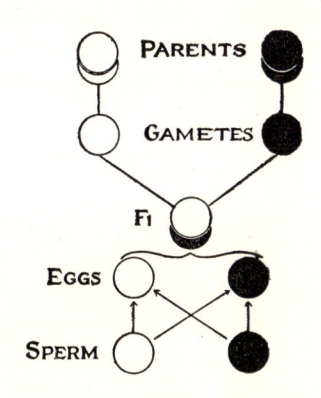

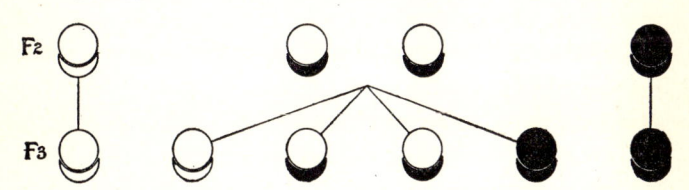

Fig. 81. — Diagram to illustrate Mendel's law of segregation. Individuals (zygotes) are represented by superimposed circles, whose colors stand for the factors involved. Gametes (germ cells) are represented by single circles. (*From Morgan, 1914.*)

cessive character and yellow a dominant character. As a result of breeding the (F_2) second generation it was found that all of the green seeds produced plants which bore green seeds; that is, these plants were pure green and "homozygous" as regards color; whereas the plants which bore yellow seeds could be separated into two groups; one, containing on the average one-third of these plants, was pure yellow and homozygous as regards color; the other two-thirds, although yellow, contained green in a latent condition and were therefore impure yellows and "heterozygous" as regards color. The conclusion reached was that the eggs and spermatozoa produced by the first (F_1) generation (see Fig. 81) were pure yellow or pure green and that chance combinations during fertilization resulted in the three classes of individuals in the second (F_2) generation; that is, one-fourth pure yellow, one-fourth pure green, and one-half with dominant yellow and green recessive. Evidently the factors for yellow and green repulsed each other during the maturation so that they became localized in different germ cells.

Such a characteristic as the color of the seeds of these peas is known as a *unit character*, and the separation of the factors of such a character during maturation is referred to as the *principle of segregation*. Mendel further discovered that if the seeds were also wrinkled or round, such characters behaved independently of the color characters. These and other experiments described by Mendel opened the way for new lines of investigation which have yielded results of vast importance from the standpoint of heredity and evolution.[1]

Soon after Mendel's results were "rediscovered"

[1] For more detailed accounts of experiments and theories that have been published within the past fourteen years the reader is referred to the books of Bateson (1909, 1913) and Punnet (1911).

THE GERM-PLASM THEORY

it was pointed out by Guyer (1902), Sutton (1903), and others that the distribution of the adult characteristics of hybrids which were found by Mendel to reappear in the offspring in rather definite propor-

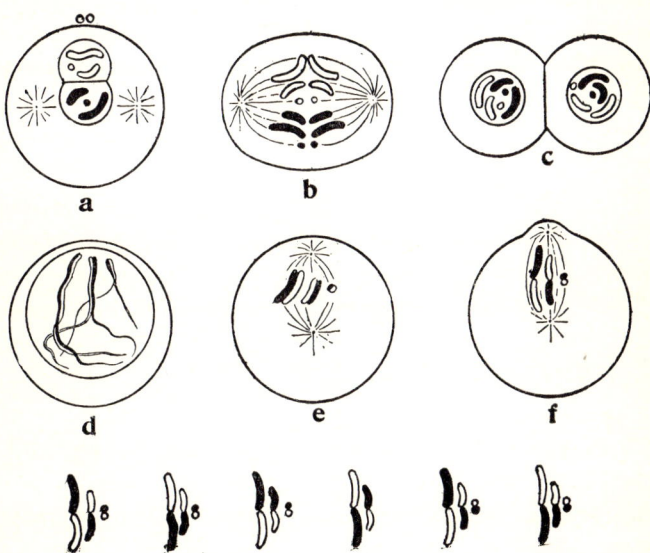

Fig. 82. — Diagrams to show the pairs of chromosomes and their behavior at the time of maturation of the egg. Three pairs of chromosomes are represented; three from one parent, three from the other. The six possible modes of separation of these three are shown in the lowest line. (*From Morgan, 1914.*)

tions, could be explained if these characteristics are located in the chromosomes. During synapsis, as already explained (p. 44), homologous maternal and paternal chromosomes are supposed to pair and then separate in the reduction division. It seems probable that the pairs of chromosomes do not occupy any definite position on the spindle at this time, but, as indicated in Fig. 82, the distribution of the maternal and paternal chromosomes to the daughter cells is entirely a matter of chance. If the homologous maternal and paternal chromosomes really are distributed by chance to the eggs and spermatozoa following synapsis, then the number of combinations possible are as follows (Sutton, 1903):

SOMATIC SERIES	REDUCED SERIES	COMBINATIONS IN GAMETES	COMBINATIONS IN ZYGOTES
2	1	2	4
4	2	4	16
8	4	16	256
16	8	256	65536
24	12	4096	16777216
36	18	262144	68719476736

The only direct evidence that such distribution of chromosomes takes place is that furnished recently by Carothers (1913) from a study of the spermatogenesis of three Orthopterous insects, *Brachystola magna*, *Arphia simplex*, and *Dissosteira carolina*. Miss Carothers, while working in Professor McClung's laboratory, discovered a tetrad in the first spermatocytes of these insects which consists of two unequal dyads (Fig. 83). During the two maturation divisions the four parts of this tetrad pass to the four spermatozoa, and consequently two sorts of spermatozoa are produced so far as this chromosome is concerned, one-half with one of the larger elements of the tetrad and one-half with one of the smaller elements. These differently sized dyads are considered by Carothers as "distinct physiological individuals, representing respectively the paternal and maternal contribution to the formation of some character or characters; and, as each can be identified, they furnish an excellent means of tracing the process of segregation and recombination" (p. 499).

It was at first assumed that each of the pairs of chromosomes which unite in synapsis was responsible for a single adult character, but the number of Mendelian characters is known to be greater in certain cases than the number of chromosomes.

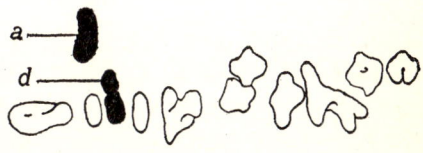

Fig. 83. — *Arphia simplex*. Chromosomes of first spermatocyte. a = accessory chromosome. b = unequal dyad. (*From Carothers, 1913.*)

Fortunately, it has been found that the characters, instead of undergoing independent assortment, may become linked so that certain of them almost always occur together in the offspring. The relation of these facts to the constitution of the chromosomes may best be illustrated by reference to the studies of Morgan and his students on the fruit-fly, *Drosophila*. Over one hundred mutants of this species have been discovered by these investigators. So far as studied, the characters of these flies seem to form three groups. "The characters in the first group show sex-linked inheritance. They follow the sex-chromosomes. The second group is less extensive. Since the characters in this group are linked to each other, we say that they lie in a second chromosome. The characters of the third group have not as yet been so fully studied, except to show that they are linked. We place them in the third chromosome without any pretensions as to which of the pairs of chromosomes are numbered II and III.

"The arrangement of these characters in groups is based on a general fact in regard to their behavior in heredity, viz., *A member of any group shows linkage with all other members of that group, but shows independent assortment with any member of any other group.*" If the factors which determine these groups of characters are situated in the chromosomes, as the hypothesis demands, we should expect each group to act as a unit in heredity. Occasionally, however, the characters of a group appear to act independently, and there must thus be an interchange of factors at the time of synapsis. As already stated (p. 254), an interchange of substances between chromosome pairs during synapsis is possible and even probable. Morgan explains the degree of crossing over of characters in the following way: The factors which determine the characters are arranged in the chromosomes in a linear series; those factors that are near together will have less chance of being separated than those that lie farther apart. The relative distances between these factors can be judged by the frequency of interchange as determined by breeding experiments. It has thus been possible to locate certain factors in the chromosomes more or less accurately and to predict with some degree of certainty the results of hybridization. Thus if the position of a newly discovered factor is determined by comparison with another particular known factor, it is possible to "calculate the results for all other known factors in the same chromosome." Morgan's ideas regarding the organization of the chromosomes coincide with those expressed by Weismann in one respect, that is, they are assumed "to have definite structures and not to be simply bags filled with a homogeneous fluid." Wilson (1912, p. 63) also regards the chromosomes as "compound bodies, consisting of different constituents which undergo different modes of segregation in different species."

Students of genetics now consider the individual as built up of a number of unit characters represented in the germ-plasm by factors, and when two different germ-plasms unite (amphimixis) the factors do not mix, but remain uncontaminated. The germ-plasm of offspring which develop from fertilized eggs is supposed to consist of an assortment of factors brought about during synapsis and reduction as indicated in Fig. 84. The factors (or genes) in the germ-plasm occur in pairs called allelomorphs,[1] and one of the pair may be regarded as dominant, the other recessive, as, for example, the yellow and green colors of pea seeds. Thus the appearance of the individual depends upon the character of its dominant factors. Any attempt to account for the origin of new species

[1] According to some investigators, especially in England, the presence of a factor should be considered one allelomorph and its absence as the contrasting factor.

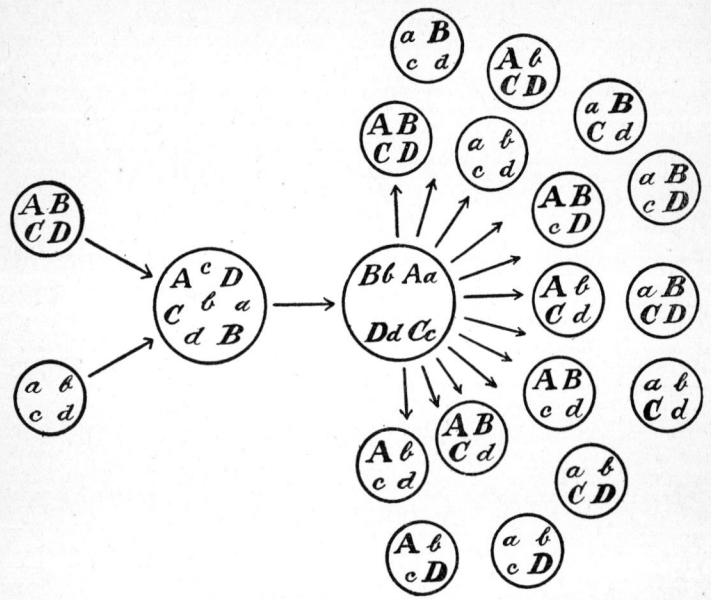

FIG. 84. — Diagrams illustrating the union of two stocks with paired factors *A, B, C, D,* and *a, b, c, d,* to form pairs *Aa, Bb, Cc, Dd.* Their possible recombinations are shown in the sixteen smaller circles. (*After Wilson.*)

must accept these facts of heredity as a basis. If evolution is a fact, new species must have arisen from time to time. This may have occurred by the dropping out of old factors or the addition of new factors. There seems to be sufficient evidence that factors are sometimes left out, but there are very few cases of the addition of new factors. Our ideas of a progressive evolution demand the addition of new factors, but whether this is brought about by changes within the germ-plasm or is the result of external influences is not known.

REFERENCES TO LITERATURE

Allen, B. M. 1906. The Origin of the Sex-cells of Chrysemys. Anat. Anz. Bd. 29.

—— 1907a. A Statistical Study of the Sex-cells of Chrysemys marginata. Anat. Anz. Bd. 30.

—— 1907b. An Important Period in the History of the Sex-cells of Rana pipiens. Anat. Anz. Bd. 31.

—— 1909. The Origin of the Sex-cells of Amia and Lepidosteus. Anat. Record. Vol. 3.

—— 1911. The Origin of the Sex-cells of Amia and Lepidosteus. Journ. Morph. Vol. 22.

Altmann, R. 1890. Die Elementarorganismen und ihre Beziehungen zu den Zellen. Leipzig.

Amma, K. 1911. Ueber die Differenzierung der Keimbahnzellen bei den Copepoden. Arch. Zellf. Bd. 6.

Ancel, P. 1903. Histogénèse et structure de la glande hermaphrodite d'Helix pomatia. Arch. Biol. T. 19.

Balbiani, E. G. 1864. Sur les mouvements qui se manifestent dans la tache germinative chez quelques animaux. C. R. Soc. Biol. Paris.

—— 1882. Sur la signification des cellules polaires des insects. C. R. Acad. Sci. Paris. T. 95.

—— 1885. Contribution à l'étude de la formation des organes sexuelles chez les insects. Receuil. Zool. Suisse. T. 2.

Bambeke, C. van. 1893. Contribution à l'histoire de la constitution de l'œuf. 2. Elimination d'éléments nucléaires dans l'œuf ovarien de Scorpæna scrofa. Bul. Acad. Belg. (3). T. 25.

Bardeleben, K. von. 1892. Über Spermatogenesis bei Säugetieren. Verb. Anat. Ges. Wien.

Bartelmez, G. W. 1912. The Bilaterality of the Pigeon's Egg. Journ. Morph. Vol. 23.

BATESON, W. 1909. Mendel's Principles of Heredity. Cambridge.

—— 1913. Problems of Genetics. New Haven.

BEARD, J. 1900. The Morphological Continuity of the Germ Cells of Raja batis. Anat. Anz. Bd. 18.

—— 1902*a*. The Germ Cells of Pristiurus. Id. 21.

—— 1902*b*. The Numerical Law of Germ Cells. Id.

—— 1902*c*. The Germ Cells. Part I. Raja batis. Zool. Jahrb. Bd. 16.

—— 1902*d*. Heredity and the Epicycle of the Germ Cells. Biol. Centrlb. Bd. 22.

BECKWITH, C. J. 1909. Preliminary Report on the Early History of the Egg and Embryos of Certain Hydroids. Biol. Bull. Vol. 16.

BENDA, C. 1897. Neuere Mitteilungen über die Histogenese des Saugetierspermatozoon. Verh. d. Phys. Ges. Berlin.

—— 1898. Über die Spermatogenese der Vertebraten und höherer Evertebraten. 2. Die Histogenese des Spermien. Verh. d. Phys. Ges. Berlin.

—— 1899. Weitere Beobachtungen über die Mitochondria und ihr Verhältnis zu Secretgranulationen, nebs kritischen Bemerkungen. Verh. d. Phys. Ges. Berlin.

—— 1903. Die Mitochondria. Ergebn. Anat. und Entwickl. Bd. 12.

BERENBERG-GOSSLER, H. VON. 1912*a*. Die Urgeschlechtszellen des Hühnerembryos u. s. w. Arch. mikr. Anat. Bd. 81.

—— 1912*b*. Geschlechtszellen und Körperzellen im Tierreich. Jena.

BESSELS, E. 1867. Studien über die Entwicklung der Sexualdrüsen bei den Lepiodopteren. Zeit. wiss. Zool. Bd. 17.

BIGELOW, M. 1902. The Early Development of Lepas. Bull. Mus. Comp. Zoöl. Vol. 40.

BLOCHMANN, F. 1881. Über die Entwicklung der Neritina fluviatilis. Zeit. wiss. Zool. Bd. 36.

—— 1886. Ueber die Reifung der Eier bei Ameisen und Wespen. Festschr. Nat. Med. Vereins. Heidelberg.

―― 1887. Ueber das regelmässige Vorkommen von bakterienähnlichen Gebilden in den Geweben und den Eiern verschiedener Insekten. Zeit. Biol. Bd. 24.

BONNEVIE, K. 1901. Ueber Chromatindiminution bei Nematoden. Jena. Zeit. Nat. Bd. 36.

BOUIN, P. 1900. Histogénèse de la glande génitale femelle chez Rana temporaria (L). Arch. Biol. T. 17.

BOUIN, M. and P. 1898. Sur la présence de formations ergastoplasmiques dans l'oocyte d'Asterina gibbosa. Bibliogr. Anat. T. 6.

BOVERI, T. 1887. Über Differenzirung der Zellkerne während der Furchung des Eies von Ascaris megalocephala. Anat. Anz. Bd. 2.

―― 1890. Über Entwickelung und Verwandtschatfsbeziehungen der Actinien. Zeit. wiss. Zool. Bd. 49.

―― 1892. Die Entstehung des Gegensatzes zwischen den Geschlechtszellen und den somatischen Zellen bei Ascaris megalocephala. Sitz. Ges. Morph. Phys. München. Bd. 8.

―― 1904. Ergebnisse über die Konstitution der chromatischen Substanz des Zellkerns. Jena.

―― 1910a. Ueber die Theilung centrifugirter Eier von Ascaris megalocephala. Arch. Entw. Bd. 30.

―― 1910b. Die Potenzen der Ascaris-Blastomeren bei abgeänderter Furchung. Festschr. R. Hertwig. Bd. 3.

―― 1911. Über das Verhalten der Geschlechschromosomen bei Hermaphroditismus. Beobachtungen an Rhabditis nigrovenosa. Verh. Phys. Med. Ges. Würzburg. Bd. 41.

BRANDT, A. 1878. Ueber das Ei und seine Bildungsstätte. Leipzig.

BRAUER, A. 1891. Ueber die Entwicklung von Hydra. Zeit. wiss. Zool. Bd. 52.

BROWNE, E. N. 1913. Study of the Male Germ Cells in Notonecta. Journ. Exp. Zoöl. Vol. 14.

BUCHNER, P. 1909. Das akzessorische Chromosomen in Spermatogenese und Ovogenese der Orthopteren, zugleich ein Beitrag zur Kenntniss der Reduktion. Arch. Zellf. Bd. 3.

―― 1910a. Keimbahn und Ovogenese von Sagitta. Anat. Anz. Bd. 35.

BUCHNER, P. 1910b. Die Schicksale des Keimplasmasder Sagitten in Reifung, Befruchtung, Keimbahn, Oogenese und Spermatogenese. Festschr. R. Hertwig. Bd. I. Jena.

—— 1912. Studien an intracellularen Symbionten. Arch. Protist. Bd. 26.

BUNTING, M. 1894. The Origin of Sex-Cells in Hydractinia and Podocoryne, and the Development of Hydractinia. Journ. Morph. Vol. 9.

BURESCH, I. 1911. Untersuchungen über die Zwitterdrüse der Pulmonaten. Arch. Zellf. Bd. 7.

CALKINS, G. N. 1911. Protozoön Germ Plasm. Pop. Sci. Monthly.

CAROTHERS, E. E. 1913. The Mendelian Ratio in Relation to Certain Orthopteran Chromosomes. Journ. Morph. Vol. 24.

CARTER, H. J. 1849. A Descriptive Account of the Freshwater Sponges, etc. Ann. Mag. Nat. Hist. (2). Vol. 4.

CASTLE, W. E. 1896. The Early Embryology of Ciona intestinales. Bull. Mus. Comp. Zoöl. Vol. 27.

CAULLERY, M. 1913. Les Problèmes de la Sexualité. Paris.

CHAMPY, C. 1913. Recherches sur la Spermatogénèse des Batraciens et les éléments accessoires du testicule. Arch. Zool. Exp. T. 52.

CHILD, C. M. 1900. The Early Development of Arenicola and Sternapsis. Arch. Entwick. Bd. 9.

—— 1904. Amitosis in Moniezia. Anat. Anz. Bd. 25.

—— 1906. The Development of Germ Cells from Differentiated Somatic Cells in Moniezia. Anat. Anz. Bd. 29.

—— 1907a. Studies on the Relation between Amitosis and Mitosis, I and II, in Biol. Bull. Vol. 12. III in Anat. Anz. Bd. 30.

—— 1907b. Amitosis as a Factor in Normal and Regulatory Growth. Anat. Anz. Bd. 30.

—— 1910. The Occurrence of Amitosis in Moniezia. Biol. Bull. Vol. 18.

—— 1911. The Method of Cell Division in Moniezia. Biol. Bull. Vol. 21.

REFERENCES TO LITERATURE

—— 1912. The Process of Reproduction in Organisms. Biol. Bull. Vol. 23.

CHUN, C. 1891. Die canarischen Siphonophoren in monographischen Darstellungen. Abh. Senc. Nat. Ges. Frankf. Bd. 16.

COLE, F. J. 1895. A case of Hermaphroditism in Rana temporaria. Anat. Anz. Bd. 11.

—— 1905. Notes on Myxine. Anat. Anz. Bd. 27.

CONKLIN, E. G. 1902. Karyokinesis and Cytokinesis, etc. Journ. Acad. Nat. Sci. Phil. Vol. 12.

—— 1905. Organization and Cell Lineage of the Ascidian Egg. Id. Vol. 13.

—— 1910. The Effects of Centrifugal Force upon the Organization and Development of the Eggs of Fresh-Water Pulmonates. Journ. Exp. Zoöl. Vol. 9.

—— 1911. The Organization of the Egg and the Development of Single Blastomeres of Phallusia mamillata. Id. Vol. 10.

—— 1912. Experimental Studies on Nuclear and Cell Division in the Eggs of Crepidula. Journ. Acad. Nat. Sci. Phil. Vol. 15.

CORRENS, C. G. 1900. Mendels Regel über das Verhalten der Nackkommenschaft der Rassenbastarde. Ber. D. Bot. Ges. Bd. 18.

COWDRY, E. V. 1914. The Development of the Cytoplasmic Constituents of the Nerve Cells of the Chick. I. Mitochondria and Neurofibrils. Amer. Journ. Anat. Vol. 15.

CUNNINGHAM, J. T. 1886. On the Structure and Development of the Reproductive Elements in Myxine glutinosa. Quart. Journ. Mic. Sci. Vol. 27.

DAHLGREN, U., and KEPNER, W. A. 1908. A Text-Book of the Principles of Animal Histology. New York.

DEBAISIEUX, P. 1909. Les débuts de l'ovogenèse dans le Dytiscus marginalis. La Cellule. T. 25.

DELAGE, Y. 1884. Evolution de la Sacculine (Sacculina carcini). Arch. Zool. Exp. (2). T. 2.

DELLA VALLE, P. 1912. La morfologia della cromatina dal punto di vista fisico. Arch. Z. Naples. Vol. 6.

DEMOLL, R. 1912a. Die Spermatogenese von Helix pomatia. Zool. Jahrb. Suppl. 15.

—— 1912b. Über Geschlechtsbestimmung, etc. Zool. Jahrb. Bd. 33.

DÉSÖ, B. 1879–1880. Die Histologie und sprossenentwicklung der Tethyen. Arch. mikr. Anat. Bd. 16 and 17.

DICKEL, O. 1904. Entwicklungsgeschichtliche Studien am Bienenei. Zeit. wiss. Zool. Bd. 77.

DIGBY, L. 1914. A Critical Study of the Cytology of Crepis virens. Arch. Zellf. Bd. 12.

DOBELL, C. C. 1908. Chromidia and the Binuclearity Hypotheses. Quart. Journ. Mic. Sci. Vol. 53.

DODDS, G. 1910. Segregation of the Germ Cells of the Teleost, Lophius. Journ. Morph. Vol. 21.

DONCASTER, L. 1914. Chromosomes, Heredity and Sex. Id. Vol. 59.

DOWNING, E. R. 1905. The Spermatogenesis of Hydra. Zool. Jahrb. Bd. 21.

—— 1909. The Ovogenesis of Hydra. Id. Bd. 28.

—— 1911. The Formation of the Spermatophore in Arenicola, etc. Journ. Morph. Vol. 22.

DRIESCH, H. 1892. Entwicklungsmechanische Studien. I, II. Zeit. wiss. Zool. Bd. 53.

DUESBERG, J. 1908. La Spermiogénèse chez le Rat. Arch. Zellf. Bd. 2.

—— 1910. Les chondriosomes des cellules embryonnaires du Poulet, etc. Arch. Zellf. Bd. 4.

—— 1912. Plastosomen, "Apparato reticolare interno," und Chromidialapparat. Ergebn. Anat. u. Entwick. Bd. 20.

—— 1913. Ueber die Verteilung der Plastosomen und der "Organ-forming Substances" Conklins bei den Ascidien. Verh. Anat. Ges. Bd. 27.

—— and HOVEN, H. 1910. Observations sur la structure du protoplasme des cellules végétales. Anat. Anz. Bd. 36.

DURME, M. VAN. 1914. Nouvelles recherches sur la vitellogenèse des œufs d'oiseaux, etc. Arch. Biol. T. 29.

DUSTIN, A. P. 1907. Recherches sur l'origine des gonocytes chez les Amphibiens. Arch. Biol. T. 23.

EHRENBERG, C. G. 1836. Ueber des Massenverhältnis der jetzt lebenden Kieselinfusorien, etc. Abh. Akad. Wiss. Berlin.

EIGENMANN, C. 1892. On the Precocious Segregation of the Sex-Cells of Micrometrus aggregatus. Journ. Morph. Vol. 5.

—— 1896a. Sex Differentiation in the Viviparous Teleost, Cymatogaster. Arch. Entwick. Bd. 4.

—— 1896b. The Bearing of the Origin and Differentiation of the Sex-Cells of Cymatogaster on the Idea of the Continuity of the Germ Plasm. Amer. Nat. Vol. 30.

ELPATIEWSKY, W. 1907. Zur Fortpflanzung von Arcella vulgaris Ehrbg. Arch. Protist. Vol. 10.

—— 1909. Die Urgeschlechtszellenbildung bei Sagitta. Anat. Anz. Bd. 35.

—— 1910. Die Entwicklungsgeschichte der Genitalprodukte bei Sagitta. Biol. Zeit. Vol. 1.

ESCHERICH, K. 1900. Ueber die Bildung der Keimblätter bei den Musciden. Nova Acta Abh. Leop. Carol. deutsch. Akad. Nat. Bd. 77.

EVANS, R. 1900. A Description of Ephydatia blembingia, etc. Quart. Journ. Mic. Sci. Vol. 44.

FAURÉ-FRÉMIET, E. 1910. Étude sur les mitochondries des Protozoaires et des cellules sexuelles. Arch. d'Anat. micr. T. 11.

—— 1913. Le Cycle Germinatif chez L'Ascaris megalocephala. Id. T. 15.

——, MAYER, and SCHAFFER. 1909. Sur la constitution et le rôle des mitochondries. C. R. Soc. Biol. T. 66.

FELT, E. P. 1911. Miastor Americana Felt, an Account of Pedogenesis. N. Y. State Mus. Bull. 147.

FIEDLER, K. 1888. Über Ei- und Samenbildung bei Spongilla fluviatilis. Zeit. wiss. Zool. Bd. 47.

FIRKET, J. 1914. Recherches sur l'organogenèse des glandes sexuelles chez les oiseaux. Arch. Biol. T. 29.

FLEMMING, W. 1882. Zellsubstanz, Kern und Zelltheilung. Leipzig.

—— 1897. Ueber die Chromosomenzahl beim Menschen. Anat. Anz. Bd. 15.

FOL, H. 1880. Études sur le développement des Mollusques. Arch. Zool. Exp. T. 8.

FOOT, K; and STROBELL, E. 1911. Amitosis in the Ovary of Protenor belfragei and a Study of the Chromatin Nucleolus. Arch. Zellf. Bd. 7.

—— 1912. A Study of Chromosomes and Chromatin Nucleoli in Euschistus crassus. Id. Bd. 9.

FRIEDMANN, F. 1898. Rudimentäre Eier im Hoden von Rana viridis. Arch. mikr. Anat. Bd. 52.

FRISCHHOLZ, E. 1909. Zur Biologic von Hydra. Biol. Centrlb. Bd. 29.

FUCHS, K. 1913. Die Zellfolge der Copepoden. Zool. Anz. Bd. 42.

FUJITA, T. 1904. On the Formation of Germinal Layers in Gastropoda. Journ. Coll. Sc. Japan. Vol. 20.

FUSS, A. 1912. Über der Geschlechtszellen des Menschen und der Säugetiere. Arch. mikr. Anat. Bd. 81.

GALTON, F. 1872. On Blood-Relationship. Proc. Roy. Soc. London. Vol. 20.

GARDINER, E. G. 1895. Early Development of Polychœrus caudatus. Journ. Morph. Vol. 11.

—— 1898. The Growth of the Ovum, Formation of the Polar Bodies and Fertilization of Polychœrus caudatus. Id. Vol. 15.

GATES, R. R. 1911. Pollen Formation in Œnothera Gigas. Annals of Botany. Vol. 25.

GERHARTZ, H. 1905. Rudimentärer Hermaphroditismus bei Rana esculenta. Arch. mikr. Anat. Bd. 65.

GIARDINA, A. 1901. Origine dell' oocite e delle cellule nutrici nel Dytiscus. Internat. Monatsschr. Anat. u. Phys. Bd. 18.

—— 1902. Sui primi stadii dell' ovogenesi principalmente sulle fasi di sinapsi. Anat. Anz. Bd. 21.

GIGLIOS-TOS, E. and GRANATA, L. 1908. J. mitochondri nelle cellule seminali maschili di Pamphagus marmoratus. Biologica. Vol. 2.

GOETTE, A. 1886. Untersuchungen zur Entwicklungsgeschichte von Spongilla fluviatilis. Zool. Anz. Bd. 7 and 8.

—— 1907. Vergleichende Entwicklungsgeschichte der Geschlechtsindividuen der Hydropolypen. Zeit. wiss. Zool. Bd. 87.

GOLDSCHMIDT, R. 1904. Chromidialapparat lebhaft funktionierender Gewebszellen Histologische Untersuchungen an Nematoden. Zool. Jahrb. Bd. 21.

GÖRICH, W. 1904. Zur Kenntnis der Spermatogenese bei Poriferen und Cölenteraten, etc. Zeit. wiss. Zool. Bd. 76.

GOVAERTS, P. 1913. Recherches sur la structure de l'ovaire des Insectes, etc. Arch. Biol. T. 28.

GRABER, V. 1889. Vergleichende Studien über die Embryologie der Insekten insbesondere der Musciden. Denkschr. Akad. Wiss. Bd. 56.

—— 1891. Beiträge zur vergleichenden Embryologie der Insekten. Id. Bd. 58.

GRIMM, O. V. 1870. Die ungeschlechtliche Fortpflanzung einer Chironomusart, etc. Mém. Acad. Sc. St. Petersburg. (7). T. 15.

GROBBEN, C. 1879. Die Entwicklungsgeschichte der Moina rectirostris. Art. Zool. Inst. Wien. Bd. 1.

GROSS, J. 1901. Untersuchungen über das Ovarium der Hemipteren. Zeit. wiss. Zool. Bd. 79.

GUDERNATSCH, J. F. 1911. Hermaphroditismus Versus in Man. Amer. Journ. Anat. Vol. 2.

GUENTHER, K. 1904. Nucleolus und Synapsis. Eine Studie aus der Samenreifung von Hydra viridis. Zool. Jahrb. Suppl. 7.

GUILLIERMOND, A. 1911. Sur les mitochondries des cellules végétals. C. R. Acad. Sci. Paris. T. 153.

GÜNTHERT, T. 1910. Die Eibildung der Dytisciden. Zool. Jahrb. Bd. 30.

GUTHERZ, S. 1912. Ueber ein bemerkenswertes Strukturelement (Heterochromosome?) in der Spermiogenese des Menschen. Arch. mikr. Anat. Bd. 79.

GUYER, M. 1909a. The Spermatogenesis of the Domestic Guinea. Anat. Anz. Vol. 34.

—— 1909b. The Spermatogenesis of the Domestic Chicken. Id. Vol. 34.

—— 1910. Accessory Chromosome in Man. Biol. Bull. Vol. 19.

—— 1911. Nucleus and Cytoplasm in Heredity. Amer. Nat. Vol. 45.

HADZI, J. 1906. Vorversuche zur Biologie von Hydra. Arch. Entwick. Bd. 22.

HAECKEL, E. 1872. Die Kalkschwämme. Berlin.

HAECKER, V. 1892. Die Furchung des Eies von Aequorea forskalea. Arch. mikr. Anat. Bd. 40.

—— 1895. Die Vorstadien der Eireifung. Id. Bd. 45.

—— 1897. Die Keimbahn von Cyclops. Id. Bd. 49.

—— 1899. Die Reifungserscheinungen. Anat. Hefte. Bd. 8.

—— 1912. Allgemeine Vererbungslehre. 2d. Ed. Braunschweig.

HALLEZ, P. 1886. Loi de l'orientation de l'embryon chez les Insects. C. R. Acad. Sci. T. 103.

HARGITT, C. W. 1904a. The Early Development of Eudendrium. Zool. Jahrb. Bd. 20.

—— 1904b. The Early Development of Pennaria tiarella. Arch. Entwick. Bd. 18.

—— 1906. The Organization and Early Development of Clava leptostyla. Biol. Bull. Vol. 10.

—— 1911. Some Problems of Cœlenterate Ontogeny. Journ. Morph. Vol. 22.

HARGITT, G. T. 1913. Germ Cells of Cœlenterates. I. Campanularia flexuosa. Journ. Morph. Vol. 24.

HARM, K. 1902. Die Entwickelungsgeschichte von Clava squamata. Zeit. wiss. Zool. Bd. 73.

HARMAN, M. T. 1913. Method of Cell-Division in the Sex Cells of Tænia teniæformis. Journ. Morph. Vol. 24.

HARMER, S. F. 1893. On the Occurrence of Embryonic Fission in Cyclostomatous Polyzoa. Quart. Journ. Mic. Sci. Vol. 34.

HARTMANN, M. 1902. Ovarialei und Eireifung von Asterias glacialis. Zool. Jahrb. Bd. 15.

HASPER, M. 1911. Zur Entwicklung der Geschlechtsorgane von Chironomus. Zool. Jahrb. Bd. 31.

HEGNER, R. W. 1908. The Effects of Removing the Germ-Cell Determinants from the Eggs of Some Chrysomelid Beetles. Biol. Bull. Vol. 16.

—— 1909*a*. The Origin and Early History of the Germ Cells in Some Chrysomelid Beetles. Journ. Morph. Vol. 20.

—— 1909*b*. The Effects of Centrifugal Force on the Eggs of Some Chrysomelid Beetles. Journ. Exp. Zool. Vol. 6.

—— 1911*a*. Experiments with Chrysomelid Beetles. III. The Effects of Killing Parts of the Eggs of Leptinotarsa decemlineata. Biol. Bull. Vol. 20.

—— 1911*b*. Germ-Cell Determinants and their Significance. Amer. Nat. Vol. 45.

—— 1912. The History of the Germ Cells in the Pædogenetic Larva of Miastor. Science. Vol. 36.

—— 1914*a*. Studies on Germ Cells. I. The History of the Germ Cells in Insects with Special Reference to the Keimbahn-Determinants. II. The Origin and Significance of the Keimbahn-Determinants in Animals. Journ. Morph. Vol. 25.

—— 1914*b*. Studies on Germ Cells. III. The Origin of the Keimbahn-Determinants in a Parasitic Hymenopteron, Copidosoma. Anat. Anz. Bd. 46.

HENKING, H. 1891. Untersuchungen über die ersten Entwickelungsvorgänge in den Eiern der Insekten. Zeit. wiss. Zool. Bd. 51.

HERBST, C. 1894–1895. Ueber die Bedeutung der Reizphysiologie für de causale Auffassung von Vorgängen in der thierischen Ontogenese. Biol. Centrlb. Bd. 14, 15.

HEROLD, M. 1815. Entwicklungsgeschichte der Schmetterlinge, anatomisch und physiologisch bearbeitet. Kassel und Marburg.

HERRICK, F. H. 1895. Movements of the Nucleolus through the Action of Gravity. Anat. Anz. Bd. 10.

HERTWIG, O. 1880. Die Chaetognathen. Jena. Zeitsch. Bd. 14.

—— and HERTWIG, R. 1878. Der Organismus der Medusen und seine Stellung zur Keimblättertheorie. Jena.

HERTWIG, R. 1899. Über Encystierung und Kernvermehrung bei Arcella vulgaris Ehrbg. Festschr. Kupffer.

—— 1906. Über Knospung und Geschlechtsentwicklung der Hydra fusca. Biol. Centrlb. Bd. 26.

HEYMONS, R. 1890. Über die hermaphroditische Anlage der Sexualdrüsen beim Männchen vom Phyllodromia (Blatta) germanica. Zool. Anz. Bd. 13.

—— 1895. Die Embryonalentwicklung von Dermapteren und Orthopteren. Jena.

HODGE, C. F. 1894. A Microscopical Study of the Nerve Cell during Electrical Stimulation. Journ. Morph. Vol. 9.

HOGUE, M. J. 1910. Über die Wirkung der Centrifugalkraft auf die Eier von Ascaris megalocephala. Arch. Entwick. Bk. 29.

HOLMES, S. J. 1913. Behavior of Ectodermic Epithelium of Tadpoles when Cultivated in Plasma. Univ. Cal. Pub. Zoöl. Vol. 11.

HOOKER, D. 1912. Der Hermaphroditismus bei Fröschen. Arch. mikr. Anat. Bd. 79.

HOVEN, H. 1910. Sur l'histogénèse du système nerveux périphérique et sur le rôle des chondriosoma dans le neurofibrillation. Arch. Biol. T. 25.

ISCHIKAWA, C. 1887. Über die Abstammung der männlichen Geschlechtszellen bei Eudendrium racemosum. Zeit. wiss. Zool. Bd. 45.

JÄGER, G. 1877. Physiologische Briefe. Kosmos. Bd. 1.

JANDA, V. 1912. Die Regeneration der Geschlechtsorgane bei Criodrilus lacuum Hoffm. Arch. Entwick. Bd. 33.

JANSSENS, F. A. 1909. Spermatogénèse dans le Batraciens. V. La Théorie de la Chiasmatypie. La Cellule. T. 25.

JARVIS, M. M. 1908. Segregation of the Germ Cells of Phrynosoma cornutum. Biol. Bull. Vol. 15.

JENKINSON, J. W. 1911. On the Origin of the Polar and Bilateral Structure of the Egg of the Sea-urchin. Arch. Entwick. Bd. 32.
—— 1913. Vertebrate Embryology. Oxford.
JENNINGS, H. S. 1896. The Early Development of Asplanchna herrickii. Bull. Mus. Comp. Zoöl. Vol. 30.
JORDAN, H. E. 1910. The Relation of Nucleoli to Chromosomes in the Egg of Cribrella sanguinolenta. Arch. Zellf. Bd. 5.
—— 1911. The Spermatogenesis of the Opossum. Id. Bd. 7.
JÖRGENSEN, M. 1910. Beiträge zur Kenntnis der Eibildung, Reifung, Befruchtung und Furchung bei Schwämmen (Syconen). Arch. Zellf. Bd. 4.
KAHLE, W. 1908. Die Paedogenese der Cecidomyiden. Zoologica. Bd. 21.
KELLICOTT, W. E. 1913. A Text-Book of General Embryology. New York.
KELLOGG, V. L. 1907. Sex Differentiation in Larval Insects. Biol. Bull. Vol. 12.
KING, H. D. 1908. The Oögenesis of Bufo lentiginosus. Journ. Morph. Vol. 19.
—— 1910. Some Anomalies in the Genital Organs of Bufo lentiginosus and their Probable Significance. Amer. Journ. Anat. Vol. 10.
KITE, G. L. 1913. Studies on the Physical Properties of Protoplasm. Amer. Journ. Physiol. Vol. 32.
KLEINENBERG, N. 1872. Hydra, eine anatomisch-entwicklungsgeschichtliche Untersuchung. Leipzig.
—— 1879. The Development of the Earthworm, Lumbricus trapezoides. Quart. Journ. Mic. Sci. Vol. 19.
—— 1881. Ueber die Entstehung der Eier bei Eudendrium. Zeit. wiss. Zool. Bd. 35.
KNAPPE, E. 1886. Das Bidder'sche Organ. etc. Morph· Jahrb. Bd. 11.
KOLTZOFF, N. K. 1906. Studien über die Gestalt der Zelle. Arch. mikr. Anat. Bd. 67.
KOROTNEFF, A. 1883. Zur Kenntniss der Embryologie von Hydra. Zeit. wiss. Zool. Bd. 38.

KORSCHELT, E., and HEIDER, K. 1902.

KOWALEVSKY, A. 1886. Zur Embryonalentwicklung der Musciden. Biol. Centrlb. Bd. 6.

KRUGER, E. 1912. Die phylogenetische Entwicklung der Keimzellenbildung einer freilebenden Rhabditis. Zool. Anz. Bd. 40.

KÜHN, A. 1908. Die Entwicklung der Keimzellen in den parthenogenetischen Generationen, etc. Arch. Zellf. Bd. 1.

—— 1911. Über determinierte Entwicklung bei Cladoceren. Zool. Anz. Bd. 38.

—— 1913. Die Sonderung der Keimbezirke in der Entwickelung der Sommereier von Polyphemus pediculus De Geer. Zool. Jahrb. Bd. 35.

KULESCH, L. 1914. Der Netzapparat von Golgi in den Zellen des Eierstockes. Arch. mikr. Anat. Bd. 84.

KÜNSTLER, J. 1882. Contribution à l'étude des Flagellés. Bull. Soc. Zool. France. 7. Année.

KUSCHAKEWITSCH, S. 1908. Ueber den Ursprung der Urgeschlechtszellen bei Rana esculenta. Sitz. math.-phys. Kl. bayer. Akad. Wiss. Bd. 38.

—— 1910. Die Entwicklungsgeschichte der Keimdrüsen von Rana esculenta. Festschr. R. Hertwig. Bd. 2.

LAMS, H. 1907. Contribution à l'étude de la génèse du vitellus dans l'ovule des Amphibiens. Arch. d'anat. micr. T. 9.

LANG, A. 1884. Die Polycladen des Golfes von Neapel. Fauna Flora Golf. Neapel. 11 Monographie.

LA VALLETT ST. GEORGE, A. VON. 1886. Spermatologische Beiträge. Arch. mikr. Anat. Bd. 27.

—— 1895. Zwitterbildung beim kleinen Wassermolch (Triton tæniatus S.). Arch. mikr. Anat. Bd. 45.

LECAILLON, A. 1898. Recherches sur l'œuf et sur le développement embryonnaire de quelques Chrysomelides. Paris.

LEE, A. B. 1905. The Microtomist's Vade-Mecum. 6th ed. Phila.

LEUCKART, R. 1865. Die ungeschlechtliche Fortpflanzung der Cecidomyienlarven. Arch. Naturg. Berlin. Bd. 1.

LEWIS, M. R. and W. H. 1914. Mitochondria in Tissue Culture. Science. Vol. 39.

LEYDIG, F. 1848. Die Dotterfurchung nach ihrem Vorkommen in der Thierwelt und nach ihrer Bedeutung.

LIEBERKÜHN, N. 1856. Beiträge zur Entwicklungsgeschichte der Spongillen. Muller's Arch. Anat. Phys.

LILLIE, F. R. 1906. Observations and Experiments concerning the Elementary Phenomena of Embryonic Development in Chætopterus. Journ. Exp. Zoöl. Vol. 8.

—— 1909a. Karyokinetic Figures of Centrifuged Eggs. Biol. Bull. Vol. 17.

—— 1909b. Polarity and Bilaterality of the Annelid Egg. Id. Vol. 16.

LILLIE, R. S. 1905. The Structure and Development of the Nephridia of Arenicola cristata. Mitth. Zoöl. Sta. Naples. Bd. 17.

LOEB, J. 1912. The Mechanistic Conception of Life. Chicago.

—— 1913. Artificial Parthenogenesis and Fertilization. Chicago.

—— and BANCROFT, F. W. 1912. Can the Spermatozoön Develop Outside the Egg? Journ. Exp. Zoöl. Vol. 12.

LOEWENTHAL, N. 1888. Zur Kenntnis des Keimfleckes im Ureie einiger Säuger. Anat. Anz. Bd. 3.

LOYEZ, M. 1909. Les premiers stades de la vitellogénèse chez quelques Tuniciers. C. R. Assoc. Anat. Nancy.

LUBARSCH, O. 1896. Über das Vorkommen krystallinischer und krystalloider Bildungen in den Zellen des menschlichen Hodens. Arch. Path. Anat. Bd. 145.

LUBOSCH, W. 1902. Über die Eireifung der Metazoen, etc. Anat. Hefte. Bd. 11.

MAAS, O. 1893. Die Embryonalentwicklung und Metamorphose der Cornacuspongien. Zoöl. Jahrb. Vol. 7.

—— 1910. Über Involutionserscheinungen bei Schwämmen, etc. Festschr. R. Hertwig. Bd. 3.

MCCLENDON, J. F. 1906a. On the Development of Parasitic Copepods. Biol. Bull. Vol. 12.

—— 1906b. Myzostoma. Amer. Mus. Bull. Vol. 22.

MCCLUNG, C. F. 1899. A Peculiar Nuclear Element in the Male Reproductive Cells of Insects. Zoöl. Bull. Vol. 2.

McClung, C. F. 1902. The Accessory Chromosome — Sex-Determinant? Biol. Bull. Vol. 3.

—— 1905. The Chromosome Complex of Orthopteron Spermatocytes. Biol. Bull. Vol. 9.

McGregor, J. H. 1899. The Spermatogenesis of Amphiuma. Journ. Morph. Vol. 15 (suppl.).

Mangan, J. 1909. The Entry of Zoöxanthellæ into the Ovum of Millepora, etc. Quart. Journ. Micr. Sci. Vol. 53.

Marchal, P. 1904. Recherches sur la biologie et le développement des Hyménoptères parasites. Arch. Zoöl. Exp. (4). T. 2.

Marcora, F. 1911. Über die Histogenese des Centralnerven systems, etc. Folia Neurobiol. Haarlem. Bd. 5.

Marshall, A. M. 1884. On Certain Abnormal Conditions of the Reproductive Organs in the Frog. Journ. Anat. Phys. Vol. 18.

Marshall, W. 1884. Vorl. Bemerkungen über die Fortpflanzungsverhältnisse von Spongilla lacustris. Sitz. Nat. Ges. Leipzig. Jahrg. 11.

Marshall, W. M. 1907. Contributions toward the Embryology and Anatomy of Polistes pallipes. Zeit. wiss. Zool. Bd. 86.

Maupas, M. 1900. Modes et formes de reproduction des Nematodes. Arch. Zoöl. Exper. (3). T. 8.

Megusar, F. 1906. Einfluss abnormale Gravitationswirkung auf die Embryonalentwicklung bei Hydrophilus aterrimus. Arch. Entwick. Bd. 22.

Meinert, F. R. 1864. Miastor metraloas. Natur. Tidsskrift.

Mendel, G. 1866. Versuche ueber Pflanzenhybriden. Verh. naturf. Vereins in Brünn. IV.

Metchnikoff, E. 1865. Ueber die Entwicklung der Cecidomyienlarven aus dem Pseudovum. Arch. Naturg. Bd. 1.

—— 1866. Embryologische Studien an Insekten. Zeit. wiss. Zool. Bd. 16.

—— 1886. Embryologische Studien an Medusen. Wien.

Meves, F. 1891. Über amitotische Kerntheilung i. d. Spermatogonien, etc. Anat. Anz. Bd. 6.

―― 1895. Über eigenthümliche mitotische Processe in jungen Ovocyten von Salamandra maculosa. Anat. Anz. Bd. 10.

―― 1904. Über das Vorkommen von Mitochondrien bzw. Chondriomiten in Pflanzenzellen. Ber. d. Deutsch. Bot. Ges. Bd. 22.

―― 1907a. Über Mitochondrien bzw. Chondriokonten in dem Zellen junger Embryonen. Anat. Anz. Bd. 31.

―― 1907b. Die Spermatocytenteilungen bei der Honigbiene nebst Bemerkungen über Chromatin-reduktion. Arch. mikr. Anat. Bd. 70.

―― 1908. Die Chondriosomen als Träger erblicher Anlagen. Id. Bd. 72.

―― 1910. Über Structuren in dem Zelles des embryonalen Stützgewebes, etc. Id. Bd. 75.

―― 1911. Über die Beteilung der Plastochondrien an der Befruchtung des Eies von Ascaris megalocephala. Id. Bd. 76.

―― 1914. Die Plastochondrien in dem sich teilenden Ei von Ascaris megalocephala. Id. Bd. 84.

―― 1914. Verfolgung des Mittelstückes des Echinidenspermiums durch die ersten Zellgenerationen des befruchteten Eies. Arch. mikr. Anat. Bd. 85.

MEYER, O. 1895. Celluläre Untersuchungen an Nematoden-Eiern. Jena. Zeit. Bd. 29.

MINCHIN, E. A. 1900. Porifera. In Lankester's Treatise on Zoölogy. Part II. London.

MONTGOMERY, T. H. 1895. On Successive Protandric and Proterogynic Hermaphroditism in Animals. Amer. Nat. Vol. 29.

―― 1898. The Spermatogenesis in Pentatoma up to the Formation of the Spermatid. Zool. Jahrb. Vol. 12.

―― 1899. Comparative Cytological Studies. Journ. Morph. Vol. 15.

―― 1906. The Analysis of Racial Descent in Animals. New York.

―― 1910. Are Particular Chromosomes Sex Determinants? Biol. Bull. Vol. 19.

MONTGOMERY, T. H. 1911. Spermatogenesis of an Hemipteron, Euschistus. Journ. Morph. Vol. 22.
—— 1911. Differentiation of the Human Cells of Sertoli. Biol. Bull. Vol. 21.
—— 1912. Complete Discharge of Mitochondria from the Spermatozoön of Peripatus. Biol. Bull. Vol. 22.
—— 1912. Human Spermatogenesis, etc. Journ. Acad. Nat. Sci. Phila. Vol. 15.
MOORE, J. E., and ARNOLD, G. 1906. On the Existence of Permanent Forms among the Chromosomes, etc. Proc. Roy. Soc. Vol. 77.
MORGAN, T. H. 1905. Some Further Experiments on Self-Fertilization in Ciona. Biol. Bull. Vol. 8.
—— 1907. Experimental Zoölogy. New York.
—— 1909a. The Effects Produced by Centrifuging Eggs before and during Development. Anat. Rec. Vol. 3.
—— 1909b. A Biological and Cytological Study of Sex-Determination in Phylloxerans and Aphids. Journ. Exp. Zoöl. Vol. 7.
—— 1911. An Attempt to Analyze the Constitution of the Chromosomes on the Basis of Sex-limited Inheritance in Drosophila. Journ. Exp. Zoöl. Vol. 11.
—— 1913. Heredity and Sex. New York.
—— 1914. The Mechanism of Heredity as Indicated by the Inheritance of Linked Characters. Pop. Sci. Monthly. Vol. 84.
—— and SPOONER, G. B. 1909. The Polarity of the Centrifuged Egg. Arch. Entwick. Bd. 28.
MORSE, M. 1909. The Nuclear Components of the Sex Cells of Four Species of Cockroaches. Arch. Zellf. Bd. 3.
—— 1911. Cestode Cells in Vitro. Science. Vol. 34.
MÜLLER, F. 1885. Die Zwitterbildung im Thierreich. Kosmos. Bd. 17.
MÜLLER, K. 1911. Das Regenerationsvermögen der Süsswasserschwämme, etc. Arch. Entwick. Bd. 32.
MULLER-CALÉ, C. 1913. Über die Entwicklung von Cypris incongruens. Zool. Jahrb. Bd. 36.

Munson, J. P. 1912. A Comparative Study of the Structure and Origin of the Yolk Nucleus. Arch. Zellf. Bd. 8.

Nachtsheim, H. 1913. Cytologische Studien über die Geschlechtsbestimmung bei der Honigbiene (Apis mellifica L). Arch. Zellf. Bd. 11.

Nansen, F. 1886. Forelöbig Meddelelse om Undersögelser, etc. Bergens Mus. Aarsberetning. (Ann. Mag. N. H. (5). Vol. 18.)

Noack, W. 1901. Beiträge zur Entwicklungsgeschichte der Musciden. Zeit. wiss. Zool. Bd. 70.

Nussbaum, M. 1880. Zur Differenzierung des Geschlechts im Thierreich. Arch. mikr. Anat. Bd. 18.

—— 1887. Ueber die Theilbarkeit der lebendigen Materie. II. Id. Bd. 29.

—— 1901. Zur Entwickelung des Geschlechts beim Huhn. Verh. Anat. Ges. Jena.

Ognew, S. J. 1906. Ein Fall von Hermaphroditismus bei Rana temporaria. Anat. Anz. Bd. 29.

Okkelberg, P. 1914. Hermaphroditism in the Brook Lamprey. Sci. Vol. 39.

Owen, R. 1849. On Parthenogenesis. London.

Patterson, J. T. 1912. The Early Development of Graffilla gemellipara. Biol. Bull. Vol. 22.

—— 1913. Polyembryonic Development in Tatusia novemcincta. Journ. Morph. Vol. 24.

—— and Wieman, H. L. 1912. The Uterine Spindle of the Polyclad, Planocera inquilina. Biol. Bull. Vol. 23.

Paulcke, W. 1900. Ueber die Differenzierung der Zellenelemente im Ovarium der Bienenköniginen. Zool. Jahrb. Bd. 14.

Paulmier, F. C. 1899. The Spermatogenesis of Anasa tristis. Journ. Morph. Vol. 15.

Payne, F. 1912. A Further Study of Chromosomes in Reduviidæ. Journ. Morph. Vol. 23.

Pelseneer, P. 1894. Hermaphroditism in Mollusca. Quart. Journ. Mic. Sci. Vol. 37.

PETRUNKEWITSCH, A. 1901. Die Richtungskörper und ihr Schicksal im befruchteten und unbefruchteten Bienenei. Zool. Jahrb. Bd. 14.

—— 1903. Das Schicksal der Richtungskörper im Drohnenel. Zool. Jahrb. Bd. 17.

PICK, L. 1914. Über den wahren Hermaphroditismus des Menschen und der Sängetiere. Arch. mikr. Anat. Bd. 84.

PRENANT, A. 1910. Les mitochondries et l'ergastoplasme. Journ. de l'Anat. et Phys. T. 46.

PREUSSE, F. 1895. Ueber die amitotische Kerntheilung in den Ovarien der Hemipteren. Zeit. wiss. Zool. Bd. 59.

PUNNET, R. C. 1911. Mendelism.

RATH, O. VOM. 1891. Ueber die Bedeutung der amitotischen Kerntheilung in Hoden. Zool. Anz. Bd. 14.

—— 1893. Beiträge zur Kenntnis der Spermatogenese von Salamandra maculosa. Zeit. wiss. Zool. Bd. 57.

REGAUD, C. 1908. Sur les mitochondries de l'epithélium séminal. 3. C. R. Soc. Biol. Paris. T. 64.

—— 1909. Attribution aux "formations mitochondriales" de la fonction générale d'extraction et de fixation électives, etc. C. R. Soc. Biol.

RHODE, E. 1911. Histogenetische Untersuchungen. II. Zeit. wiss. Zool. Bd. 98.

RICHARDS, A. 1909. On the Method of Cell Division in Tænia. Biol. Bull. Vol. 17.

—— 1911. The Method of Cell Division in the Development of the Female Sex Organs of Moniezia. Id. Vol. 20.

RITTER, R. 1890. Die Entwicklung der Geschlechtsorgane und des Darmes bei Chironomus. Zeit. wiss. Zool. Bd. 50.

ROBERTSON, A. 1903. Embryology and Embryonic Fission in the Genus Crisia. Univ. Cal. Pub. Zoöl. Vol. 1.

ROBIN, C. 1862a. Mémoire sur les globules polaires de l'ovale et sur le mode de leur production. C. R. Acad. Sci. Paris. T. 54.

—— 1862b. Mémoire sur la production des cellules du blastoderme sans segmentation du vitellus chez quelques articulés. Id.

REFERENCES TO LITERATURE

Rösel v. Rosenhoff, A. J. 1755. Insecten-Belustigung, III. Nuremberg.

Rosner, M. A. 1901. Sur la genèse de la grossesse gémellaria monochoriale. Bull. Acad. Sci. Cracovie.

Rubaschkin, W. 1907. Über das erste Auftreten und Migration der Keimzellen bei Vögelembryonen. Anat. Hefte. Bd. 31.

—— 1909. Über die Urgeschlechtszellen bei Säugetieren. Id. Bd. 39.

—— 1910. Chondriosomen und Differenzierungsprozesse bei Säugetierembryonen. Id. Bd. 41.

—— 1912. Zur Lehre von der Keimbahn bei Säugetieren. Id. Bd. 46.

Rückert, J. 1888. Ueber die Entstehung der Excretionsorgane bei Selachiern. Arch. Anat. Phys.

Russo, A. 1907. Sull' origine dei mitocondri, etc. Boll. R. Accad. dei Lincei. Roma.

Samassa, P. 1893. Die Keimblätterbildung bei den Cladoceren. Arch. mikr. Anat. Bd. 41.

Sauerbeck, E. 1909. Über den Hermaphroditismus verus, etc. Frankf. Zeit. Path. Bd. 3.

Schapitz, R. 1912. Die Urgeschlechtszellen von Amblystoma. Arch. mikr. Anat. Bd. 79.

Schaxel, J. 1910. Die Eibildung der Meduse, Pelagia noctiluca. Festschr. R. Hertwig. Bd. 1.

Schleip, W. 1911. Das Verhalten des Chromatins bei Angiostomum (Rhabdonema) nigrovenosum. Arch. Zellf. Bd. 7.

—— 1913. Geschlechtsbestimmende Ursachen im Tierreich. Ergebn. u. Forts. Zool. Bd. 3.

Schmidt-Marcel, W. 1908. Über Pseudo-Hermaphroditismus bei Rana temp. Arch. mikr. Anat. Bd. 72.

Schneider, K. C. 1890. Histologie von Hydra fusca, etc. Arch. mikr. Anat. Bd. 35.

Schönemund, E. 1912. Zur Biologie und Morphologie einiger Perlaarten. Zool. Jahrb. Bd. 34.

Schönfeld, H. 1901. La spermatogénèse chez le Taureau et chez les Mammifères en général. Arch. Biol. T. 18.

Schreiner, K. E. 1904. Über das generationsorgan von Myxine glutinosa. Biol. Centrlb. Bd. 24.

Schultze, O. 1903. Zur Frage von den geschlecht's-bildenden Ursachen. Arch. mikr. Anat. Bd. 63.

Schulze, F. E. 1871. Ueber den Bau und die Entwicklung von Cordylophora lacustris. Leipzig.

—— 1875. Untersuchungen über den Bau und die Entwicklung der Spongien. Zeit. wiss. Zool. Bd. 25.

—— 1904. Hexactinellida. Wiss. Ergeb. D. Tiefsee Exp. Bd. 4.

Selenka, E. 1881. Über eine eigentümliche Art der Kernmetamorphose. Biol. Centrlb. Bd. 1.

Semon, R. 1891. Studien über den Bauplan des Urogenitalsystems der Wirbelthiere. Jena. Zeit. Nat. Bd. 26.

Siebolt, C. T. E. v. 1864. Ueber Zwitterbienen. Zeit. wiss. Zool. Bd. 14.

Silvestri, F. 1906 and 1908. Contribuzioni alla conoscenza biologica degli Imenotteri parassiti. I–IV. Boll. Scuola sup. Agric. Portici. Vol. I and III.

Simon, W. 1903. Hermaphroditismus verus. Virchow's Arch. Bd. 172.

Smallwood, W. M. 1899. A Contribution to the Morphology of Pennaria tiarella. Amer. Nat. Vol. 33.

—— 1909. A Reëxamination of the Cytology of Hydractinia and Pennaria. Biol. Bull. Vol. 17.

Stevens, N. M. 1904. Further Studies on the Oögenesis of Sagitta. Zool. Jahrb. Bd. 21.

—— 1905. A Study of the Germ Cells of Aphis rosæ and Aphis œnotheræ. Journ. Exp. Zoöl. Vol. 2.

—— 1906. Studies in Spermatogenesis. Carnegie Inst. Pub. 36.

—— 1910a. Chromosomes in the Germ Cells of Culex. Journ. Exp. Zoöl. Vol. 8.

—— 1910b. Further Studies on Reproduction in Sagitta. Journ. Morph. Vol. 21.

Strasburger, E. 1895. Karyokinetische Probleme. Jahr. wiss. Bot. Bd. 28.

REFERENCES TO LITERATURE

STRICHT, O. VAN DER. 1904. La couche vitellogène et les mitochondries de l'œuf des Mammifères. Verh. Anat. Ges. Jena.

—— 1909. La Structure de l'œuf des Mammifères. Mém. Acad. Sci. Belg. (2). T. 2.

STUHLMANN, F. 1886. Die Reifung des Arthropodeneis, etc. Ber. Nat. Ges. Freiburg. Bd. 1.

SUCKOW, F. 1828. Geschlechtsorgane der Insekten. Hensinger's Zeit. organ. Physik. Bd. 2.

SURFACE, F. M. 1907. The Early Development of a Polyclad, Planocera inquilina. Proc. Acad. Nat. Sci. Phila. Vol. 59.

SUTTON, W. S. 1903. The Chromosomes in Heredity. Biol. Bull. Vol. 4.

SWAREZEWSKY, B. 1908. Über die Fortpflanzungerscheinungen bei Arcella vulgaris. Arch. Protist. Bd. 12.

SWIFT, C. H. 1914. Origin and Early History of the Primordial Germ Cells in the Chick. Amer. Journ. Anat. Vol. 15.

TANNREUTHER, G. W. 1908. The Development of Hydra. Biol. Bull. Vol. 14.

—— 1909. Observations on the Germ Cells of Hydra. Biol. Bull. Vol. 16.

THALLWITZ, J. 1885. Über die Entwicklung der männlichen Keimzellen bei den Hydroiden. Jena. Zeit. Naturw. Bd. 18.

TREMBLEY, A. 1744. Mémoires pour servir à l'histoire de Polypes d'eau douce. Leide.

TSCHASCHKIN, S. 1910. Über die Chondriosomen der Urgeschlechtszellen bei Vögelembryonen. Anat. Anz. Bd. 37.

TSCHERMAK, E. 1900. Über künstliche Kreuzung bei Pisum sativum. Zeit. Landw. Versuchu. in Österreich.

UFFREDUZZI, O. 1910. Ermafroditismo vero nell' uomo. Archiv. per le Scienze Mediche. Vol. 34.

VANDER STRICHT, R. 1911. Vitellogénèse dans l'ovule de Chatte. Arch. Biol. T. 26.

VARENNE, A. DE. 1882. Recherches sur la reproduction des Polypes Hydraires. Arch. Zool. Exp. T. 10.

VEJDOVSKY, F. 1911–1912. Zum Problem der Vererbungsträger. Prag.

VOELTZKOW, A. 1889a. Entwicklung im Ei von Musca vomitoria. Art. Zool.-Zoot. Inst. Würzburg. Bd. 9.

—— 1889b. Melolontha vulgaris. Ein Beitrag zur Entwicklung im Ei bei Insekten. Id.

VOLLMER, C. 1912. Zur Entwicklung der Cladoceren aus dem Dauerei. Zeit. wiss. Zool. Bd. 102.

VOSS, H. VON. 1914. Cytologische Studien an Mesostoma ehrenbergi. Arch. Zellf. Bd. 12.

VRIES, H. DE. 1900. Sur le loi de disjonction des hybrides. C. R. T. 130.

WAGER, R. E. 1909. The Oögenesis and Early Development of Hydra. Biol. Bull. Vol. 17.

WAGNER, N. 1862. Ueber spontane Fortpflanzung der Larven bei dem Insekten (Russian). Kasan. Fol. 50.

WALDEYER, W. 1870. Eierstock und Ei. Leipzig.

—— 1906. Die Geschlechtszellen. Hertwig's Handbuch der Entw. Bd. 1. Jena.

WALKER, C. E. 1907. Observations on the Life-Cycle of Leucocytes. Part III. Proc. Roy. Soc. London. (B). Vol. 79.

WEISMANN, A. 1863. Die Entwicklung der Dipteren im Ei. Zeit. wiss. Zool. Bd. 13.

—— 1882. Beiträge zur Kenntnis der ersten Entwicklungsvorgänge im Insektenei. Festschr. Henle.

—— 1883. Die Entstehung der Sexualzellen bei den Hydromedusen, etc. Jena.

—— 1884. Die Entstehung der Sexualzellen bei den Hydromedusen. Biol. Centrlb. Bd. 4.

—— 1885. Die Continuität des Keimplasmas als Grundlage einer Theorie der Vererbung. Jena.

—— 1904. The Evolution Theory. 2 vols. London.

—— and ISCHIKAWA. 1889. Ueber die Parakopulation im Daphnidenei, etc. Zool. Jahrb. Bd. 4.

WELTNER, W. 1892. Bemerkungen über den Bau und die Entwicklung der Gemmulä der Spongilliden. Biol. Centrlb. Bd. 13.

REFERENCES TO LITERATURE

—— 1907. Spongillidenstudien. 5. Arch. Naturg. Bd. 73.
WHEELER, W. M. 1889. The Embryology of Blatta germanica and Doryphora decemlineata. Journ. Morph. Vol. 3.
—— 1893. A Contribution to Insect Embryology. Id. Vol. 8.
—— 1894. Protandric Hermaphroditism in Myzostoma. Zool. Anz. Bd. 17.
—— 1894. Planocera inquilina, a Polyclad Inhabiting the Branchial Chamber of Sycotypus canaliculatus. Journ. Morph. Vol. 9.
—— 1896. The Sexual Phases of Myzostoma. Mitth. Zool. Sta. Naples. Bd. 12.
—— 1897. The Maturation, Fecundation and Early Cleavage in Myzostoma. Arch. Biol. T. 15.
—— 1900. The Development of the Urinogenital Organs of the Lamprey. Zool. Jahrb. Bd. 13.
—— 1904. Dr. Castle and the Dzierzon Theory. Science. Vol. 19.
WHITMAN, C. O. 1893. The Inadequacy of the Cell-Theory of Development. Journ. Morph. Vol. 8.
WIEMAN, H. L. 1910a. The Pole Disc of Chrysomelid Eggs. Biol. Bull. Vol. 18.
—— 1910b. A Study of the Germ Cells of Leptinotarsa signaticollis. Journ. Morph. Vol. 21.
—— 1910c. The Degenerated Cells in the Testis of Leptinotarsa signaticollis. Id.
—— 1913. Chromosomes in Man. Amer. Journ. Anat. Vol. 14.
WIERZEJSKI, A. 1886. Le développement des gemmules des Éponges d'eau douce d'Europe. Arch. Biol. Slav. Vol. 1.
—— 1906. Embryologie von Physa fontinalis. Zeit. wiss. Zool. Bd. 83.
WIJHE, J. W. VAN. 1889. Ueber die Mesodermsegmente des Rumpfes, und die Entwicklung des Excretions-systems bei Selachiern. Arch. mikr. Anat. Bd. 33.
WILCOX, E. V. 1900. Human Spermatogenesis. Anat. Anz. Bd. 17.
WILDMAN, E. E. 1913. The Spermatogenesis of Ascaris megalocephala, etc. Journ. Morph. Vol. 24.

Wilke, G. 1912. Zur Frage nach der Herkunft der Mitochondrien in den Geschlechtszellen. Anat. Anz. Bd. 42.

Wilson, E. B. 1895. Archoplasm, Centrosome, and Chromatin in the Sea-Urchin Egg. Journ. Morph. Vol. 11.

—— 1900. The Cell in Development and Inheritance. New York.

—— 1903. Experiments on Cleavage and Localization in the Nemertine Egg. Arch. Entwick. Bd. 16.

—— 1905–1912. Studies on Chromosomes I–VIII. Journ. Exp. Zoöl. Vol. 2, 3, 6, 9, 13. Journ. Morph. Vol. 22.

—— 1912. Some Aspects of Cytology in Relation to the Study of Genetics. Am. Nat. Vol. 46.

Wilson, H. V. 1902. On the Asexual Origin of the Ciliated Sponge Larva. Amer. Nat. Vol. 36.

—— 1907. On Some Phenomena of Coalescence and Regeneration in Sponges. Journ. Exp. Zoöl. Vol. 5.

—— 1911. Development of Sponges from Dissociated Tissue Cells. Bull. U. S. Bur. Fisheries. Vol. 30.

Winiwarter, H. von. 1901. Recherches sur l'ovogenèse et l'organogenèse de l'ovaire des Mammifères. Arch. Biol. T. 17.

—— 1912. Etudes sur la spermatogenèse humaine. Id. 27.

Woods, F. A. 1902. Origin and Migration of the Germ-Cells in Acanthias. Amer. Journ. Anat. Vol. 1.

Wulfert, J. 1902. Die Embryonalentwickelung von Gonothyrea loveni. Zeit. wiss. Zool. Bd. 71.

Yung, E. 1907. Sur un cas d'hermaphrodisme chez la Grenouille. Revue Suisse Z. T. 15.

Zarnik, B. 1911. Über den Chromosomenzyklus bei Pteropoden. Verh. Deutsch. Zool. Ges.

Zeleny, C. 1904. Experiments on the Localization of Developmental Factors in the Nemertine Egg. Journ. Exp. Zoöl. Vol. 1.

Zoja, L. and R. 1891. Über die fuchsinophilen Plastidulen. Arch. Anat. u. Entwick.

Zykoff, W. 1892. Die Entwicklung der Gemmulae der Ephydatia fluviatilis. Zool. Anz. Bd. 25.

INDEX OF AUTHORS

All numbers refer to pages. An asterisk (*) after a page number indicates that the title of a contribution by the author will be found on that page.

Allen, B. M., 32, 100, 102, 206, 311.*
Altmann, 276, 282, 311.*
Amma, 140, 163 ff., 216, 228, 311.*
Ancel, 195–197, 311.*

Baer, van, 192.
Balbiani, 107, 214, 229, 311.*
Baltzer, 261.
Bambeke, van, 222, 311.*
Bancroft, 21.
Bardeleben, 273, 311.*
Bartelmez, 232, 311.*
Bateson, 312.*
Beard, 100, 312.*
Beckwith, 135, 312.*
Benda, 40, 276, 277, 279, 282, 312.*
Beneden, van, 80, 82, 87, 88.
Berenberg-Gossler, 98, 100, 102, 312.*
Bessels, 118, 312.*
Bigelow, 172, 186, 225, 312.*
Blockmann, 185, 221, 225, 312.*
Bonnevie, 177, 286, 313.*
Bouin, 206, 276, 313.*
Boveri, 174 ff., 184, 193, 195, 217, 230, 268, 301, 313.*
Brandt, 118, 313.*
Brauer, 83, 313.*
Brown, 3.
Browne, 285, 313.*
Buchner, 123, 140, 180, 187, 195, 222, 286, 313.*
Bunting, 87, 314.*
Buresch, 195, 199 ff., 226, 314.*

Calkins, 26, 314.*
Carothers, 306, 307, 314.*
Carter, 74, 314.*
Castle, 192, 314.*
Caullery, 195, 314.*
Champy, 195, 206, 209, 314.*
Child, 136, 188, 297, 314.*
Chun, 184, 315.*
Cohn, 3.
Cole, 207, 209, 315.*
Conklin, 218, 232, 233, 234, 315.*
Correns, 302, 315.*
Cowdry, 280, 285, 315.*
Cunningham, 209, 315.*

Debaisieux, 120, 121, 122, 315.*
Delage, 195, 315.*
Della Valle, 12, 315.*
Demoll, 195, 202 ff., 316.
Désö, 70, 76, 316.*
Dickel, 144, 316.*
Digby, 299, 316.*
Dobell, 28, 316.*
Dodds, 102–103, 316.*
Doncaster, 275, 316.*
Downing, 83–85, 97, 188, 316.*
Driesch, 161, 231, 316.*
Duesberg, 104, 233, 273, 280, 283, 316.*
Dujardin, 3.
Durme, van, 286, 316.*
Dustin, 99, 206, 317.*

Ehrenberg, 82, 317.*
Eigenmann, 100, 243, 297, 317.*

INDEX OF AUTHORS

Elpatiewsky, 26, 140, 179 *ff.*, 195, 228, 317.*
Escherich, 107, 317.*
Evans, 75, 317.*

Farmer, 273.
Fauré-Frémiet, 13, 279, 283, 285, 317.*
Feistmantel, 207.
Felt, 52, 317.*
Fiedler, 73, 317.*
Firket, 99, 317.*
Fischer, 12.
Flemming, 214, 273, 318.*
Fol, 186, 318.*
Foot, 123, 137, 214, 318.*
Friedmann, 207, 318.*
Frischholz, 97, 318.*
Fuchs, 163, 169, 318.*
Fujita, 186, 225, 318.*
Fuss, 100, 318.*

Galton, 290, 318.*
Gardiner, 157, 318.*
Gates, 160, 318.*
Gerhartz, 207, 318.*
Giardina, 120–122, 223, 231, 318.*
Giglios-Tos, 279, 319.*
Goette, 75, 95, 319.*
Goldschmidt, 222, 279, 286, 319.*
Görich, 73, 319.*
Govaerts, 120, 123, 128, 319.*
Graber, 107, 319.*
Granata, 279.
Grimm, 107, 310.*
Grobben, 163, 170, 319.*
Gross, 137, 319.*
Gudernatsch, 194, 319.*
Guenther, 83, 319.*
Günthert, 121, 122, 128, 319.*
Guilliermond, 277, 319.*
Gutherz, 273, 320.*
Guyer, 272, 300, 305, 320.*

Hadzi, 83, 320.*
Haeckel, 320.*

Haecker, 36, 73, 124, 140, 163 *ff.*, 184, 215, 320.*
Hallez, 112, 320.*
Hargitt, C. W., 86, 88, 95, 296, 320.*
Hargitt, G. T., 96, 320.*
Harm, 88, 89, 98, 320.*
Harman, 136, 320.*
Harmer, 161, 321.*
Hartmann, 216, 321.*
Harvey, 1.
Hasper, 104, 107, 110, 140, 218, 230, 235, 321.*
Hegner, 33, 51, 107, 140, 219, 225, 235, 286, 294, 321.*
Heider, 79.
Henking, 106, 256, 321.*
Herbst, 216, 321.*
Herold, 118, 321.*
Herrick, 215, 322.*
Hertwig, O., 82, 231, 322.*
Hertwig, R., 83, 222, 322.*
Heymons, 186, 194, 322.*
His, 231.
Hodge, 214, 322.*
Hogue, 179, 322.*
Holmes, 137, 322.*
Hooke, 2, 207, 322.*
Hoven, 277, 280, 322.*

Ijima, 76.
Ischikawa, 86, 163, 170, 322.*

Jäger, 291, 322.*
Janda, 297, 322.*
Janssens, 254, 255, 322.*
Jarvis, 100, 322.*
Jenkinson, 50, 232, 323.*
Jennings, 186, 225, 323.*
Jordan, 214, 288, 323.*
Jörgensen, 72, 74, 78, 323.*

Kahle, 51, 107, 140, 230, 235, 294, 323.*
Kellicott, 50, 323.*
Kellogg, 118, 323.*
King, 195, 206, 208, 323.*

INDEX OF AUTHORS

Kite, 6, 323.*
Kleinenberg, 80, 82, 83, 161, 323.*
Knappe, 208, 323.*
Kölliker, 373.
Koltzoff, 323.*
Korotneff, 83, 323.*
Korschelt, 79, 324.*
Kossel, 8.
Kowalevsky, 107, 324.*
Kruger, 195, 267, 324.*
Kühn, 140, 163 *ff.*, 225, 236, 324.*
Kulesch, 105, 324.*
Künstler, 276, 324.*
Kuschakewitsch, 100, 195, 206, 324.*

Lams, 286, 324.*
Lang, 157, 324.*
La Valette St. George, 207, 276, 324.*
Lecaillon, 109, 111, 324.*
Lewis, 281, 324.*
Leuckart, 51, 107, 324.*
Levene, 11.
Leydig, 82, 325.*
Lieberkühn, 73, 325.*
Lillie, 188, 232, 234, 325.*
Loeb, 13, 21, 325.*
Loewenthal, 222, 325.*
Loyez, 286, 325.*
Lubarsch, 130, 325.*
Lubosch, 214, 325.*

Maas, 73, 76, 78, 325.*
McClendon, 172, 185, 325.*
McClung, 256, 325.*
McGregor, 134, 135, 326.*
Malpighi, 3.
Mangan, 187, 326.*
Marchal, 161, 326.*
Marcora, 280, 326.*
Marshall, A, 326.*
Marshall, W., 75, 326.*
Marshall, W. M., 222, 326.*
Maupas, 267, 326.*
Mayer, 283.
Megusar, 113, 326.*
Meinert, 51, 326.*

Mendel, 302 *ff.*, 326.*
Metschnikoff, 51, 107, 183, 224, 326.*
Meves, 134, 216, 244, 266, 284, 287, 326.*
Meyer, 176, 327.*
Minchin, 70, 72, 327.*
Mohl, von, 3.
Montgomery, 129, 131, 195, 214, 241, 285, 297, 300, 327.*
Moore, 273, 328.*
Morgan, 192, 232, 255, 265, 302, 307, 309, 328.*
Morse, 137, 244, 328.*
Müller, F., 195, 328.*
Müller, K., 77, 80, 328.*
Muller-Calé, 172, 328.*
Mulsow, 256, 257.
Munson, 226, 329.*

Nachtsheim, 143, 145, 265, 266, 329.*
Noack, 107, 109, 111, 225, 235, 329.*
Nussbaum, 83, 100, 291, 329.*

Ognew, 208, 329.*
Okkeberg, 209, 329.*
Ostwald, 9.
Owen, 290, 329.*

Patterson, 157, 161, 329.*
Paulcke, 120, 122, 222, 329.*
Paulmier, 256, 329.*
Payne, 138, 329.*
Pelseneer, 195, 329.*
Petrunkewitsch, 143, 145, 265, 266, 330.*
Pflüger, 205, 231.
Pick, 194, 330.*
Prenant, 279, 283, 330.*
Preusse, 137, 330.*
Punnet, 330.*

Rath, vom, 134, 135, 330.*
Regaud, 279, 282, 330.*
Rhode, 218, 330.*
Richards, 136, 330.*
Ritter, 107, 108, 229, 235, 330.*
Robertson, 161, 330.*
Robin, 107, 330.*

INDEX OF AUTHORS

Rösel V. Rosenhoff, 72, 331.*
Rosner, 161, 331.*
Roux, 141.
Rubaschkin, 98, 100, 103, 226, 283, 331.*
Rückert, 99, 331.*
Russo, 286, 331.*

Samassa, 170, 172, 331.*
Sauerbeck, 194, 331.*
Schapitz, 100, 331.*
Schaxel, 214, 331.*
Schäffer, 283.
Schleip, 195, 268, 331.*
Schleiden, 3.
Schmidt-Marcel, 205, 207, 331.*
Schmiedeberg, 12.
Schneider, 83, 331.*
Schönemund, 194, 331.*
Schönfeld, 237, 331.*
Schreiner, 209, 332.*
Schulze, 76, 80, 193, 332.*
Schwann, 3.
Selenka, 157, 332.*
Semon, 206, 332.*
Siebolt, von, 193, 332.*
Silvestri, 143, 145, 215, 332.*
Simon, 194, 332.*
Smallwood, 87, 98, 332.*
Spooner, 234.
Steudel, 12.
Stevens, 140, 180, 195, 228, 256, 332.*
Strasburger, 214, 332.*
Stricht, van der, 188, 286, 333.*
Strobell, 123, 137, 214.
Stuhlmann, 221, 333.*
Suckow, 118, 333.*
Surface, 157, 333.*
Sutton, 305, 306, 333.*
Swarezewsky, 26, 333.*
Swift, 33, 103, 226, 333.*

Tannreuther, 83, 333.*
Tennent, 261.
Thallowitz, 88, 333.*
Trembley, 82, 333.*

Tschaschkin, 98, 102, 226, 302, 333.*
Tschermak, 333.*

Uffreduzzi, 194, 333.*

Vander Stricht, 187, 333.*
Varenne, 82, 333.*
Vejdovsky, 334.*
Voeltzkow, 107, 334.*
Vollmer, 172, 334.*
Voss, von, 204, 334.*
Vries, de, 302, 334.*

Wager, 83, 334.*
Wagner, 51, 334.*
Waldeyer, 98, 130, 334.*
Walker, 159, 334.*
Wassilieff, 286.
Weismann, 25, 82, 88, 97, 107, 113, 144, 296, 309, 334.*
Weltner, 73, 75, 77, 334.*
Wheeler, 33, 100, 109, 144, 157, 185, 193, 335.*
Whitman, 231, 335.*
Wieman, 124, 138, 225, 273, 335.*
Wierzejski, 75, 186, 225, 335.*
Wijhe, van, 99, 335.*
Wilcox, 273, 335.*
Wildman, 279, 335.*
Wilke, 285, 336.*
Wilson, E. B., 4, 21, 133, 224, 232, 250, 301, 309, 336.*
Wilson, H. V., 75, 77, 80, 336.*
Winiwarter, 129, 132, 251, 273, 336.*
Winter, de, 119, 120.
Woods, 100, 336.*
Wolff, 2.
Wulfert, 89, 98, 336.*

Youngman, 207.
Yung, 207, 336.*

Zarnik, 195, 269, 336.*
Zeigler, 237.
Zeleny, 232, 336.*
Zoja, 287, 336.*
Zykoff, 75, 336.*

INDEX OF SUBJECTS

All numbers refer to pages. Words in italics are names of families, genera, species, or of higher divisions. Numbers in thick type are numbers of pages on which there are figures.

Aborting spindle, 157.
Accessory chromosome, 134, 202.
Acidophile, 11.
Actinospherium, 222.
Ageniaspis, 146.
Allelomorph, 309.
Alternation of generations, 23.
Alveolar structure of protoplasm, 4.
Amœbocyte, 71, 73, 79.
Amia, **32**, **33**.
Amitosis, **13–14**, 133–139, 250.
Amphiaster, **15**.
Amphibia, amitosis, 134–135; hermaphroditism, 205 *ff.*
Amphimixis, 309.
Amphiuma, 135.
Amyloplastid, 7.
Anaphase, **15**, **16**.
Anello cromatico, **121**, **123**, **223**.
Animal pole, 20.
Aptera, life cycle, 22.
Arcella, **26**.
Archæocyte, 70–73.
Archoplasm, **5**, **7**.
Arenicola, 188.
Armadillo, polyembryony in, 161.
Arphia, **307**.
Arthropoda, 212.
Ascaris, 122, 174 *ff.*, 217 *ff.*, 230, 241, 301; maturation in, 261, **263**; mitochondria in, **284**.
Asexual larvæ, 149.
Asplanchna, 186, 225.

Aster, **15**.
Asterias, 6.
Attraction-sphere, 5, **7**, **227**.
Aurelia, 183.
Aussenkörnchen, **164**, 213, 216, **228**.
Axolotl, 159, 208.

Bacteria, 4, 186–187.
Basophile, 11.
Bat, 188.
Besondere Körper, **180**, 181 *ff.*, 213, 228, 239.
Bidder's organ, 207.
Binary fission, 17.
Binuclearity hypothesis, 27.
Bioblast, 276.
Bivalent chromosomes, 44.
Blastotomy, 161.
Bryozoa, 161.
Budding, 17, 22, 23, 69, 161, 297.

Calligrapha, 109, 111, 230.
Calliphora, 107, **111** *ff.*, 235.
Camponotus, 221.
Canthocamptus, 165.
Cat, 187.
Cell, 2–16; definition, 3; division, 13–16; lineage, 29; shape, 4; size, 4; theory, 3.
Centrifuged eggs, 173.
Centrosome, **5**, **7**, 14, **15**, 164, 169, 237, 238.
Cerebratulus, 232.
Cestoda, 136–137.

INDEX OF SUBJECTS

Chætognatha, 212.
Characters, dominant, 303; linked, 307; recessive, 303; unit 303.
Chiasmatype theory, 254.
Chick, 33, 100, **103**, 227, 281.
Chironomus, 108–109, **110**, 224, 229, 235.
Chloroplastid, 7.
Cholesterin, 8, 12, 13.
Chorion, 113.
Chondriodiérèse, 279.
Chondriokont, 279.
Chondriosome, 7, 102, **103**, 168, 227 *ff.*, 275, 277.
Chondriotaxis, 279.
Chromatin, **5**, 7, 11–12; as germplasm, 299; as keimbahn-determinants, 211 *ff.*
Chromatin-diminution, 47, **56**, **57**, 139–141, 174 *ff.*, 217 *ff.*, 249.
Chromatin-nucleolus, **5**, 7.
Chromidia, **26**, 123, 168, 221 *ff.*, 279.
Chromidial net, **26**.
Chromosome, 6, 7, 14, **15**, 243, 299; accessory, 106; cycle, 245–275; diploid, 43; division, 248; in fertilization, 49; haploid, 43; individuality, 255; in man, 272 *ff.*; and Mendelism, **305**; number, 246; from nucleolus, 214; in parthenogenesis, 246; univalent, 249.
Chrysemys, **32**.
Chrysomelidæ, 109.
Ciona, 192.
Cladocera, 163 *ff.*
Clathrina, 70.
Clava, 88, 135.
Cleavage, 29, 115.
Cockroach, 194.
Cœlenterata, 80–98, 212.
Coleoptera, 109–143.
Colloid, 9.
Colony, 17.

Compsilura, 107, 109.
Conjugation, 17.
Copepoda, 165 *ff.*
Copidosoma, 146 *ff.*
Copulationszelle, 163.
Corps enigmatique, 187.
Crepidula, 218.
Crustacea, 163–173.
Crystalloid, 9.
Cyclops, 124, 164 *ff.*, 228, **247**.
Cymatogaster, 100.
Cynthia, 233, 280.
Cyst formation, 125–129.
Cytomicrosome, 276.
Cytoplasm, 6, 143, 179, 224 *ff.*, 300 *ff.*

Daphnidæ, 163.
Death, natural, 25.
Determination of sex, 118.
Determiner, 302.
Diaptomus, 165.
Differentiation, 76, 141–143.
Diœcious, 18, 190.
Diploid, chromosomes, 248.
Diplotene, **252**.
Diptera, 107.
Dispermic, 177, **178**.
Dominance, 303.
Dotterplatte, 109, 115, 225, 235.
Drosophila, 307 *ff.*
Dyad, **45**, 46, 306, **307**.
Dytiscus, 120–124, **121**, 223.
Dzierzon theory, 143.

Earthworm, 161, **190**, 191.
Eclectosome, 279.
Ectosome, **166**, 167 *ff.*, 213, 237.
Egg, **19**, **20**.
Encyrtus, 145.
Enzyme, 300.
Ephydatia, 75.
Epigenesis, 2, 243.
Ergastoplasma, 276.
Eudendrium, 86.

INDEX OF SUBJECTS

Euschistis, 281.
Evolution, 310.

Factor, 302, 309.
Female sex, 18.
Fertilization, 44, 47–49, 256, *ff*.
Fission, 22.
Frog, hermaphroditism in, 205 *ff*.
Fusion, of chromosomes, 254; of oöcytes, 152, 155 *ff*.

Gel, 5, 6, 9.
Gemmule, 18, 74–75, 76, 79.
Genes, 302, 309, 310.
Genetics, 309.
Genetic-continuity of chromosomes, 255.
Germ cell, 19–22, 101, *v.s.* somatic cell, 296–297.
Germ-cell cycle, 28–49.
Germinal continuity, 292.
Germinal epithelium theory, 98.
Germinal localization, 231.
Germinal spot, 214.
Germinal vesicle, 19, 20, 54.
Germ-plasm, in *Ascaris*, 177, in *Hydra*, 83–85; in *Miastor*, 293; in polyembryony, 162; in sponges, 80.
Germ-plasm theory, 290–310.
Gonochorism, 18, 191.
Gonocyte, 71, 73.
Gonothyræa, 89.
Gonotome theory, 97.
Graffilla, 157.
Gryllus, 123, 244.
Guinea-pig, 102, **103**, **104**, 227.
Gynandromorph, 193–194.

Haploid, 247.
Hauptnucleolus, 214.
Helix, 195, 196 *ff*., 226.
Hemiptera, amitosis in, 137.
Hermaphrodite, 18, 189–210, 269.
Heterocope, 165.

Heterotypic mitosis, 46, **252**, 253.
Heterozygous, 304.
Homologous chromosomes, 253.
Homotypic mitosis, 46.
Homozygous, 303.
Honey-bee, 143–144, 261 *ff*., **266**.
Hyaloplasm, 4, **5**.
Hydra, 82–85, 159.
Hydractinia, 87.
Hydroid, life cycle of, 23.
Hydrophilus, 113.
Hydrozoa, 85–98.
Hymenoptera, 143–163, 221, **235**.

Idiochromatin, 28.
Individuality of chromosomes, 255.
Interkinesis, 299.
Isotropism, 231.

Jelly-fish, 23.

Karyochondria, 279.
Karyokinesis, 13, 14, **15**.
Karyolymph, 6.
Karyosome, **5**, 7, 213.
Keimbahn, in *Æquorea*, 183, **184**; *Amphibia*, 206 *ff*.; *Cladocera*, 163 *ff*.; *Copepoda*, 165 *ff*.; insects, 106–163; nematodes, 174–179; *Sagitta*, 179 *ff*.
Keimbahn-determinants, 19, 211–244, 296, 301; genesis, 211–234; localization, 234–240; fate, 240–244.
Keimbahnchromidien, 223.
Keimbahnchromatin, 152 *ff*., 223.
Keimbahnplasma, 108, **110**, 115, 230, 235.
Keimbahnzelle, 104.
Keimfleck, 214.
Keimhautblastem, 113, **114**.
Keimstätte, 95.
Keimwulst, 108, **110**, 115, 235.
Keimzone, 95.

INDEX OF SUBJECTS

Kinetochromidia, 214.
Kinoplasm, 214.

Lamprey, 100, 209.
Larva, 23.
Lecithin, 8, 12.
Lepas, 172, 225.
Lepidoptera, 118.
Lepidosteus, **32**, 33, 101.
Leptinotarsa, 37–41, 111, 125–129, 138–139.
Leptotene, 251, **252**.
Life cycles, 22 *ff*.
Linin, **5**, 7.
Linked characters, 307.
Locust, 23.
Lophius, 102.
Lygæus, 259.
Lymnæa, 192.

Macrogamete, 27.
Male, 18.
Man, chromosomes of, 272 *ff*.; hermaphroditism in, 194.
Maturation, 41–47, 129, 256 *ff*.
Medusa, 23.
Mesostoma, 204.
Metabolism, and sex, 275; and Keimbahn-determinants, 228.
Metagenesis, 23.
Metanucleolus, 183, 215.
Metaplasm, **5**, 7, 8.
Metaphase, **15**, 16.
Metazoa, 1, 18.
Miastor, 51–68, 107, 217 *ff*., 235, 293–294.
Microgamete, 27.
Microsome, 6.
Middle piece, of sperm, 21, 216.
Migration, of germ cells, 31–34, 101–102, 116, 226.
Mitochondria, **5**, 13, **39**, 40, 226 *ff*., 275–289; methods, 282–283; Ascaris, **284**; chick, **278**; division of, **281**, 284; function of, 286 *ff*.; in living cells, 280, **281**; in plants, 277, **280**; reduction of, 285; and sex, 285.
Mitosis, 13, 14–16.
Mitrocoma, 183.
Mixochromosomes, 251.
Moina, 163.
Mollusk, 185, 191.
Monad, chromosome, **45**, 46.
Moniezia, 136, 297.
Monœcious, 18, 191.
Monospermy, 48.
Mosaic development, 233.
Moulting, 23.
Musca, 107.
Myofibril, 280.
Myxine, 209.
Myzostoma, 37, 185, 193.

Nahrzellenkern, 170.
Nebenkern, **203**, 221, 285.
Nebennucleolus, 214.
Nematodes, chromosomes of, 267 *ff*.
Nepa, 137.
Neratina, 186, 225.
Netzapparat, **103**, 104.
Neurofibril, 280.
Nuclear sap, 6.
Nucleic acid, 11.
Nuclein, 11.
Nucleolo of Silvestri, 145 *ff*.
Nucleolus, **5**, 6, 13, 167, 213 *ff*.
Nucleoprotein, 8, 11.
Nucleus, 3, 13–16.
Nurse cells, 35–36, **53**, 119–**121**, **150**, 151, **201**, 202.
Nutritive substances, 225 *ff*.

Œnothera, 160.
Oncopeltus, 261, **262**.
Oöcyte, **38**, **39**, 40–41.
Oögenesis, **42**, 256 *ff*.
Oöpthora, 145, **146**.
Ophryotrocha, 37.
Opossum, 288.

INDEX OF SUBJECTS

Organ-forming substances, 233.
Organization of egg, 19, 29, 228 *ff.*
Oxyphile, 11.

Pachytene, 252.
Pædogenesis, 18, 52.
Paracopulationszelle, 212, 225.
Paramecium, 27.
Paranucleus, 163.
Paraplasm, 7.
Parasitism, 191–192.
Parasynapsis, 254.
Parthenogenesis, 18, 47, 145, 246, 265.
Pea, 302, **303**.
Pecten, 191.
Pennaria, 87.
Peripatus, 285, 288.
Petromyzon, 33.
Phallusia, 233.
Phosphatid, 8, 12.
Phylloxera, 265 *ff.*
Physa, 186, 225.
Pig, 194.
Planocera, 157.
Planorbis, 186.
Plasmodia, artificial, 77–78.
Plasmosome, **5**, 7, 102, **103**, 213.
Plastid, **5**, 7.
Plastochondria, 279.
Plastokonta, 279.
Plastosome, 7, 244, 275, 279.
Polar body, 47, 143–144.
Polares Plasma (*see* pole-plasm).
Polarity, 19, 107, 124, 179, 231 *ff.*
Pole-cell, **110**, **111**, **117**.
Pole-disc, 109, **114**, **117**, 142, 219, 225, 229, 235.
Pole-plasm, 53–55, 228, 230, 235, 294–295.
Polistes, 222.
Polychœrus, 157.
Polyembryony, 145 *ff.*, 161.
Polyp, 23.
Polyphemus, **170** *ff.*, 236.

Polyspermy, 48, 115, 299.
Porifera, 69 *ff.*
Potato beetle (*see Leptinotarsa*).
Preblastodermic nuclei, **114**.
Predetermination, 2.
Preformation, 2, 243.
Prochromosome, 299.
Progerminative cell, 196, **197**.
Promorphology, 19.
Prophase, 14.
Protandry, 193.
Protein, 8, 10.
Protenor, 123, 258.
Protogyny, 192–193.
Protoplasm, 3–13.
Protozoa, 1, 17, 25.
Pteropod, 269, **271**.
Pupa, 23.
Pyrrhocoris, 256.

Rana, 32.
Recessive character, 304.
Reduction of chromosomes, 43, 253.
Regeneration, 79–80, 297.
Reproduction, 17–18.
Rotifera, 186.
Rhabditis, 267, **270**.
Richtungscopulationskern, 144.

Sagitta, 179 *ff.*, 195, 228.
Salamandra, 134.
Sarcode, 3.
Scorpœna, 222.
Sea urchin, 216.
Secondary sex characters, 189.
Segregation of germ cells, 29.
Self-copulation, 192.
Self-fertilization, 192.
Sertoli cell, 35, 129–133.
Sex, 18, 189.
Sex chromosome, 255 *ff.*
Sex determination, 274.
Sol, 5, 6, 9.
Sorite, 76, 79.

Spermatogenesis, **42**, 256 *ff*.
Spermatogonia, **127**.
Spermatozoön, **19–22**, 48.
Sphérule, 276.
Spireme, 14, **15**.
Spongilla, 73.
Spongioplasm, 4, **5**.
Sporulation, 17.
Squash bug, 256.
Starfish, 6.
Statoblast, 18.
Statocyte, 70, 71, 73.
Stem-cell, **175**.
Stone-fly, hermaphroditic, 194.
Synapsis, 44, 122, 250 *ff*., **305**.
Synaptene, 251, **252**.
Synizesis, 43, 237, 251, **252**.

Tænia, 136, 137.
Telophase, **15**, 16.
Telosynapsis, 254.
Testis, 41.
Tethya, 70, 76, 79.

Tetrad, 44, **45**.
Tipulides, 107.
Toad, hermaphroditic, 207–208.
Tokocyte, 71, 73, 79.
Trophochromatin, 28.

Unit character, 304.
Uterine spindle, 157.

Vacuole, **5**, 8.
Vegetative pole, 20.
Vertebrate, **32**, 95–105, 212.
Vitelline membrane, 113, **114**.
Vitellophag, **114**.

X-chromosome, 255 *ff*., **264**, 299.

Y-chromosome, 259 *ff*., **264**.
Yolk, in germ cells, 101, 224.
Yolk nucleus, 19, **226**, 285.

Zygosome, 251.
Zygote, 1, 48.

THE following pages contain advertisements of books by the same author or on kindred subjects

An Introduction to Zoölogy

By

ROBERT W. HEGNER, Ph.D.

Assistant Professor of Zoölogy in the University of Michigan

A TEXT-BOOK INTENDED FOR THE USE OF STUDENTS IN COLLEGES AND UNIVERSITIES

Illustrated, 12mo, $ 1.90 net

"There are some interesting distinctive features in this new introduction to zoölogy. Only a few types are studied (all of them Invertebrates); they are discussed so as to illustrate the principles of the science; the morphological aspect is not especially emphasized, but is coördinated with the physiological aspect (which, of course, includes the study of interrelations and behavior)."

"The author shows a keen educative instinct; there is a marked freshness and individuality of treatment, and the assistance of a number of experts, who have read particular chapters, has secured an enviable freedom from mistakes. There is a very useful bibliography, and a glossary."

"It is a work which it has been a pleasure to read, and which deserves a career of much usefulness." — *Nature.*

"The book is cordially recommended as giving a thorough preparation for advanced courses in the subject."
— *American Journal of Science.*

"The attempt is made to present the newer zoölogy to the beginner. Here we find the figures of Jennings, Yerkes, Morgan — in fact, it may be called an American product from cover to cover. Consequently, the student finds himself at home at once among American forms and American names. It is not to be understood, however, that the view is circumscribed and that the data from foreign sources are eliminated."

"It may be said that the result is excellent in the light of the labor set before the author. The book-making is good, the illustrations are carefully selected, and there is a unity in the volume which appeals very strongly to the reviewer." — *Science.*

THE MACMILLAN COMPANY
Publishers   64-66 Fifth Avenue   **New York**

COLLEGE ZOÖLOGY

By

ROBERT W. HEGNER, Ph.D.

Assistant Professor of Zoölogy in the University of Michigan

Illustrated, Cloth, 12mo, xxiv + 733 pp., $2.60 net

This book is intended to serve as a text for beginning students in universities and colleges, or for students who have already taken a course in general biology and wish to gain a more comprehensive view of the animal kingdom. It differs from many of the college text-books of zoölogy now on the market in several important respects: (1) the animals and their organs are not only described, but their functions are pointed out; (2) the animals described are in most cases native species; and (3) the relations of the animals to man are emphasized. Besides serving as a text-book, it is believed that this book will be of interest to the general reader, since it gives a bird's-eye view of the entire animal kingdom as we know it at the present time.

Within the past decade there has been a tendency for teachers of zoölogy to pay less attention to morphology and more to physiology. As a prominent morphologist recently said, "Morphology . . . is no longer in favor . . . and among a section of the zoölogical world has almost fallen into disgrace" (Bourne). The study of the form and structure of animals is, however, of fundamental importance, and is absolutely necessary before physiological processes can be fully understood; but a course which is built up on the "old-fashioned morphological lines" is no longer adequate for the presentation of zoölogical principles.

The present volume has not been made by merely adding a description of the vertebrates to the author's "Introduction to Zoölogy" (for a brief description of which see the preceding advertisement). On the contrary, it is a new work throughout, although the same general method of treatment, which proved so successful in the earlier book, has been employed in this one. Similarly, in the preparation of this book the author has submitted the manuscript of each chapter to a scholar and teacher of unquestioned authority in the particular field. The criticisms and suggestions thus secured have greatly increased both the accuracy and the practicability of the text.

THE MACMILLAN COMPANY

Publishers   64–66 Fifth Avenue   New York

Genetics. An Introduction to the Study of Heredity

By HERBERT EUGENE WALTER

Associate Professor of Biology, Brown University

Cloth, 12mo, $1.50 net

In his "Genetics" Professor Walter summarizes the more recent phases of the study of heredity and gives to the non-technical readers a clear introduction to questions that are at present agitating the biological world.

Professor Walter's conception of sexual reproduction is that it is a device for doubling the possible variations in the offspring, by the mingling of two strains of germ plasm. The weight of probability, he concludes, is decidedly against the time-honored belief in the inheritance of acquired characters. Professor Walter also predicts that the key to this whole problem will be furnished by the chemist, and that the final analysis of the matter of the "heritage carriers" will be seen to be chemical rather than morphological in nature. In the practical application of this theory to human conservation or eugenics, it would follow that the only control that a man has over the inheritance of his children is in selecting his wife. Professor Walter holds, if only modifications of the germ plasm can count in inheritance, and if these modifications come wholly from the combination of two germ plasms, then the only method of hereditary influence is in this selection.

"I find that it is a very useful study for an introduction to the subject. Professor Walter has certainly made one of the clearest statements of the matters involved that I have seen, and has made a book which students will find very useful because he keeps everything in such entirely simple and clear outlines, and at the same time he has brought the book up to date." — PROFESSOR LOOMIS of Amherst College.

"I am much pleased with it and congratulate you upon securing so excellent a treatment. It is one of the most readable scientific books I have, and goes unerringly to the fundamentals of our most recent advances in the experimental study of heredity as well as those of the older studies." — PROFESSOR GEORGE H. SHULL, Cold Spring Harbor, Long Island, N. Y.

"There was a decided need for just such a work. The book strikes me as most excellently done." — PROFESSOR H. S. JENNINGS, Johns Hopkins University.

THE MACMILLAN COMPANY

Publishers   **64-66 Fifth Avenue**   **New York**

An Outline of the Theory of Organic Evolution

With a Description of some of the Phenomena which it explains

By MAYNARD M. METCALF, Ph.D.
Professor of Zoölogy, Oberlin College, Oberlin, Ohio

THIRD EDITION, FUNDAMENTALLY REVISED

Cloth, 8vo, Colored Plates, $2.50 net

The lectures out of which this book has grown were written for the author's students at the Woman's College of Baltimore, and for others in the college not familiar with biology who had expressed a desire to attend such a course of lectures. The book is, therefore, not intended for biologists, but rather for those who would like a brief introductory outline of this important phase of biological theory.

It has been the author's endeavor to avoid technicality so far as possible, and present the subject in a way that will be intelligible to those unfamiliar with biological phenomena. The subject, however, is somewhat intricate, and cannot be presented in so simple a manner as to require no thought on the reader's part; but it is hoped that the interest of the subject will make the few hours spent in the perusal of this book a pleasure rather than a burden.

In many instances matter that might have been elaborated in the text has been treated in the pictures, which, with their appended explanations, form an essential part of the presentation of the subject. This method of treatment has been chosen both for the sake of the greater vividness thus secured and because it enables the book to be reduced to the limits desired. Many of the illustrations have been obtained from books with which the reader may wish later to become familiar.

THE MACMILLAN COMPANY
Publishers   64-66 Fifth Avenue   New York

By S. HERBERT, M.D. (Vienna), M.R.C.S. (Eng.),
L.R.C.P. (Lond.)

The First Principles of Heredity

Cloth, 199 pp., Ill., 8vo, $2.00 net

The purpose of this book is to supply in a simple and yet scientific manner all that may be desirable for the average student to know about Heredity and related questions, without at the same time assuming any previous knowledge of the subject on the reader's part.

The First Principles of Evolution

By S. HERBERT

Cloth, 8vo, 346 pp., containing 90 illustrations and tables, $1.60 net

Though there are hosts of books dealing with Evolution, they are either too compendious and specialized, or, if intended for the average reader, too limited in their treatment of the subject. In a simple, yet scientific, manner, the author here presents the problem of Evolution comprehensively in all its aspects.

CONTENTS

INTRODUCTION — Evolution in General.
SECTION I — Inorganic Evolution.
    The Evolution of Matter.
SECTION II — Organic Evolution.
PART I — The Facts of Evolution.
    Morphology.
    Embryology.
    Classification.
    Palæontology.
    Geographical Distribution
PART II — Theories of Evolution.
SECTION III — Superorganic Evolution.
    Social Evolution.
CONCLUSION — The Formula of Evolution.
    The Philosophy of Change.

THE MACMILLAN COMPANY

Publishers   **64–66 Fifth Avenue**   **New York**